Perspectives
on
Communication
in
Social Conflict

PRENTICE-HALL SERIES IN SPEECH COMMUNICATION
Larry L. Barker and Robert J. Kibler, *Consulting Editors*

ARGUMENT: AN ALTERNATIVE TO VIOLENCE
Abne Eisenberg and Joseph Ilardo

ARGUMENTATION: INQUIRY AND ADVOCACY
George W. Ziegelmueller and Charles A. Dause

BEYOND WORDS
Randall Harrison

COMMUNICATION: CONCEPTS AND PROCESSES
Joseph A. DeVito

COMMUNICATION VIBRATIONS
Larry L. Barker

DESIGNS FOR PERSUASIVE COMMUNICATION
Otto Lerbinger

GROUP COMMUNICATION
Alvin Goldberg and Carl Larson

LANGUAGE: CONCEPTS AND PROCESSES
Joseph A. DeVito

MASS NEWS: PRACTICES, CONTROVERSIES, AND ALTERNATIVES
David J. LeRoy and Christopher H. Sterling

MONOLOGUE TO DIALOGUE: AN EXPLORATION OF
INTERPERSONAL COMMUNICATION
Charles T. Brown and Paul W. Keller

ORGANIZING A SPEECH: A PROGRAMMED GUIDE
Judy Haynes

PERSPECTIVES ON COMMUNICATION IN SOCIAL CONFLICT
Gerald R. Miller and Herbert W. Simons

PERSUASION: COMMUNICATION AND INTERPERSONAL RELATIONS
Raymond S. Ross

THE PROSPECT OF RHETORIC
Lloyd F. Bitzer and Edwin Black

SPEECH COMMUNICATION: FUNDAMENTALS AND PRACTICE, third edition
Raymond S. Ross

TRANSRACIAL COMMUNICATION
Arthur L. Smith

GERALD R. MILLER
Michigan State University

HERBERT W. SIMONS
Temple University

Perspectives

on

Communication

in

Social Conflict

SPONSORED BY

*Speech
Communication
Association*

Prentice-Hall, Inc., Englewood Cliffs, New Jersey

Library of Congress Cataloging in Publication Data
Main entry under title:

Perspectives on communication in social conflict.

(The Prentice-Hall series in speech communication)
"Sponsored by [the] Speech Communication Association."
Bibliography: p.
1. Social conflict.   2. Communication in the social
sciences.   I. Miller, Gerald R., ed.   II. Simons,
Herbert W., 1935-   ed.   III. Speech Communication
Association.
HM136.P56   301.6'3   74-3263
ISBN 0-13-660399-8

© **1974 by Prentice-Hall, Inc., Englewood Cliffs, New Jersey**

PRINTED IN THE UNITED STATES OF AMERICA

10 9 8 7 6 5 4 3 2 1

PRENTICE-HALL INTERNATIONAL, INC., LONDON
PRENTICE-HALL OF AUSTRALIA, PTY. LTD., SYDNEY
PRENTICE-HALL OF CANADA, LTD., TORONTO
PRENTICE-HALL OF INDIA PRIVATE LIMITED, NEW DELHI
PRENTICE-HALL OF JAPAN, INC., TOKYO

3-1303-0004 4-2690

Table of Contents

5

COMMUNICATION STRATEGIES IN CONFLICTS BETWEEN INSTITUTIONS AND THEIR CLIENTS   125

John Waite Bowers

6

CONFLICT AND COMMUNICATION WITHIN THE UNIVERSITY   153

Phillip K. Tompkins / Jeanne Y. Fisher
Dominic A. Infante / Elaine V. Tompkins

7

THE CARROT AND STICK AS HANDMAIDENS OF PERSUASION IN CONFLICT SITUATIONS   172

Herbert W. Simons

8

Preface

Within the social sciences in general, and within speech communication, in particular, there has been growing recognition that communication theory and conflict theory cannot continue to go their separate ways. The attempt at integration is most noticeable in recent journal articles (e.g., the special issue of *Speech Monographs* for March, 1974), but it is also manifest at the curricular level. Within departments of speech communication, graduate and undergraduate courses bearing on social conflict are now commonplace. The large department may list one course entitled "Communication and Conflict" (or "Persuasion in Social Conflicts" or "The Rhetoric of Conflict"), several courses dealing with one or another species of conflict (e.g., protest rhetoric, political communication, campaigns and movements, organizational communication), and several "standard" courses (e.g., persuasion, discussion, communication theory, interpersonal communication), in which segments of the course are reserved for the study of social conflict. Correspondingly, courses in or about conflict within departments of political science, sociology, and psychology now seem to increasingly emphasize the role of communication in conflict situations.

Although this book was not designed as a textbook, it might well be used as required reading in courses dealing directly with communication and conflict or as collateral reading in other related courses. In the process of presenting and defending their own perspectives, the contributors to this volume provide an introduction to major concepts, theories, methods, and research in the area. For example, rather than assuming knowledge of the workings of the Prisoner's Dilemma game, Steinfatt and Miller have described this gaming procedure in some detail. In this way, the book has been adapted to beginning graduate students and advanced undergraduates.

A great many people helped make this book possible, not the least of whom were the contributors themselves. All but three of the contributors (the exceptions are Jeanne Fisher, Dominic Infante, and Elaine Tompkins) were also participants at a conference on communication and conflict, held March 2–4, 1972, at which time many of the ideas expressed in this volume were first discussed. We wish to thank the Speech Communication Association for sponsoring both the conference and this book. In particular, we wish to thank Patrick Kennicott and William Work of the national office and Lloyd Bitzer, a fellow member of the SCA Research Board, which supervised the project. Also deserving thanks are Donald Zacharias of the University of Texas and two political scientists who served as critic-consultants at the conference, Peter Bachrach of Temple University and Jack Nagel of the University of Pennsylvania. Credit is also given to Temple University, which provided its Sugarloaf conference center facilities for the conference at reduced cost. In addition, we thank Art Rittenberg of Prentice-Hall for his continued support of projects such as this one. Finally, we owe special thanks to our wives and children, whose patience during the period of writing and editing made our tasks considerably easier.

Contributors

JOHN WAITE BOWERS (PhD, University of Iowa, 1962) is head professor of the Communication Research Division, Department of Speech and Dramatic Art, University of Iowa. His many publications in communication theory and research include *Designing the Communication Experiment;* and, with Donovan J. Ochs, *The Rhetoric of Agitation and Control.*

JEANNE Y. FISHER (PhD, University of Michigan, 1970) is Assistant Professor of Rhetoric and Communication, State University of New York, Albany. Her major research interests lie in Burkeian theory, persuasion theory, and communication theory. She has recently completed articles dealing with communication anxiety and with a Burkeian analysis of a multiple murder and suicide.

DOMINIC A. INFANTE (PhD, Kent State University, 1971) is Assistant Professor of Speech Communication, University of South Florida. His major research interests are in persuasion and communication theory. Professor Infante has authored several articles for journals in speech and communication.

FRED E. JANDT (PhD, Bowling Green State University, 1970) is Associate Professor of Speech Communication at State University of New York, Brockport. His areas of special research interest are interpersonal communication, particularly cross-cultural communication, and the development of self-concept. The developer of several simulation exercises employing principles of communication, Professor Jandt has recently edited a volume entitled *Conflict Resolution Through Communication.*

GERALD R. MILLER (PhD, University of Iowa, 1961) is Professor of Communication at Michigan State University. His major research interests are in the areas of interpersonal communication and persuasion. The author of three books and over sixty articles in journals of communication, speech, and psychology, Professor Miller has held numerous offices in the Speech Communication Association and International Communication Association and is a recipient of the Distinguished Faculty Award from Michigan State University.

C. DAVID MORTENSEN (PhD, University of Minnesota, 1967) is Associate Professor of Communication Arts, University of Wisconsin, Madison. His major research interests are in the areas of interpersonal and small group communication. The author of numerous articles appearing in journals of speech and communication, Professor Mortensen has edited several volumes of readings dealing with communication theory and research and has authored a work titled *Communication: The Study of Human Interaction.*

HERBERT W. SIMONS (PhD, Purdue University, 1961) is Professor of Speech at Temple University. He has served as chairman of the Speech Communication Association's Research Board and also as chairman of the Rhetoric and Communication Theory Division of that Association. A recipient of several awards for outstanding scholarly papers, Professor Simons has concentrated his research in the area of persuasion, specializing in political persuasion, protest, and social conflict.

THOMAS M. STEINFATT (PhD, Michigan State University, 1970) is Assistant Professor of Communication, Queens College of the City University of New York. His major research interests are in interpersonal and small group communication, especially persuasion, inducing resistance to persuasion, and the effects of communication in conflicts and game simulations. The author of several articles appearing in journals of psychology and communication, Professor Steinfatt is currently studying the effects of communication in game-simulated situations under the auspices of a grant from the Research Foundation of the City University of New York.

ELAINE V. TOMPKINS (MA, University of Iowa, 1966) is a Lecturer in Speech at the New York State Police Academy. The co-author of *Communication Crisis at Kent State,* Ms. Tompkins lives in the foothills of the Helderberg Mountains with six ducks, six cats, and one of the co-authors of the article in this volume, entitled "Conflict and Communication within the University."

PHILLIP K. TOMPKINS (PhD, Purdue University, 1962) is Professor and Chairman, Department of Rhetoric and Communication, State University of New York, Albany. The author of numerous articles in journals of speech, communication, and psychology, Professor Tompkins is also the co-author of *Communication Crisis at Kent State.* He lives in the foothills of the Helderberg Mountains with six ducks, six cats, and one of the co-authors of the article in this volume, entitled "Conflict and Communication within the University."

1

Prologue

HERBERT W. SIMONS

This book was born of a conference on communication and conflict sponsored by the Research Board of the Speech Communication Association. The conference took place March 2–4, 1972 at Sugarloaf, a conference center belonging to Temple University. The charge to the conferees was to bring forth fresh perspectives or to enliven old ones, and to disseminate the fruits of their labors to students of communication and conflict, both within and outside the field of speech communication. In this chapter, I should like to report informally on the Sugarloaf conference, provide a preview of this book, and interject some comments of my own about possible directions for research and theory in the area of communication and conflict.

In many ways, the field's increased attention to social conflict represents a logical extension of trends that have been developing over a period of many years. For those unfamiliar with the discipline, speech communication is at once among the oldest and youngest of academic fields. Its roots extend to the rhetoricians of ancient Greece, yet its emergence as a scientific discipline dates back no earlier than the 1930s. For two thousand years, it was the exclusive province of the humanities, a cousin of poetics and dialectics committed almost entirely to the study of oratory. Even as the science of speech communication made its debut as a kind of applied social psychology, its preoccupation was with measures of the immediate effects of speeches or other verbal messages that had been delivered to passive audiences in contexts, such as classrooms, in which power relationships could be minimized or ignored. Gradually, the field has enlarged its scope to include two-way communication situations, multistage interactions, nonverbal messages, more extensive and more extended measures of effect, and a concern for the impact of situational variables, including power variables. Still, not until the dramatic, highly visible conflicts of the sixties had impressed themselves upon the collective consciousness of academe did speech communication scholars begin questioning the appropriateness of their conceptual armament for the study of conflict and begin looking in earnest at the contributions of conflict theorists.

This brings me to the common concerns which inspired the creation of this book. It became apparent that the conferees were united, not by any agreement on a method of study, or theory, or even on a definition of conflict, but by a set of shared dissatisfactions with the current state of knowledge and theory. Let me comment briefly on what I believe were the chief complaints.

SOME SHARED DISSATISFACTIONS

Dissatisfaction with Game-Theoretic Treatments of Communication in Social Conflicts

Game theory and game theoretic research continue to occupy center stage among conflict theorists, and while the conferees acknowledged their debt to the "gamesmen," they uniformly deplored—or at least regretted—the paucity of attention to communication variables in experimental gaming research, an oversight discussed more fully in the next chapter.

That inattention is, of course, understandable. Conflict is difficult enough to study without allowing all manner of communication variables to enter in. If one is to develop elegant models of social interaction applicable to broad classes of behavior, some restrictions on variables are inevitable. Moreover, the study of conflict presents special problems. Whereas some areas of social inquiry involve actors and reactors whose behaviors can be modeled mechanistically and sequentially, conflicts involve co-acting entities whose behaviors must be modeled dynamically and relationally. Whereas some forms of interaction are highly transient, involving relatively brief time spans and definite beginnings and endings, most interesting conflicts involve ongoing relationships over extended periods in which the researcher must at best punctuate the sequence of events. And whereas it is often possible to experimentally manipulate social relationships without incurring ethical objections, if a researcher experimentally creates rip-roaring conflicts in his classroom or laboratory, he risks immediate moral censure.

Still, the conferees were apparently convinced that in their efforts to avoid "muddle-headed" treatments of social conflict, the game theorists had gone to the other extreme of presenting "simple-minded" accounts of the phenomenon. Communication, after all, is the means by which conflicts get socially defined, the instrument through which influence in conflicts is exercised, and the vehicle by which partisans or third parties may prevent, manage, or resolve conflicts. Outside the gaming laboratory, communication is not confined to moves on a board.

Several contributors to this volume have proposed alternative perspectives and/or other methods for studying communication in social conflicts. Mortensen offers a transactional paradigm and urges the study of relational variables. Jandt proposes the use of simulation techniques, a compromise of sorts between gaming techniques and traditional "deception" experiments in social psychology. Both Bowers and Tompkins et al. rely on case studies and interviews. All offer criticisms of game theoretic research.

Alone among the contributors, Steinfatt and Miller remain faithful to the gaming perspective but seek to encourage more research on communication variables as a way of rectifying current deficiencies. Toward that end, they have clarified game theoretic terms, provided an extensive review of research on communication variables in gaming research, and reported on some original research conducted by Steinfatt.

Dissatisfaction with Exclusively Objectivist Treatments of Social Conflict

Are conflicts in the eye of the beholder or do they exist independent of the perceiver? Among conflict theorists, the prevailing tendency seems to be to treat them as though they had an objective, "out-there" existence. This approach has the advantage of enabling nonparticipants to observe, characterize, and in some cases, manipulate the situation without always asking those in conflict to tell them what is "really" going on. Indeed, it is sometimes useful to characterize a situation as conflictful even when both parties *deny* that it is a conflict. The Freudian may insist, for example, that father and son are in a conflict over mother though neither is aware of it. The Marxist may insist that the workers are in conflict with the capitalists but that they are unaware of their "real" interests.

If enough is known about the "objective" conflict situation, it is presumably possible for the researcher, as omniscient observer, to characterize the "logic" of the situation, to develop a theory of rational decision-making for that situation, and to compare actual behavior with behavior considered rational on an a priori basis. Given these assumptions, a Marxist, for example, may erect a theory of history and conclude that such and such a revolutionary strategy is "correct" in light of his theory, or a military gamesman may decide that his army's invasion should take place at Location A rather than Location B.

Despite the apparent advantages of objectivist approaches to social conflict, most contributors to this volume underscore its perceptual or phenomenological aspects. They recognize, however, that the "subjective-objective" controversy does not require the taking of extreme positions, and indeed that they would be retreating into solipsisms were they to deny the existence of situational factors which at least give rise to perceived conflict and which may be altered by actions following from those perceptions. The quarrel, it would seem, is one of emphasis, but it is nevertheless important. The professional bias of communication theorists is that meaning is ultimately in people, and especially in the receiver of messages. That bias leads them to ask questions that exclusively objectivist theorists would not ask—questions about the subjective meaning of a hypothetical payoff to the players of an experimental game and not just its assigned payoff; questions about the symbolic significance of an act of violence and not just its physical impact; and so on.

Probably the most ambitious attempt in this volume to deal with the objectivist-subjectivist controversy is Mortensen's transactional approach. It invokes such notions as "knowing-knowns" as ways of avoiding subject-object dualisms. No doubt many behaviorists, game theorists, and others reared in a positivist tradition will find his approach much too vague for their liking. Still another approach is to speak of stages of conflict or types of conflict, and by means of such categories, to reflect an awareness of the interactions between objective (i.e., external) and subjective (i.e., internal) forces. In one way or another, this is what other contributors to this volume have done.

Dissatisfaction with Anti-Conflict Biases in System Orientations

Coser (1956), Skolnick (1969), and others have observed that many social scientists either deny the existence of social conflicts (asserting, for example, that all apparent conflicts are "really" breakdowns in communication) or dilute the concept's meaning by lumping conflicts together with mere differences of opinion. Generally speaking, such theorists have an "anti-conflict" bias; they tend to regard conflicts as "deviations" from a "normal" state of "harmony," "order," or "system equilibrium" (Coser, 1956). The pathology metaphor is most often employed by theorists with what Gamson (1968) calls a "social control" or "system perspective." As compared with "influence-oriented" or "actor-oriented" social scientists, system-oriented theorists tend to view conflicts as bad because they prevent the system (a government, a business, or any other such collectivity) from realizing its supraordinate interests. From an actor-oriented perspective, conflicts are good (or at least necessary and inevitable) because they help the actor realize his individual interests. From a system perspective, conflicts are to be prevented, resolved, or controlled; the emphasis is on the similarities that unite individuals, and the chief operating assumption is that scarce resources can be equitably shared and indeed enlarged through cooperative efforts. From the perspective of those with an actor orientation, however, there are *real*, not just *apparent* differences of interest among men, and each combatant must fight for his own share of a limited resource pie.

Although the issue is not stressed in this volume, the conferees expressed dismay at the anti-conflict biases manifested by some scholars within their own discipline. This is not to say that system orientations are themselves indefensible, only that they become excessive when conflict is treated as an aberration: when it is assumed that it is always preferable to preserve existing systems rather than supplant them, or that conflicts are necessarily dysfunctional *for* systems, or that dialogue is sufficient to resolve conflicts, or that Machiavellian studies of how to "win" in conflicts are inherently evil. While recognizing that system orientations and actor orientations *both* yield unique and rewarding insights, participants at the conference emphasized in particular the need to examine communication strategies for conflicts from an actor orientation. The chapters contributed by Bowers and by Steinfatt and

Miller do just that. Although I devote considerable space to communication strategies, my primary interests are in analyzing relationships among types of influence and in identifying conceptual and normative implications that follow from such an analysis. Other contributors focus on the perceived effects of actor-initiated conflict behaviors or on identifying antecedents and mapping dimensions of these behaviors.

Dissatisfaction with Popular Conceptions of Persuasion in Social Conflicts

I must confess that this is my own pet peeve (see Simons, 1972), but it was also voiced by others at the conference. Within speech communication (and elsewhere besides), the effective persuader tends to be stereotypically depicted as a marvelously adaptable soul, one who, although not necessarily becoming a chameleon, nevertheless manages to move toward his audience psychologically in ways that cause his audience to move toward him. Attitudinal convergence is accomplished by appeals to common ground. The speaker may offer rational arguments to his audience but they are grounded on shared premises. He may advertise his own expertise but he assures himself first that the image he sells is one his audience wants. Bribes and threats are foresworn; indeed, persuasion and coercion are said to be conceptually antithetical and psychologically incompatible. Finally, the model, having been fashioned from observations of orators addressing relatively passive audiences, is geared more to speech-making or essay-writing than to situations in which two or more persons alternately seek to persuade each other.

The conferees complained that this is not a model for social conflict, or at the very least, that it is by no means the only model. Adherence to the model may help to explain why the field has contributed so little to our understanding of collective bargaining, international diplomacy, militant confrontations, or other activities in which interacting parties, each with vested interests, typically combine reasoned arguments with the power of the carrot and the stick.

One can only speculate as to why other, more realistic models have not been developed. I suspect that this has something to do with the fear that in identifying effective means of persuasion, the field will be charged with being manipulative and exploitative. I suspect, too, that it may have something to do with our aversion toward social conflict, and with the tendency, noted earlier, to treat conflicts as mere disagreements. Perhaps our sense of etiquette is another contributing factor. Conflict behaviors are frequently indecorous, uncivil, and impolite. In fact, as

Schelling (1960) has repeatedly observed, it is often a rational strategy in conflict situations to act as though you are irrational. From a system-oriented perspective, and even from a personal, humanistic perspective, these are not behaviors one is naturally inclined to promote.

Still, if a science of communication in social conflicts is to be developed, professional fears and personal tastes must be put aside. My own chapter explores some of the ways in which persuasive appeals are combined with inducements and constraints. Bowers looks at a variety of persuasive strategies commonly used by agents of commercial institutions and by those consumers who challenge the policies or practices of these institutions. All of the contributors consider persuasion in social conflicts as a genuinely interactive process.

SOME TOUGH QUESTIONS

I said earlier that the conferees were in far greater agreement on what they did not like than on what they did like. As can be expected in a developing social science, they were not agreed on what to study, how to study it, and how to make sense of it once it has been studied. This is especially predictable since the contributors were chosen, in part, for the diversity of their interests. At this stage of our development, exploration of alternative perspectives seems eminently preferable to feigned or forced consensus on a single perspective.

Still, if we are not simply to go our separate ways, we will have to face up to some tough questions. Here, let me preview some of the questions confronted in this book as well as others that were discussed at the conference.

Defining Key Terms

How shall "conflict" be defined? How shall it be differentiated, if at all, from such related terms as "hostility," "disagreement," "incompatibility," "competition," and "misunderstanding"? Is conflict a process, a relational state, a feeling, a set of behaviors, or what? And because there is a conflict over how to define "conflict," how should that conflict be resolved?

From all appearances, the contributors to this volume are in no greater agreement on these issues than were those early conflict theorists whose definitions and distinctions were examined by Mack and Snyder (1957) over fifteen years ago. Not all contributors define "conflict," although all of them at least hint at a definition. Steinfatt and Miller, for example, suggest what they mean by the term in their discussion of types of conflict. Mortensen defines "conflicts" as "expressed struggles over incompatible interests in the distribution of limited resources." Similarly, I define "conflict" as "that state of a social relationship in which incompatible interests between two or more parties give rise to a struggle between them." However, our operationalizations of these definitions are quite different.

How shall "communication" be defined? Is any behavior to be classified as communication or should this term be restricted to symbolic acts (whatever they are) and/or verbal messages? Although the word goes undefined by most contributors, they generally seem to take the broad view of it while focusing on verbal messages and their gestural and inflectional accompaniments. To take a restricted view, of course, would have the effect of denying contributors the opportunity to comment on acts, such as riots, which are of particular significance in terms of the meanings they generate in conflict situations. On the other hand, taking the broad view entails the risk that our own study of conflict will be no different from that of other social scientists. More about that later.

Then, too, there are the many terms in the influence family: "power," "authority," "social control," "cooptation," "coercion," "persuasion," "force," "legitimate influence," and the like. Each term is slippery and confusion is compounded by inconsistent usage. As with the many ambiguous terms in the conflict and communication families, one sometimes wishes for a terminological arbiter who would resolve all disputes. I would be happy to perform the function, but I suspect that my colleagues would not be sympathetic to the idea.

Selecting Levels and Types of Generalization

A. R. Louch (1969) has lamented that generalizations in the social sciences tend either to be trivial, circular, or untrue. He adds that broad generalizations billed as explanations are almost always indictable on one or more of these counts.

Those who deal in *conflict theory,* as opposed to theories about familiar categories of conflict such as marital conflict or labor-management conflict, must be particularly sensitive to Louch's charge. To theorize about conflict per se is to ignore differences between these conventional types, and as a result, perhaps, to miss out on those nuances and subtleties which might help to give generalizations explanatory power. On the other hand, to become too problem- or context-oriented is to risk pitching one's constructs and statements at such a low level of abstraction that few meaningful theoretic propositions are ever generated.

The problem is especially acute for those who wish to theorize about *communication* in conflicts. Communication strategies and effects are invariably governed by the very contextual factors which, for example, make marital conflicts different from labor-management conflicts. For this reason, perhaps, several contributors have narrowed their sights. Bowers confines his chapter to conflicts between individuals and institutions, Tompkins et al. restrict their interest to conflicts within universities, while I focus primarily on political conflicts.

It may be that the real issue is not one of *level* of generalization but rather *type* of generalization. Even among those striving to develop highly abstract, mathematical models of conflict, contingent variables are taken into account. The mathematically oriented game theorists, for example, concede that marital conflicts are different in important ways from labor-management conflicts. They insist, however, that other variables are more significant. For them, it is more important whether the "game" is constant sum or variable sum, involves only two players or several players, perfect information or imperfect information, and so on (Rapoport, 1970). Certainly, one of the great virtues of game theory is its unique way of categorizing conflicts, a classification scheme which permits insightful comparisons between (once again) marital conflicts and labor-management conflicts.

The Quest for Identity

We come now to what may well be the toughest of all questions for a field that has long suffered from problems of identity. Leaving aside issues which do not bear directly on the subject matter of this book, let us simply ask whether there are distinctive contributions for speech communication to make to the study of conflict—contributions for which we are, or can be, better equipped than other disciplines.

Ironically, the problem of self-definition has been aggravated by our increased breadth and sophistication. There was a time, for example, when we so overestimated the significance of platform speaking in political conflicts that some rhetorical critics came close to advocating a theory of oratorical determinism. There was a time, too, when we naively accepted the notion that most conflicts were simply misunderstandings which could be resolved through better listening, or through the use of such semantic devices as indexing, dating, and bracketing. These notions were distinctive in some ways but they were also myopic. Now we have enlarged our scope to include such notions as informal interactions, pseudo-events, coercive persuasion, and body rhetoric, and we have come to appreciate the importance, in conflicts, of such "non-communication" factors as money and physical force. In so doing, however, our interests have merged more closely with those of the political scientist, the economist, the sociologist, and the social psychologist.

The question of identity was discussed at the conference but was left unresolved. Rather than presuming to speak for the others, let me briefly indicate two important tasks which I believe our field is especially equipped to perform.

Identifying Patterns of Interaction in Social Conflicts. Drawing on their rich rhetorical heritage as well as on recent contributions to rhetorical theory and communication theory, scholars in speech communication are in a unique position to characterize *message patterns* in conflict interactions. Until relatively recently our attention to message patterns was confined largely to sequences of arguments and structural arrangements in individual messages. Contemporary theorists have extended that interest to include patterns of action and reaction. This is reflected in the notions of positive and negative feedback loops, in the conception of redundancy in human communication (Watzlawick et al., 1967), and in Mortensen's (1972) double interact. As I suggested earlier, communication in social conflicts is inherently interactive. Unfortunately, we do not as yet have a language of description which can adequately characterize the complex patterns of interaction generally found in social conflicts.

Especially intriguing to me is the Burkeian notion of rhetorical communication as dramatistic. Jumping off from Burke, let me suggest that we attempt to identify *communication scenarios* in social conflicts. By a "communication scenario" I mean *an extended and recurring stochastic process of social interaction.* An example should help to clarify the definition.

During the late sixties, campus confrontations were *recurring* and *extended* processes in the sense that they displayed striking similarities on campus after campus and involved not just two stages but a complex *chain of events* (Simons, 1969). The fact of recurrence made any one chain of events on a given campus relatively predictable. But beyond that, predictability was enhanced by the apparent *internal logic* of the interactive process. Each stage in the chain of events seemed to unfold, and to give impetus to the next stage. Like a Greek tragedy, it almost seemed as though the outcome was inexorable. But not quite! Unlike a computer program, something was left to art and skill—to rhetoric, if you will. It is in this sense that the confrontations could be described as *stochastic processes:* they were chains of events exhibiting lawfulness but not complete predictability.

I believe the concept of a communication scenario can prove to be extremely useful. With careful observation and some imagination we should be able to describe escalation and deescalation scenarios (whether between nations or spouses), collusion scenarios (for example, when management and labor stage a breakdown in contract negotiations in order to wrest benefits from government), and many others. One advantage of attempting to identify complex patterns of events is that, divorced from such contexts, isolated acts often seem to make little sense. Imagine, for example, trying to make sense, acontextually, of the Yippies bringing a pig to Chicago in 1968 or of President S. I. Hayakawa of San Francisco State ripping wires from an outdoor sound system. Another advantage of such accounts is that they do not require additional explanation. As Watzlawick et al. (1967) point out, the lawfulness displayed by a stochastic process is its own best explanation.

Describing and Assessing Conflict Strategies. This point was made earlier in the chapter but let me elaborate upon it here. Schelling (1960) has correctly observed that the subject of conflict strategy is an academic no-man's land. There are any number of approaches, to be sure, but none of the disciplines has as yet succeeded in translating the art of influence in social conflicts into a systematized set of rules. In the sense in which I am using the term, the "art" of influence includes those devices which professional practitioners (e.g., labor mediators, diplomats, etc.) label as "tricks of the trade," and especially those stratagems which rule-makers and rule-breakers devise and implement, as opposed to practices engineered by more ordinary folk. Because of the constraints imposed upon the players, the gaming and simulation laboratories are not the most ideal places for the study of that art. But there are other avenues for such study, and scholars in speech communication are in a unique position to travel them. Conflict stratagems are, after all, eminently rhetorical in nature, and the effort to discover and systematize rules of rhetoric has long been our principal mission.

How shall we approach the study of conflict strategy? Let me suggest that we begin at a descriptive level, by observing what practitioners, especially successful ones, say and do. There are, for example, any number of manuals on conflict strategy: manuals for labor negotiators, political campaigners, right-of-way agents, grantsmen, and military planners. Some have even enjoyed considerable popularity—see, for example, Alinsky's (1971) entertaining yet provocative *Rules for Radicals*. There are, in addition, a great many books and pamphlets written for law enforcement officials as well as for those who would challenge existing laws and practices. Then too, there are biographies and other descriptions of the stratagems employed by noted trial lawyers, political bosses, and robber barons. On this last point, Schelling (1960) has convincingly argued that there is much to be learned about the art of conflict strategy from representatives of the underworld. His book is generously spiced with anecdotes about blackmailers, pirates, con artists, and other assorted lawbreakers. Finally, of course, we can observe practitioners of the art at work, and we can get additional information through interviews. I would propose that we examine these materials with an eye toward discovering unity in diversity—rhetorical devices which conflict strategists in quite different spheres of activity jointly recommend or implement. We will find, I suspect, that there are common threads and that the strategies of influence recommended for social conflicts are not mere carbon copies of those recommended in our own handbooks on persuasion.

The task of assessing stratagems in terms of their effects is, admittedly, much more difficult. One problem is that successful influence cannot be defined in terms of any single criterion. In addition to the test of immediate compliance, one ought probably to consider long-range effects, weigh benefits produced against costs incurred, and estimate attitudinal effects (the latter bear directly on the enforceability of conflict outcomes). For any one act of influence, morever, there are likely to be behavioral and attitudinal effects on a number of subsidiary issues. Conflicts, in general, tend to have spillover effects.

Apart from the question of what dependent variables to study, there is also the problem of isolating independent variables. On this matter I have two brief suggestions. First, it is often possible to make at least crude causal inferences about conflict stratagems through field studies. Such studies are especially fruitful when the researcher is privy to what is being said behind closed doors, when he has access to participants and witnesses at the time of the conflict, and when the practices in question are dramatic enough to have registered as isolated events on the interviewee's consciousness. Whyte's (1951) *Pattern for Industrial Peace* and Tompkins and Anderson's (1971) *Communication Crisis at Kent State* are examples of what I mean, and I would encourage more of the same.

My second suggestion, related to the first, is that we utilize our own classrooms as "fields" for field studies of conflict. Within our classrooms there are potential conflicts and not just academic controversies—conflicts about course methods and goals, conflicts of authority, and conflicts about such procedural issues as whether smoking is to be permitted. Rather than creating game-type conflicts or manipulating subjects into believing they are in conflict when they are not, we can fasten upon already experienced conflicts and utilize our positions to manipulate and study independent variables. I have tried this approach with the smoking issue—pitting smokers against nonsmokers—and I have found, invariably, that I could foment real involvement and have an opportunity to observe conflict stratagems in operation.

A FINAL NOTE

Quite apart from whatever tangible contributions it may offer, this book—as well as the Sugarloaf Conference which nurtured it—has symbolic significance: its sponsorship by the Speech Communication Association bespeaks an institutionalized commitment toward encouraging research and theory on communication in social conflicts by SCA's membership. The need for such study should by now be apparent. It also should be apparent that the field is wide open and that we in speech communication can make a distinctive contribution.

REFERENCES

ALINSKY, S. D., *Rules for Radicals*. New York: Random House, 1971.

COSER, L. A., *The Functions of Social Conflict*. New York: Free Press of Glencoe, 1956.

GAMSON, W. A., *Power and Discontent*. Homewood, Ill.: Dorsey Press, 1968.

LOUCH, A. R., *Explanation and Human Action*. Berkeley and Los Angeles: University of California Press, 1969.

MACK, R. W., and R. C. SNYDER, "The Analysis of Social Conflict—Toward an Overview and Synthesis," *Journal of Conflict Resolution*, 1 (1957), 212–48.

RAPOPORT, A., "Conflict Resolution in the Light of Game Theory and Beyond," in *The Structure of Conflict*, P. Swingle, ed. New York: Academic Press, 1970, pp. 1–43.

SCHELLING, T. C., *The Strategy of Conflict*. Cambridge, Mass.: Harvard University Press, 1960.

SIMONS, H. W., "Confrontation as a Pattern of Persuasion in University Settings," *Central States Speech Journal*, 20 (1969), 163–70.

————, "Persuasion in Social Conflicts: A Critique of Prevailing Conceptions and a Framework for Future Research," *Speech Monographs*, 39 (1972), 227–47.

SKOLNICK, J. H., *The Politics of Protest: A Task Force Report Submitted to The National Commission on the Causes and Prevention of Violence*. New York: Simon and Schuster, 1969.

TOMPKINS, P. K., and E. V. B. ANDERSON, *Communication Crisis at Kent State*. New York: Gordon and Breach, 1971.

WATZLAWICK, P., J. H. BEAVIN, and D. D. JACKSON, *Pragmatics of Human Communication*. New York: W. W. Norton & Co., 1967.

WHYTE, W. F., *Pattern for Industrial Peace*. New York: Harper, 1951.

2

Communication
in
Game Theoretic Models
of
Conflict

THOMAS M. STEINFATT
GERALD R. MILLER

The word "conflict" is ambiguous. When we refer to a conflict, to what class, or classes, of events are we referring? Who is in conflict, and about what? If we approach conflict with an eye toward answering the question, "Who is in conflict?" we can list many conflict types, one for each kind of participant with each other kind of participant. The individual, the family, the clan, the community, the town, the state, the political party, the race, the religion, the work group, the industry, the nation, the guards, the prisoners: if we list all possible antagonists in a conflict and pair each with every possible opponent, there would be $\frac{n^2 - n}{2}$ types of conflict, given n types of antagonists. Thus, our incomplete list of 14 participants yields 91 different types of conflicts. This is not a fruitful way to proceed, for if we define a conflict with respect to its antagonists there will be far too many types of conflict to study. Besides, do all these conflicts differ, or do they all share common characteristics? Although this question must ultimately be answered by research, many approaches to the study of conflict assume that because families, clans, races, nations, and work groups consist of individuals, all conflicts are basically between individuals, and the study of individuals in conflict will shed light on the nature of conflict itself. This is not to deny the many situational variables that influence specialized conflict situations, but only to assert that numerous variables operate similarly across many different types of conflict situations.

Perhaps the basis of the conflict—"*What* is the conflict about?"— affords a more useful approach. Bernard (1957), Rapoport (1960), and Raven and Kruglanski (1970) offer conflict classifications based primarily on features of the conflict situation itself. Although there are several important differences between each of these classification schemes (see Fink, 1968, pp. 426–28), they all distinguish certain basic conflicts.

Conflicts may occur over *ends* or *means*. Ends-conflict is usually more serious: one way of reducing its severity is to redefine the situation so that ends are seen as ultimately common, with the conflict centered on means. Incompatibility of goals suggests conflict grounded in an *impersonal base. Personal bases* of conflict are also possible: these involve questions about the personal attractiveness of the antagonist. Conflict can arise from either source, but the two are often so intertwined that it is impossible for the antagonists to separate them. It is difficult to admire the personal characteristics of an individual who strongly opposes one's achievement of a cherished goal.

Conflicts about ends are sometimes called *conflicts of value* or *goal conflicts.* Aubert (1963) distinguishes between *conflicts of value* and *conflicts of interest:* conflicts of value keep the antagonists apart while conflicts of interest draw them together. A conflict of interest implies at least some minimum consensus about what is valuable, with the conflict stemming from a scarcity of the valued commodity. The parties in an interest conflict have at least one common need or aspiration which tends to draw together to resolve the conflict, as in a market situation or the case of two politicians who compete fiercely for office but get along well when not opposing each other in an election. In contrast, conflicts of value imply dissension over what is to be valued. The parties in a value conflict often move away from each other because people tend to associate with others of similar value structure (Rokeach, 1967). A somewhat similar distinction emerges in Rapoport's (1960) discussion of *fights,* characterized by mutual fear and hostility; *games,* typified by agreement on goals and rules; and *debates,* disagreements about what is or what ought to be. A fight might result from a conflict of values, while the consensus in an interest conflict would lead the parties toward an agreement on goals and rules as in a game.

Bernard (1957) singles out verbal or conceptual misunderstanding, a *semantic* conflict, as a separate type. Finally, Deutsch (1969) differentiates *manifest* and *underlying* conflict. Manifest conflict represents the stated reason for controversy. Sometimes manifest conflict may resemble the impersonal conflict situation mentioned above. A family sits down to dinner; there is little talk; they eat quietly. Suddenly the husband accidently spills his coffee when reaching for the salt. The wife explodes and castigates him for causing her more work. He responds by attacking her cooking. Although the manifest conflict is obvious, the underlying conflict may be deeply buried in the couple's relationship.

There are numerous approaches to the study of conflict, several of which are discussed in other chapters of this book. The approach that underlies this chapter is labeled *game theory*. Game theory recognizes all types of bases of conflict, but concentrates on *rational* features of the conflict situation; i.e., on rational self-interests pursued by the conflicting parties through their choices of alternative courses of action with different potential payoffs for the parties. Not surprisingly, it deals primarily with game-type conflicts rather than debates or outright fights. Its concern is with manifest, impersonal conflict over means or goals, not with semantic misunderstandings or intrapersonal tensions.

Game theory is concerned with how to win a game, with strategies of move sequences that maximize the player's chance for gain and minimize his chance for loss. Because a major ingredient in conflict situations is the desire to gain something one does not possess and to hold onto that which one does possess, certain games are analogous to particular conflict situations and game theory serves as a model to predict the behavior of persons in such conflict situations attempting to gain those ends. The rational features of the conflict situation serve as the independent variables or predictors for this model, which states the probabilities that a move or move sequence will be in a player's best self-interest.

Game theory is not concerned with the psychological makeup of the players, the reduction of hostility, the redefinition of goals and interests that would change the value of certain payoffs to the players, or like matters. As students of the communication behavior of human beings we are interested in such matters. We choose to employ game theory as a model to predict behavior in conflict situations because it considers the point of view of the individual faced with the conflict situation. A model such as systems theory ignores this point of view and treats the conflict as the outcome of the interaction of forces and stresses which define the structure and dynamics of large social organizations. But having made this choice we do not feel constrained by it to the extent that we would ignore the beliefs, attitudes, and values of the participants. Our principal concern is with communication and the behaviors it produces, and we feel free to add relevant communication variables to the game theory model of human behavior in a conflict situation. We call this approach *game theoretic* and distinguish it from *game theory,* the purely rational theory of games.

THE TERMINOLOGY
OF GAME THEORY

Game theory deals with rationally conducted conflicts between players *(actors, participants, parties)* each of whom (1) pursues well-defined *interests,* and (2) chooses between at least two alternative courses of action *(choices, moves).* These interests are represented by the numbers in the cells in Figure 1 which are the payoffs resulting from particular choices by each player such as *a* and *c.* Ideally, no time limit is imposed upon the moves. This allows each player to ponder thoroughly the consequences of his moves.

Three types of games may be distinguished: games of *physical skill,* games of *chance,* and games of *strategy.* Some complex games have all three elements; for instance, tennis and football are primarily games of strategy and physical skill, but chance enters into each. Game theory is principally concerned with games of strategy. In games of strategy, players make a sequence of choices or moves whose consequences are conditional upon the choices of other players. Although games of pure chance or pure strategy seldom occur in real life, chance may be conceptualized as a player in a game of strategy whose choices (moves) are perfectly random, resulting in a game of chance and strategy. If chance is the only player who can make real choices, the game becomes one of pure chance, because chance has no interests and no strategic skills.

Games of strategy are classified as either *two-person* or n-*person* games and as either *constant sum* or *nonconstant sum* games. Constant sum games are either *zero sum* or *non-zero sum,* though in practice this distinction is minor. In zero sum games, the *reward (payoff)* for both players must sum to zero, while in non-zero constant sum games, the reward total for both players is any constant but non-zero number such as 1 or 53.572. For one player to win in a zero sum game, the other must lose by an equal amount. In any constant sum game, zero or non-zero, the interests of the players are diametrically opposed, for any payoff received by one necessarily reduces the payoff to the others (see Figure 1).

This pure opposition of interests sets apart most constant sum

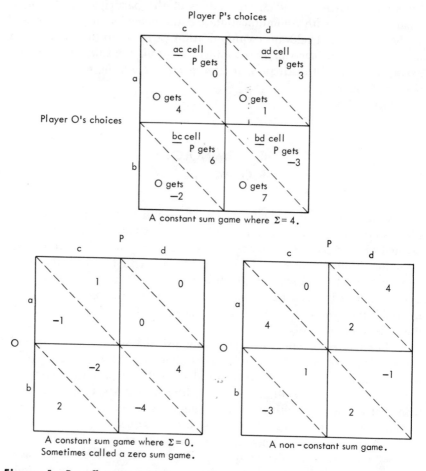

Figure 1   Payoff matrices for three experimental games.

games. In nonconstant sum games, the interests of all players are partially opposed and partially congruent, a situation more closely akin to most real-life conflicts. Nonconstant sum games are often called mixed-motive if and only if at least two distinct motives exist, each suggesting a different move by a given player.

If the strategies (sequence of choices) of various players in non-constant sum games are *joint*—i.e., if they take into account the interests and payoffs of other players in consideration for reciprocal choices on their part—the game is characterized as *cooperative;* if not, the game is *noncooperative.* Cooperative games are occasionally referred to as *games of communication,* while noncooperative games are called *games of no communication.* This distinction is not strictly correct, because symbolic communication may or may not occur when strategies are joint.

Agreement on a joint strategy by two or more players is called an *alliance.* Such agreement may occur in two different ways. If communication is defined as the use of mutually understood symbolic behavior, an alliance may result from mutual observation and response to actual moves or from communication of proposed move sequences or strategies. Phillips (1967) specifies five types of alliances. In a *coordinating social unit* each member's actions maintain or increase the expected payoff for all other members, but no actual communication toward this end occurs. A *cooperative social unit* is a coordinating social unit which reaches its agreement via communication but which does not allow side payments. A *common-fate alliance* embraces both communication and side payments.

The preceding three alliances are possible in both two-person and *n*-person groups of greater than two: a *collusion* is a cooperative social unit with an opponent while a *coalition* is a common-fate alliance with an opponent. Finally, for the sake of completeness, a sixth type of alliance, a *coordinating social unit with an opponent,* should be added to Phillips' five.

Side payments constitute one form of creative solution to a game. If communication occurs, it sometimes takes the form of *bargaining* as to the apportionment of gains and losses obtained by the coalition. Agreements reached through bargaining, communication, or the formation of a coordinating social unit are instances of conflict resolution. In formal game theory, the conflict resolved involves only rational conflict over proposed distributions of payoffs and ignores the emotions of the players and their attitudes toward ultimate goals that are apart from the immediate conflict situation.

All games have *rules* that specify whose move it is, what alternatives are open in each situation, and what situations signify the game's end. A *rational player* chooses a strategy that maximizes his gains and minimizes his losses given the rules of the game and the alternatives open to other players. Strategies may be pure or mixed: a strategy selected before the beginning of play which specifies the alternative to be chosen in any given situation is said to be pure, while if more than one pure strategy is open to a player, a mixed strategy specifies the probability of a move from a pure strategy being chosen in a particular situation. Depending on the rules of the game, there may exist for each player either a pure or a mixed strategy which is the *best strategy* or *optimal strategy;* i.e., it yields the best payoff in a statistical sense over many trials. *Games of nonperfect information,* such as card games, which begin with an arrangement of cards that is unknown to a player, usually, but not always, have a best mixed strategy for that player. Usually chance is the only player who knows the card arrangement, because she shuffled them.

Given this brief introduction to the terminology of game theory, we may now discuss certain studies which have examined conflict situations from a game theoretic perspective. First, we will review the literature of gaming studies of conflict in which communication has not been allowed or has been severely restricted. Then, using these studies as a background, we will define what we mean by communication in a game conflict and go on to review studies of conflict in which communication has been treated as a variable.

TYPICAL STUDIES
INVOLVING GAME THEORY
IN CONFLICT SITUATIONS [1]

Game theory's formal existence can be traced to the publication of *Theory of Games and Economic Behavior* by Von Neumann and Morganstern, in 1944, but evidence of interest in many game theoretic problems may be found in writings as early as the 1700s. The mathematicians Waldgrove and Bernouilli were aware of the concept of a mixed strategy as early as 1713. Since 1944, there has been considerable work using a game theory paradigm, and there are at least fourteen journals currently publishing articles directly related to behavior in games. Initial research concentrated on zero sum and other constant sum two-person games, partly because the mathematics of linear programming bears a strong relationship to the solution of such games.

Cooperation and Competition

Beginning with a study by Mintz (1951), research emphasis began to shift to studies of cooperation and competition in mixed-motive games. Mintz attached strings to cones placed in a bottle with a narrow neck. He then asked each subject to pull a cone out of the bottle before it got wet, since the bottle was slowly filling with water. Although sufficient time was allowed for all cones to be pulled out without becoming soggy, few were actually extricated due to traffic jams at the bottleneck. Instructions emphasizing coordination within the group increased the number of successes.

[1] The authors wish to thank Jerry K. Frye, of SUNY, Buffalo, for his assistance in compiling the bibliography.

In a related experiment, Kelley (1953) found that increased threat of punishment for failure resulted in correspondingly fewer successful escapes from the situation. This phenomenon has frequently been demonstrated under nonexperimental conditions. The Cocoanut Grove fire in Boston during World War II, which took almost 500 lives, is a case in point; such tragedies as this graphically illustrate why fire codes specify that doors must open outward in public establishments.

In a mixed-motive game, a player has a reason, or motive, for wanting to play either of two or more of his alternatives. If both players have motives which support either choice, then their interests usually partly conflict and partly coincide. Most game theory research has used mixed-motive games in which the maximum gain choice for an individual player results in losses to everyone when all players choose it. Such games punish competition and reward cooperation; a "cooperative" choice is built into the reward matrix. Gallo and McClintock (1965) defend this approach, asserting that "mutually cooperative behavior between members leads to the formation and maintenance of groups, and mutually competitive behavior results in the disruption of groups. . . . The fundamental assumption made in [international politics] is that cooperation leads to the resolution of conflict, whereas competition leads to a continuation and intensification of conflict" (pp. 68–69).

Criticism of
Cooperation Versus Competition

Coser (1956), who built upon the work of the German sociologist, Simmel, would probably question the view expressed by Gallo and McClintock. Quoting from the writings of Machiavelli, Marx, and Whitehead, Coser suggests that [2]

> Far from being only a "negative" factor which "tears apart," social conflict may fulfill a number of determinate functions in groups and other interpersonal relations; it may, for example, contribute to the maintenance of group boundaries and prevent the withdrawal of members from a group. Commitment to the view that social conflict is necessarily destructive to the relationship within which it occurs leads, as we shall see, to highly deficient interpretations. (p. 8)

Later, he adds that

> The absence of conflict cannot be taken as an index of the strength and stability of a relationship. Stable relationships may be characterized by

[2] Alfred North Whitehead wrote, "The clash of doctrines is not a disaster, it is an opportunity," in *Science and the Modern World*.

conflicting behavior. Closeness gives rise to frequent occasions for conflict, but if the participants feel that their relationships are tenuous, they will avoid conflict, fearing that it might endanger the continuance of the relation. When close relationships are characterized by frequent conflicts rather than by the accumulation of hostile and ambivalent feelings, we may be justified, given that such conflicts are not likely to concern basic consensus, in taking these frequent conflicts as an index of the stability of these relationships. (p. 85)

Thus, as long as consensus is maintained, conflict may be functional as well as dysfunctional.

Phillips and Conner (1970) also criticize the heavy emphasis on cooperative behavior in most gaming research, typified by the Prisoner's Dilemma game which is discussed below. Their criticism stems from different grounds than Coser's and is twofold. First, they argue that knowledge of the way a conflict is generated provides a crucial key to its resolution and that Prisoner's Dilemma experiments involve artificial conflict. Thus, its method of resolution may be unrelated to methods of resolving rationally created conflict. Second, the Prisoner's Dilemma reward matrix contains a cooperative solution that provides each player with a satisfactory payoff. Phillips and Conner object to excessive concern with conflicts which can be resolved cooperatively with mutual satisfaction by a simple readjustment of behavior. They point out that conflict over a narrow band of issues may be noncompromisible and the search for a cooperative solution in such cases is meaningless.

Conflict of this latter form may be termed *uelative conflict.* Its prototype is the *duel;* for Aaron Burr and Alexander Hamilton, a cooperative solution was impossible. The expansion of a duel to three-person situations, where only one player at most can gain a positive payoff, is labeled a *truel.* The n-person duel is called an n-*uel,* thus the term *uelative conflict.* The payoff structure in uelative conflict is such that at best only one of the n-players can achieve a gain, although such a gain is by no means guaranteed. The game of Chicken provides one example of a uelative conflict. Rapoport and Chammah (1965) and Swingle (1970) discuss the structure of Chicken and other so-called dangerous games.

Two kinds of outcomes may result from a uelative conflict such as Chicken. *Status quo instability* is characterized by the period of time during a game of Chicken when each player attempts to bluff the other. When one player finally weakens and swerves, the outcome may be called a *forced solution.*

As in much of the gaming research to be discussed below, uelative conflicts such as Chicken rest on an assumption of no communication. Phillips and Conner argue that attention should be refocused on creative alternatives to status quo instabilities and forced solutions. Rather than structuring the game so that a cooperative solution is inherent in the situation, they suggest the addition of an interactive process (communication) between the participants. Such an addition would allow the participants to create new solutions to the conflict which do not exist in the structural framework.

Cooperation and Competition in Prisoner's Dilemma

Even if one grants the validity of the preceding criticisms, the conditions fostering cooperation or competition are still of great interest. Regarding one form of mutual mixed-motive games, Prisoner's Dilemma, Gallo and McClintock (1965) believe that

> It answers the long-felt need in social psychology of a well-controlled interaction situation with an easily quantifiable and unambiguous dependent variable, the number of cooperative responses made by each subject. In addition, it provides an excellent framework within which problems of motivation, decision making, personality, and perception of persons can be studied.
> Perhaps even more important is the fact that the decisions that have to be made by the subjects in the game are very similar to decisions that are made in real life bargaining and conflict situations. The players have a real stake in cooperating, and yet at the same time there are realistic reasons why they should compete. Many researchers see the decisions and strategies in the Prisoner's Dilemma as prototypes of the more complex decisions and strategies in labor-management bargaining and international negotiations. (p. 70)

This section on cooperation and competition concentrates largely on research generated in Prisoner's Dilemma (PD) games, because more carefully controlled, internally valid studies are available for PD than for any other single game. Their availability facilitates comparison of results across different studies and avoids confusion over different findings from different game matrices. Certain non-PD games will be discussed, but these will be carefully labeled as games different in form from the Prisoner's Dilemma.

Figure 2 displays a payoff matrix for Prisoner's Dilemma. Player O has two possible moves, a and b. If O plays a, he receives either $+1$ or -2 units of reward, depending on P's choice. If O chooses b, he gets $+2$ or -1 units of reward, depending on P's move. P's payoffs are similarly determined by a combination of both players' moves. Given this matrix, a and c are the cooperative choices, b and d the competitive. Each player

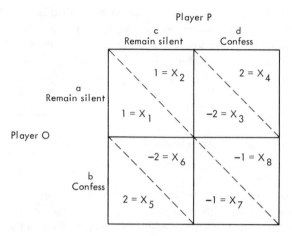

Figure 2 A typical Prisoner's Dilemma payoff matrix.

realizes that the competitive strategy is best for him personally, for it offers the possibility of the greatest gain with the least loss. But if both players make the competitive choice, both will lose. Any game matrix which takes the following form represents a PD game:

$$X_1 = X_2, \ X_7 = X_8, \ X_3 = X_6, \ X_4 = X_5.$$

$$2X_1 > X_3 + X_4 > 2X_8, \ X_5 > X_1, \ X_5 > X_6, \text{ and } X_8 > X_6.$$

Any game for which these inequalities do not hold is not a PD game (see Figure 2).

The name "Prisoner's Dilemma" is derived from one explanation of the game given to persons who play it. Suppose P and O are two prisoners just apprehended by the local police. They are separated and told they have two choices: remain silent or confess. The two choices are displayed in Figure 2. The dilemma centers on whether each can trust the other to remain silent. For if one confesses, he will go free and be rewarded by the police while the other will receive a heavy sentence. If both confess, both will go to jail, but they will receive relatively light sentences. Finally, if each remains silent, trusting the other will also do so, the police will have no case, and both will be released after only a few days in jail.

By definition, the *rational solution* to any game is to play the move that maximizes gains and minimizes losses. In Figure 2 the *b* and *d* choices provide the greatest possibility for gain and the least possibility for loss. Thus, game theory holds that two rational players in a PD game should both confess, whereby both lose. This prediction considers only the rational (self-interest) features of the game from one player's viewpoint. When played over multiple trials the game theory prediction remains the same: the only rational solution is for both players to defect from their trust of the other and to confess. Consequently, the *a* and *c* choices in Figure 2 are sometimes called the *trusting* or *cooperative* choices, while the *b* and *d* choices are called *defecting* or *competitive*.

Although game theory predicts the rational solution, early students of PD games (e.g., Luce and Raiffa, 1957) suggested that after numerous trials players might settle on the cooperative (*ac*) choice because of the punishment associated with the competitive (*bd*) choice. Early studies (e.g., Flood, 1958; Scodel et al., 1959) yielded no support for this position. Instead, the game theory prediction was usually supported, with fewer than 50 percent cooperative choices reported in almost every experiment published before 1965. Typically, 60 to 80 percent of the choices were competitive, demonstrating that players did not eventually settle on a joint cooperative strategy that would maximize their payoffs.

Given that PD players tend to choose a competitive rather than a cooperative strategy, it seems natural to ask if certain kinds of players vary in competitiveness, and if other variables affect the general level of competition or cooperation. Rapoport and Chammah (1965) emphasize the importance of the number of trials, or iterations, of the game. They believe that in order to produce important differences in game-playing behavior, a series of at least 100 trials is necessary. Their reasoning is based on what Rapoport (1965) calls the *equilibrium trap*. If fewer than 100 trials are played, subjects may become bored or apprehensive but still feel they can "hang on" for a few more trials. As the number of trials rises steadily past 100, the subjects experience more pressure. They become uncertain that the game will end soon, and the pressure to escape from the equilibrium trap increases.

At least two major factors emerge in long runs that are not revealed in a shorter series of trials. First, cooperative choice behavior usually begins at a level somewhat below 50 percent. There is an initial decline in cooperation, usually up to thirty to fifty trials. If the trials continue, this decline is reversed and the level of cooperation reaches or, in some cases, exceeds the initial level of cooperation. McClintock and McNeel (1966) used Belgian students in a *Maximizing Difference* (MD) game and found a decline in cooperation followed by a recovery, indicating that the finding is apparently not culture-bound. (The MD game is similar to the PD, except that the cooperative choice results in the greatest payoff for both players. For example, the matrix in Figure 2 would depict an MD game if the values in the *ac* box were both +3 instead of +1). Game theory would predict a rational strategy of complete cooperation under MD conditions, but "apparently the subjects would rather compete than ride the gravy train, even though competition punishes both" (Rapoport, 1966, p. 87).

The second factor that emerges in long runs is differences in amount of cooperation as a function of the sex of the players. For mixed pairs (male-female), there are no apparent differences in long or short runs. When long runs of male pairs are compared with long runs of female pairs, the women consistently make about half as many cooperative choices as the men. In other words, over a long number of trials, women are more likely than men to defect from a trusting strategy when playing against an opponent of the same sex (Rapoport and Chammah, 1965).

Possibly, this sex difference results from different socialization patterns. In our society men are brought up to be more interested than women in playing most games. This difference in interest manifests itself in a generally more active style of play by men. In PD, it requires action or initiative to break out of a *bd* response pattern with cooperative choices or to play a reciprocating cooperation (tit-for-tat) strategy. Using a non-PD game, Vincent and Schwerin (1971) found that women played more cooperatively than men. As Rapoport (1971) suggests, an explanation of sex differences based on different levels of activity may also be applicable to this finding. In Vincent and Schwerin's game, men were found to be generally more active than women. This activity may have manifested itself in a more aggressive style of play by men, producing the misleading conclusion that females were more cooperative than males, just as a more aggressive style of play might yield more cooperative choices by men in PD games.

Although many other variables have been investigated, few have been shown to be related to cooperative choice behavior. If subjects play against a strategy preprogrammed by the experimenter, though they are told they are playing against another person whom they cannot see, neither a preprogrammed strategy of 100 percent cooperative nor 100 percent defecting responses has much effect on the level of subjects' cooperative responses, although the 100 percent cooperative program produces significantly more cooperation during early trials. The subject's usual response is to guess (correctly) that he is not playing against another person.

The only preprogrammed strategy shown to be consistently effective in increasing the proportion of cooperative responses is a *tit-for-tat* strategy in which the response matches whatever the subject played on the previous trial (Solomon, 1960; Rapoport et al., 1965). Playing 300 trials against a tit-for-tat strategy, both men and women produce 70 to 80 percent cooperative responses (Rapoport, 1966). Comparing individual players with pairs of players (who had to agree on the move their side would make) over 150 trials, Pylyshyn, Agnew, and Illingsworth

(1966) reported 64 percent cooperative responses by the former to a tit-for-tat strategy and 80 percent cooperative responses by the latter.

Bixenstine and Gaebelein (1971) studied the effects over 150 trials of five strategies that were contingent upon the moves of the subject. Tit-for-tat is a contingent strategy which follows each subject's play with a like response from the other on the following play. Bixenstine and Gaebelein called tit-for-tat a Quick-Quick strategy, because any play by a subject was answered in kind immediately. In addition they investigated a Quick (to cooperate)-Slow (to compete) strategy, a Slow-Quick strategy, a Slow-Slow strategy, and a Trap-Slow strategy. A Slow strategy was defined as a .6 probability of responding in kind on the first response after the subject's move, a .8 probability of responding in kind to the second consecutive subject response of a kind, and a 1.0 probability of responding in kind to three or more consecutive subject responses of a kind. A Trap strategy was defined as a 1.0, .8, and .6 probability of responding in kind to a move by the subject after one, two, and three or more consecutive responses of a kind, respectively. This Trap strategy tended to lull the subject into making cooperative responses so the other could take advantage of him.

Results indicated that the Slow-Slow strategy was even more effective in producing cooperative responses than the Quick-Quick (tit-for-tat) strategy. There was no significant difference between the Quick-Quick and Quick-Slow strategies in producing cooperation, but both were significantly better than the Slow-Quick and Trap-Slow strategies. The Slow-Slow strategy evoked a level of cooperation approaching 80 percent, the highest level of cooperative choice reported for individuals playing a PD game. The lesson, according to Bixenstine and Gaebelein is that

> Turning the other cheek (or being slow-to-compete) is fine, but for maximum influence in producing mutually gainful behavior, it is best wed to a cautious exposure of one's cheek to begin with! Or stated differently: to induce maximum cooperation in another, be suspicious and enter into trusting behavior gradually, but at the same time, be tolerant of and slow to retaliate to his acts of untrustworthiness. (p. 164)

Other PD studies have demonstrated that runs of five or more cooperative or competitive responses in a row produce a locking-in effect on the subject's responses that is difficult to break (Rapoport and Chammah, 1965). Moreover, there is some evidence that a preprogrammed strategy which moves from primarily uncooperative to primarily cooperative responses is more effective in producing cooperation than is the reverse strategy (Scodel, 1962, 1963; Bixenstine and Wilson, 1963). Scodel also found that pregame discussions of how to play the game increased cooperation, and Deutsch (1958) achieved over 70 percent co-operation by using instructions stressing that the goal of the subjects should be to obtain the maximum joint payoff. The Deutsch and the Scodel studies will be discussed at greater length below.

Finally, Oskamp (1971) conducted post hoc analyses of his own and other researchers' PD data and concluded that persons who (1) experience an *ac* outcome on the first trial, (2) receive a fairly high level of early cooperation, (3) give a fairly high level of early cooperation without witnessing a dramatic defection from the other, or (4) establish a mutually cooperative relationship during the game are more likely to become highly cooperative toward the end of the game.

A word of caution concerning the interpretation of the cooperation and competition results is in order. Rapoport (1971) has suggested that cooperation is partially defined by the game situation in which a player finds himself. In a game with a nonsymmetrical payoff matrix, for example, cooperation by Player X may require him to submit to the will of Player Y, while cooperation by Player Y may involve voluntarily giving up part of his payoff to X if X does submit. Clearly then, cooperation means different things in different situations, and any conclusions about variables which enhance the level of cooperation should be drawn across studies where the operational definition of cooperation is clearly specified and constant.

HIGH AND LOW PAYOFFS AS REAL AND IMAGINARY REWARDS

Gallo (1963) suggested that game behavior may be quite different when subjects are playing for *imaginary* rather than *real rewards*. The terms "real" and "imaginary" are used in a phenomenological sense; i.e., they refer to the subject's perception of the nature of the reward. Gallo argues that the greater the desirability of the reward, the greater the reality of the game for the player. With perceived reward low, the payoffs, and thus the game itself, tend to be seen by the player as more imaginary.

The findings on cooperation and competition cited above were obtained almost exclusively in studies using low or imaginary rewards as payoffs to the subjects. How might these subjects perceive the characteristics of the experimental situation? Typically, the subject is told that he is going to play a game and that he will have a chance to win points. He may be asked to imagine that these points represent money, or that they may actually be exchanged for money at some very low rate of exchange at the end of the game. It does not require a mighty intellect nor a highly sophisticated game player to be aware, either from the beginning or after a few trials, that the structure of the game dictates a long, repetitious sequence of cooperative choices if the player is to maximize his own gain. In addition, however, this sequence also maximizes the other player's gain. Thus, as Gallo and McClintock (1965) point out, "If the reward has no real value to him, it would be far more interesting to invent a new game in which the object is to maximize the difference between his own payoffs and those of his opponent" (p. 76).

On the other hand, if the reward is important to the player, he may shun amusing diversions and treat the game as a "real" situation. This does not imply that laboratory research is artificial; indeed, the subject's behavior in a laboratory is every bit as real as his behavior in any other situation. But under high reward conditions, experiments in gaming behavior share common features with certain kinds of nonlaboratory situations. Chief among these features is the motivation to maximize one's own reward, as opposed to maximizing the *difference* between one's own reward and the reward of the other players. Given nonlaboratory conflicts where there is high motivation to increase the reward differential between the participants, the low reward studies may serve as the best model. But for conflicts involving self-interest without regard for the reward of the other, high reward studies seem more appropriate.

Strangely enough, certain types of cooperation are much more likely when a player concerns himself only with maximizing his own reward, instead of considering the reward level of the other players. Deutsch and Krauss (1962) used a trucking game which required pairs of subjects to learn to take turns using a narrow section of roadway. When two subjects learn to cooperate, both show a profit. But if both refuse to cooperate in using the roadway, both lose money. Deutsch and Krauss found that most pairs of players show a profit over twenty trials. However, a second group of subjects who were given gates to place in the path of the opponent's truck suffered large losses over the twenty trials and failed to learn the cooperative strategy. Both Deutsch and Krauss (1963) and Borah (1963) have replicated this second finding.

Kelley (1962, 1965) has criticized the operational ambiguity of the threat construct in the trucking game, inasmuch as the gates could be used for many different purposes (punishment, revenge, signaling). Horai and Tedeschi (1969) and Tedeschi, Bonoma, and Novison (1970) concur with Kelley that the use of the gates by trucking game participants is subject to multiple interpretations. Even with this limitation, the trucking game studies are still of interest.

Gallo (1963) extended Deutsch and Krauss' 1962 study by increasing the reward 4.5 times for all conditions and by adding a condition of real monetary rewards. Maximum payoff for any one trial was $1.15, and complete cooperation throughout resulted in a reward of $16 for each subject. All of Gallo's subjects were given barriers. Subjects in the imaginary money condition lost an amount directly comparable to the loss of the barrier group in the original Deutsch and Krauss group. Fourteen pairs in Gallo's real money condition showed a profit compared with only two in the imaginary money condition. Real money pairs improved earnings significantly over trials and decreased barrier use significantly in the barrier conditions, a style of play not found in the imaginary reward condition.

McClintock and McNeel (1966), using Belgian students in an MD game, also observed more cooperative choices in high than in low reward conditions. Thus, the level of perceived reward appears to be directly related to the motivation of subjects in these games. Highly motivated subjects apparently play to maximize their own profit, while subjects with low motivation may seek to increase their interest in the game by maximizing the difference between themselves and another player.

Shubik (1970) reaches a similar conclusion, arguing that if the real payoff to the subject is not clearly crucial, then the subject's choices should be interpreted as a reaction to boredom or as cutthroat behavior rather than as a response to the rational, observable properties of the experiment or game. It seems clear, however, that some game situations purposely investigate the effects of boredom. Rapoport (1965) argues in favor of long numbers of trials on the basis that certain differences occur only after many iterations of a game. Still, it is uncertain that findings resulting from large numbers of iterations or results of games where the real reward to a participant is low can be generalized to predict the outcomes of high reward conflict where neither party considers the situation boring.

THREE METHODS OF COMING TO KNOW

In each of the games studied, conflict exists. Nonlaboratory conflicts can occur over many things and can arise in many ways. In most of the above research, the conflict involves a problem for the player. If he is to maximize his gains and minimize his losses, he must make the move on each trial that will take best overall advantage of his opponent's move. In order to choose his best move, the player strives to know in advance what his opponent is going to do. Obviously, if he knows for sure what his opponent will do in a given instance, he will have little trouble determining his own best move.

There are three distinct ways a player may come to know his opponent's strategy. The first is to observe the opponent's behavior, to watch which responses he makes to the player's own moves. This approach fits nicely into a learning theory, stimulus-response paradigm. The player using this approach gains all the advantages and risks all the pitfalls of the strict behaviorist. The principal advantage is that he can ignore the complexities of his opponent's cognitive and affective states. The player need only observe the behavioral end product of all these cognitive and affective factors and record it accurately, a relatively simple task. The major disadvantage is that as the complexity of the opposing strategy increases, a large sample of behavior is required for accurate prediction. The number of trials required may surpass the game limits, and the player will suffer such massive losses while learning his opponent's strategy that he can never hope to recoup even if he masters it.

After the player has learned his opponent's strategy well enough to choose his own responses wisely, he may encounter another problem common to the strict behaviorist. Responses which seemed to be concomitants of a relatively simple stimulus pattern may now occur with new stimuli as part of a more complex stimulus pattern, and new responses may occur with the simple stimulus pattern. This change could result from two factors: either the opponent has learned what the player is doing and is changing his responses accordingly (a mixed strategy), in which case the player's long and patient observation goes for naught, or the opponent's strategy is pure but more complex than was originally apparent from the small sample of responses available. Either or both may be true, but the distinction between them is largely irrelevant for the player, since the practical result is about the same. He must observe more trials and continue to lose while he is doing it, for he cannot hope to learn his opponent's strategy if he makes responses based only on his own best move. This behaviorist approach to determining opposing strategy apparently occurs in many of the studies reported above. In games where no communication is allowed and the payoff matrix is not displayed, it is the only way to determine an opponent's strategy.

The second way to learn an opponent's strategy is to observe the situation. Instead of concentrating on the moves the opponent makes, the player may observe the whole situation in which his opponent finds himself and look for clues that allow for the prediction of future moves. This alternative is similar to the phenomenological approach; it seeks to determine the opponent's perception of his situation, using observations of the situation as reference points and considering the opponent's personality and general belief structure.

A simplified version of this method involves the assumptions of a unified perception of the situation by all concerned and a lack of effect for any personality variables. In this case, one need only observe the payoff matrix. The advantage of this method is that only one observation of the payoff matrix is necessary; as a result of this single observation, the various strategy possibilities of the opponent become apparent. The disadvantages stem from the extent to which the common-perception and the no-personality-effects assumptions are valid for a particular situation and the extent to which perfect information exists. Accurate assessments of personality require test results normally unavailable to a player. Educated guesses about personality types are substituted, and the results are often highly inaccurate, especially as stereotyping occurs. To use a non-game example, the stereotype of the agitator held by the administrator and the stereotype of the administrator held by the agitator often provide preconceived models for branding any action by the other side as hostile, no matter how conciliatory it may be. In fact, guesses about the antagonist's personality may themselves sow the seeds for new conflict between the players.

The assumption of common perceptions of the reward structure may also be invalid, particularly as the rewards tend toward abstractions like "love" or "peace" and away from concrete rewards such as money. In such cases, perfect information about an opponent's reward structure is seldom available. Moreover, factors such as differential utility may change the value a person attaches to even such relatively concrete items as candy or cigarettes. The usual practice is to combine the observation of the reward structure and the guess as to the apparent type of opponent with observations of the adversary's moves. Combining these two methods of knowing improves chances for accurate prediction early in the game.

The third way a player may come to know his opponent's strategy is to ask him. The advantages of this method are that it takes very little time and that it potentially gives access to the opponent's perceptions of the reward structure. Also, in terms of non-game criteria, asking lowers the probability of potential violence becoming a reality. There is a reasonable chance that once lowered, this probability will not return to its former level, but this depends mainly on what takes place during communication.

Because people do not usually talk and fight simultaneously, communication may be useful even if it accomplishes nothing in the way of exchanging information about strategies. Ideally, communication makes it possible to conduct the entire conflict at the symbolic level, with each player stating how he would respond to the stated, rather than the actual moves of the other. Though some real moves may be unavoidable, many of the bad consequences of these moves may be avoided by communication. In addition, a solution reached through negotiations has a better chance of representing the interests of all the involved parties. During international conflicts, we often assume that preparatory communication has occurred before real moves are executed; for example, at the time of the mining of Haiphong Harbor, it was widely believed that Henry Kissinger had discussed this move with the North Vietnamese in Paris.

Besides avoiding the hostility, disruption, and subsequent losses resulting from actual moves, negotiations allow the parties to move away from a winner-take-all position toward a solution that provides some rewards for everyone. If the negotiators can hit upon creative solutions, mixed-motive, constant non-zero sum, and even certain zero sum games may be solved in ways such that residual hostility, tension, and conflict are kept at a level acceptable to all.

For example, a man may want his wife to attend a football game with him while she wants him to escort her to a concert which is being given at the same time. A creative solution to this form of zero sum conflict might be to find another concert and/or football game and to let the loser in the first instance become the winner in the second. This solution, impossible without communication, may even change the pay-off matrix so that football games (which were +1 for the man and −1 for the woman) and concerts (which were −1 for the man and +1 for the woman) now retain their +1 value for the man and woman respectively, but the −1 values formerly held by both change toward zero or even become slightly positive.

Obviously, reliance upon communication as a means of knowing has its potential disadvantages. The opponent may lie, be incapable of providing the needed information, or simply refuse to provide it. Some of the reasons for his refusal are discussed at length by Schelling (1960). For example, if X wishes to threaten Y but Y is either not around to be threatened or simply assures by some means that the threat cannot be communicated to him, the threat will have no force and Y's position will be strengthened. The woman who wants her husband to take out the garbage and tells him what will happen if he does not will have no real impact if he has the television turned up too loudly to hear her. The studies reported below allowed at least one form of communication or attempted communication between players. Thus, players in these studies were not mutually limited to the behavioristic or phenomenological ways of knowing about an opponent's strategy; they could also communicate.

COMMUNICATION IN
GAME-TYPE STUDIES OF CONFLICT

Watzlawick, Beavin, and Jackson (1967) have suggested that the interaction involved in PD games, particularly the mutual choice of the defecting move, is perhaps the most elegant abstract representation of a problem encountered over and over again in marriage psychotherapy. Spouses who live lives of quiet desperation, deriving minimum gratification from their joint experiences, have been known to psychiatrists for a long time. *Traditionally, however, the reason for their misery is sought in the assumed individual pathology of one or both of them.* They may be diagnosed as depressive, passive-aggressive, self-punishing, sadomasochistic, and so on. *But these diagnoses obviously fail to grasp the interdependent nature of their dilemma, which may exist quite apart from their personality structure and may reside exclusively in the nature of their relationship "game."* (p. 228) [italics ours]

Although Speer (1972) found little indication that cooperative behavior in PD games is a useful index of adequate marital communication, the point remains that treating an interaction as the unit of analysis is fundamentally different from focusing on the individual. Almost all PD studies—and for that matter, most studies of game behavior in any form—are chiefly concerned with the individual's responses to the game situation and to the behavior of other individuals. Most interaction studies are reported in terms of the rational features of the game situation, such as the number of cooperative choices by X given a particular strategy by Y. Many of these studies are interesting and meritorious; in fact, the reader has just been exposed to a brief summary of some of their major findings. Still, the interaction of the participants in terms of *communication,* the exchange of mutually understood symbolic behavior, has received very little attention.

To assert that communication has been slighted is not to say that its importance has been overlooked in gaming research. Most experiments tacitly recognize its possible effects on game outcomes by eliminating any form of communication between players. Moreover, many explicit statements on the importance of studying communication are found in the gaming literature. In their review of gaming studies, Gallo and McClintock (1965) included "Possibilities for Communication" as one of five major types of independent variables that had been studied. Editorializing in the *Journal of Conflict Resolution,* Rapoport (1966) called for a study of the effect of declaration of intent during PD games. Bostrom (1968) discussed the relationship of game theory to communication in a game theoretic setting. Bonacich (1970) declared that much experimental work on PD games is misdirected.

In not allowing or severely restricting the communication that can occur between the players, researchers have treated the Prisoner's Dilemma as a game between two isolated rational (self-interested) units, and consequently have not examined the social mechanisms that human groups develop to enable cooperation to occur when the members' interests are somewhat opposed in the interesting way that the Prisoner's Dilemma describes. (p. 379)

Shubik (1970) listed the failure to deal with problems of communication as one of the two major shortcomings of game theory applications to conflict. "The [extended PD] model is still not rich enough to capture a useful abstraction of human affairs. It fails on two counts. The first concerns survival. . . . The second concerns the problem of coding, language, and communication" (p. 190).

The use of communication as a variable in game theoretic studies of conflict poses a problem, for game theory was not designed to deal with words as moves in the actual operations of the game. Messages are often ambiguous (have more than one possible meaning) and their truth content or the degree of commitment underlying them is not easily specified. Although it is possible to translate the formal ambiguity of language into game theoretic formulations and to construct a probability model dealing with degree of commitment, application of these stochastic processes in a practical situation is almost impossible save in the most simple instances.

The first major modern attempt to deal with communication in conflict situations was launched by Schelling (1960) in *The Strategy of Conflict*. Schelling's basic outlook is that of a game theorist dissatisfied with purely rational formulations, and his work represents an initial attempt to incorporate many traditionally nonrational features of games into the theory of games.

Shubik (1970), while applauding Schelling's work on bargaining, negotiation, and conflict, criticizes *The Strategy of Conflict* as a "monument to a profound misunderstanding of the formal theory of games" (p. 191). According to Shubik, *The Strategy of Conflict* attempts to apply game theory to situations it is incapable of handling, particularly communication situations involving ambiguous meanings and unclear commitments to communication messages.

Shubik's criticism is partially correct and partially off target. Certainly, as he notes, the addition of communication variables to a gaming model as stochastic processes would be a practical impossibility, even though it is theoretically feasible. Where he errs is in the implication that communication *cannot* be studied as part of a gaming model of conflict. The study of human communication behavior is not quite the same as the study of a rock's behavior, as Shubik recognizes. The behavior of a human being is not necessarily less predictable than a rock's behavior—it simply requires more variables and more complex contingencies to describe human behavior accurately. The major problem in studying human behavior occurs when one tries to move from probabilities to certainties, to predict exactly what will happen to a particular individual in a particular situation. Given the present imperfect state of measurement of human behavior, an uncertainty principle enters into the prediction of human behavior in the same way Heisenberg's principle enters into the prediction of behavior of atomic particles. The poorer the measurement, the greater the uncertainty. Such uncertainty vastly complicates the addition of human communication variables to game theoretic predictions in practical situations.

To expect exact predictions from any model in the social sciences is unreasonable. Game theory offers exact predictions at the expense of assumptions about the nature of reality which may not hold true for the situation. Schelling does not assume that exact predictions will result from his work; consequently, he feels free to describe the realities of the situation to the best of his abilities. Thus, the Shubik-Schelling conflict is partly a semantic conflict. Shubik is a strict mathematical game theorist while Schelling is more game-theoretic as we defined the term above. Schelling's approach, therefore, does not necessarily involve a "profound misunderstanding of the formal theory of games," but reflects an emphasis on features of the game situation which are usually not discussed by the formal theory of games.

The Strategy of Conflict discusses the functional role of communication in conflict situations, as well as strategies for employing communication. Possibly, Schelling's emphasis on reasons why parties might not want to communicate and his remarks regarding the occasional advantages offered by the unilateral destruction of the possibilities for communication—e.g., "Threats are no good if they cannot be communicated to the persons for whom they are intended. . . ." (p. 146)—may have contributed to the relative lack of actual research on the role of communication in gaming studies of conflict. Though Schelling's work is of interest to any student of communication and conflict, it would certainly be more convincing if his insights were buttressed by research on the possibilities he suggests.

When stating why communication may be disadvantageous in certain conflict situations, Schelling stresses the distinction between the game's actual behavioral moves and the communication of information about these moves:

> Talk is not a substitute for moves. Moves can in some way alter the game, by incurring manifest costs, risks, or a reduced range of subsequent choice; they have an information content, or *evidence* content, of a different character from that of speech. Talk can be cheap when moves are not (except for the "talk" that takes the form of *enforceable* threats, promises, commitments, and so forth, and that is to be analyzed under the headings of *moves* rather than communication anyway). . . . While one's maneuvers are not unambiguous in their revelation of one's value systems and may even be deliberately deceptive, they nevertheless have an evidential quality that mere speech has not.[3]

3 T. C. Schelling, *The Strategy of Conflict* (Cambridge, Mass.: Harvard University Press, 1960) p. 117. By permission of the publisher.

Schelling's distinction between "talk" and "moves" forms the basis for our definition of communication. We employ the word "communication" to indicate the use of mutually understood symbolic behavior such that the probability of engaging in a particular behavior (making a given move) is altered via the exchange of symbolic move sequences which carry no *necessary* consequences for the situation (the formal game matrix). This definition contains three major features. First, communication must be symbolic in the sense that it must represent the move without carrying with it the consequences of the move. In a game, this means that any behavior which *necessarily* results in the gain or loss of points will not be regarded as communication. The actual moves of a game carry information but they also carry consequences. If X says to Y, "Your money or your life!" while brandishing a club, and this verbal and nonverbal symbolization of X hitting Y results in a change from its current value in the probability of Y engaging in a given behavior, then the statement and the brandishing of the club would qualify as communication. If X hit Y with the club, that would not be communication. The distinction is not one of information because both the *symbolic* and *actual* act have information value. But the statement carries no *necessary* consequences while the clubbing does. This is what is meant by "actual." If Y is hit with the club he has been harmed, and no future behaviors, symbolic or otherwise, can reverse that fact. But if X tells Y to hand over his money by verbal or nonverbal symbolism, Y has the opportunity to reciprocate and to send a proposed move sequence back to X. The type of return message most likely to forestall X's threat then becomes a matter of interest to communication researchers.

The second major implication of our definition is that probabilities of moves must be altered if communication has occurred. If symbolic messages are exchanged but no change in the probability of any of either participant's moves can be observed, then we cannot be sure that communication has occurred, and we refer to such a situation as an *attempt to communicate*. An example may clarify our position. Consider the case of the Israeli jets intercepting the Libyan airliner over the Sinai. By hand signals, motions of their planes, and radio messages, the Israeli pilots attempted to communicate their desire to the French pilot of the airliner that he should land his aircraft. The airliner did not change its course, and no other evidence exists to show any change in the probabilities of the airline pilot's available behaviors. Thus, by our definition, no communication occurred. A second attempt to communicate occurred when the jets fired warning shots. Again, no change in behavioral probabilities occurred on the part of the airline pilot, implying no communication. Finally, the jets attacked. The airline pilot's behavior now changed as his plane began to crash, but this is still not communication. The change in behavior resulted from a nonsymbolic act by the Israelis, shooting at and hitting the plane. The consequence of hitting the plane forms the not-so-subtle dividing line between communication and an actual move.

One advantage of our definition is that it is behavioral. That is, it becomes unnecessary to discuss whether the airline pilot "understood" or "misunderstood" the Israelis in a cognitive sense. Behaviorally he did not understand. This does not mean that no cognitive changes occurred, nor does it imply a disinterest in cognitive events. It simply allows for a determination of the occurrence of communication on a publicly observable basis.

The third implication of the definition is that although the symbolic exchange of move sequences must carry no necessary consequences for the situation, it may carry other nonsituational consequences. Actually hitting the airliner with bullets constitutes a situational change. In a game, any action that results in the payoff of points from an outcome cell constitutes a situational change. Behaviors that automatically result in situational changes are not to be considered communication, even though they may also bring about behavioral changes. But symbolic exchanges that bring about changes in behavioral probabilities are to be considered communication if the only necessary consequences of the exchanges are nonsituational. For example, the firing of the warning shots probably lowered the airline pilot's trust of the men flying the intercepting jets. In fact, this change in trust would seem to be a necessary consequence of being shot at. This necessary change in consequences is interpersonal in nature, not situational. It may be an irreversible cognitive change, but it does not imply an irreversible situational occurrence of the same nature as the first bullet to actually hit the plane. Thus, had the warning shots produced a change in the airliner's behavior, these shots would have qualified as communication because the seemingly necessary change in interpersonal trust is not a situational change. Unfortunately for 106 people, the warning shots can only be classified as an attempt to communicate.

To summarize our definition, *communication* refers to the altering of behavioral probabilities via symbolic exchanges which imply no necessary situational consequences. The definition underscores the importance of the word *symbolic*. If the communication carries with it an absolute, irrevocable commitment to a given move, then that message is no longer symbolic; it is equivalent to the move itself. An alternative way of saying this is that there can be no necessary connection between what a player says and what he does. If the connection is necessary, all the consequences following from the move will follow from the message concerning the move and no new variable will have been added to the situation.

Research on Communication in Gaming Studies of Conflict

In this section, we will refer to studies allowing attempts at communication as "studies of communication," keeping in mind that not all attempts at communication reported below produced changed probabilities of behavior. Whether the behavioral probabilities actually changed or not will be clear from the context.

Although the general plan of this section is to move from studies using only the most minimal form of communication to studies where communication possibilities are free and open, it may be instructive to begin with a study that does not involve communication between players, at least as we have defined it. Deutsch and Lewicki (1970) employed a modified version of the Deutsch and Krauss trucking game to study how the game of Chicken is affected by locking a truck in forward gear. Whenever a player used his lock, a signal informed the other player of this fact. Even though it improved coordination among cooperative players, such a signal is *not* an example of what we mean by the term *communication,* for it is simply an unambiguous, after-the-fact statement that a given move has been carried out. Communication, in our sense, is necessarily before-the-fact and not absolutely binding. No communication was allowed by Deutsch and Lewicki, for the subjects never saw each other and they were instructed not to speak to each other at any time.

Oskamp and Perlman (1965) report the findings of three experiments involving PD games. Their third experiment involved a very low level of attempted communication. Half the subjects were allowed to see each other before playing the game and half were not. This condition could be classified as pre-nonverbal communication, because subjects saw each other only before the trials began. Using thirty trials, Oskamp and Perlman found no significant differences in level of cooperation between subjects in the anonymous and pre-nonverbal groups. The only large difference between the two conditions occurred among subjects who were enrolled in introductory psychology classes at a small California college. Given the opportunity for considerable prior interaction, pre-nonverbal communication may lead to higher levels of cooperation than complete anonymity; i.e., if persons know they are playing a game with a friend, they are likely to cooperate more than if they do not know their opponent's identity. Or it is even possible that the opportunity to observe a familiar person enables the players to use nonverbal indicators to assess the type of strategy they should use. Unfortunately, nothing in Oskamp and Perlman's study tells us why this difference occurred, suggesting the possibility of further nonverbal communication research on the problem.

A slightly higher level of communication was investigated in Oskamp and Perlman's first experiment. This study examined the effects of an Asch-type pre-session—i.e., a session in which research confederates gave prearranged responses—on the cooperative play of subjects. Four confederates stated in turn that they thought everyone should cooperate, or compete, in the games, after which the two naive subjects were allowed to state their views. No attempts at communication were allowed during the actual trials. Although subjects in the competitive norm condition produced the highest level of cooperation, very little weight should be attached to this somewhat surprising finding. The effects of the conformity manipulations were confounded by the fact that the statements of the fifth person (the first naive subject) also influenced the response of the sixth (the second naive subject). The latter subject not only heard the four cooperative or four competitive statements of the confederates, he also heard either a cooperative or a competitive statement from the other naive subject. In fact, most naive subjects in both conditions (24 of 28) made a cooperative, rather than a competitive statement. Thus, the Oskamp and Perlman studies leave something to be desired, both in terms of their design and the use of some rather odd statistical procedures. They do include a very minimum level of communication and are described here for that reason. A replication of their experiments might prove interesting to students of communication and conflict.

Scodel (1962, 1963) found that a pre-game discussion of how to play the game resulted in increased cooperation. Using a 98-trial PD game, Radlow and Weidner (1966) examined the effects of allowing unenforceable commitments that were contingent on the play of the other. Subjects exchanged five different commitments, printed by the experimenter, up to fifteen times before the actual game began. The game instructions implied, but did not explicitly state, that these commitments were not to be enforced. Although this communication was entirely pre-play and limited in content and channel (all written, no chance for non-verbal), it produced a significantly higher level of cooperation (90 percent) than occurred in the noncommunication group (55 percent). Though the U-shaped curve indicating an initial decline in cooperation followed by a subsequent increase was obtained for the noncommunication group, the pattern of cooperative responses for the group allowed pre-play communication followed essentially a straight line. Radlow (1965) suggests that the U-shaped curve is generated as players try to determine the strategy and intent of the other player. As more communication is allowed, it becomes increasingly unnecessary to use the behavioral method of determining the strategy of the other, a factor which may explain the straight line generated in the pre-play communication condition.

Shure, Meeker, and Hansford (1965), using an *SMH* game, allowed a level of communication comparable to that allowed by Radlow and Weidner. The SMH game involved two players, both of whom were attempting to send a message through a communication center with limited channel capacity. In order to transmit, each player needed to occupy five of the six storage units in the channel at the same time. Players could enter only one channel storage unit at a time. After occupying three units each, neither player backed down, making it impossible to transmit a message. The objective of the game was to transmit as many messages as possible during fifteen trials.

Use of this communication-type task as the dependent variable of the study has no bearing on its inclusion in this section. The communication occurring in the SMH game itself is essentially irrelevant to the study of communication in conflict situations. Any other cover story that did not alter the task could be used to induce the players to resolve a conflict over space use. The SMH game study is relevant to communication because (1) before play began, one subject (actually the experimenter) communicated his intention to play the game as a pacifist (which involved allowing the actual subject to transmit the first five-unit message, claiming the right to transmit the second message himself, and never using an electrical shock switch that each player had available to shock the other), and (2) each actual subject was a member of a three-man team, two of whom were stooges who urged the subject to dominate the pacifist.

Intraside communication was not varied in the study. Interside communication was varied, with half the subjects assigned to the pacifist communication and half not. Two other independent variables, giving the subject biographical information about the pacifist and unilateral disarmament (giving up the ability to shock the subject) at mid-game by the pacifist, did not affect the play of the game. Two significant differences were found between the prepacifist and no-prepacifist message conditions: first, only subjects in the prepacifist message condition switched from a dominating to a sharing strategy during the game; second, subjects who remained dominant in the prepacifist message condition were more likely to indicate a belief that the pacifist was trying to trick them by making them feel guilty about their dominant strategy. Thus, the effect of this pre-message differed for different subjects. It resulted in more cooperation from some subjects, but apparently strengthened the resolve of other subjects to remain dominant.

Three studies have investigated attempted intraside communication as an independent variable in game theoretic situations. Martin (1964) used three-person teams as players in a PD game. The findings indicated that a team with consultation (intraside communication) allowed does better than an individual, who in turn does better than a team with no consultation allowed. Chammah (1966) and Pylyshyn et al. (1966) have both replicated this finding.

Although experiments involving pre-game communication or intraside communication are interesting, they do not strike at the heart of the matter. The most interesting form of communication in conflict situations occurs *between* the parties to the conflict *during* the conflict itself. There are at least three major game-type approaches to the study of people's communication behavior during the time of conflict. These approaches are generally known as (1) studies of coalition formation, (2) studies of bargaining over allocation of rewards, and (3) studies of the effects of communication on game behavior. Coalition formation and bargaining studies, though of interest to the student of communication and conflict, are generally beyond the scope of this chapter. The following studies allowed communication attempts between the parties during the actual game trials.

Todd, Hammond, and Wilkins (1966) asked pairs of subjects to make judgments about the level of democracy in various countries. The judgments were to be based on two types of information supplied to subjects by the experimenter. Participants were told they would have to agree on their judgments and that they could discuss the matter until agreement was reached. The researchers were interested in the possibility of differences resulting from ambiguous versus exact feedback concerning the correctness of judgments. Here, feedback does not imply communication in the sense we have defined it; rather, it refers to relative ambiguity of the cue stimuli associated with the situational task.

Communication attempts were not manipulated during the game; instead, all subjects were allowed to talk freely. The major finding regarding feedback was that conflicts were resolved by compromise given exact feedback and by capitulation given ambiguous feedback. From a communication perspective, it would be interesting to know if the level of communication during the game itself would influence these results, and if so, how.

Vincent and Tindell (1969) investigated a variation of the SMH game described earlier. Several electrical switches were added to the conditions of play and the description of the game was changed from a communication channel with limited capacity to a task of trying to light up five light cells. Three switches were added to the basic SMH game: one warning of intention to shock, a second announcing the wish to deescalate the number of shocks available to each side, and a third actually permitting any number of units of shocking power to be relinquished. The first two switches are essentially means of communication, for one allows players to threaten shock without necessarily acting upon the threat and the second permits players to request deescalation without necessarily making a deescalation move. By contrast, the third switch is a move switch, because its effects are direct and irrevocable. It should be noted that this is our interpretation of differences between the various switches, not Vincent and Tindell's.

All subjects played against one of two simulated strategies. Although Shure, Meeker, and Hansford had studied a pure pacifist strategy, Vincent and Tindell examined the effects of a warning pacifist and a shocking pacifist. The pure pacifist of the original SMH game promised in advance never to shock his opponent. Vincent and Tindell's warning pacifist never actually shocked his opponent, but warned that he would each time he received a shock. This warning took place while playing the game, not before, and was accomplished by means of the shock warning switch. The shocking pacifist not only warned, he shocked. But he never shocked without warning and only after being shocked by his opponent. Fourteen independent variables were studied by Vincent and Tindell, but only those basically related to the subjects' communication behavior will be considered here.

Contrary to expectations, Vincent and Tindell found that subjects with shocking pacifists for opponents gave more shocks, made fewer cooperative moves, won more points, and won more games than did subjects playing against warning pacifists. Rather than inhibiting the tendency to shock one's opponent, the shocking pacifist strategy actually increased it. No significant differences were found between the warning pacifist condition and the pure pacifist condition used originally by Shure, Meeker, and Hansford. Thus, warning aggressive subjects that they are about to be shocked without actually shocking them has about the same effect as the pure pacifist who neither warns nor shocks. Adding the shock to the warning condition only increases the aggressive subject's belligerent tendencies.

Drawing upon Berkowitz (1962), Vincent and Tindell offer three possible reasons for the heightened belligerency of subjects paired with a shocking pacifist: first, shocking is more competitive than warning; second, the returned shock is irritating; and third, there are fewer moral restraints against shocking someone who actually shocks back, rather than only issuing a warning. Thus, the results indicate that aggression against an aggressor makes him more, rather than less belligerent; unless, of course, the aggressor is put out of commission.

These findings suggest that aggression is directly tied to the behavior of players in game-type conflict situations, and that differences in type of, and opportunity for communication mediate aggressive behavior. More research dealing with the effects of communication on aggressive acts is needed and could be incorporated into studies of communication and conflict. The research of Vincent and Tindell, though interesting in its own right, sheds little light on the effects of communication in such situations. Because all subjects were always either warned but not shocked or warned and shocked, the effects of the communicated warning after several trials were almost identical with the conditions for a game move, rather than a communicated message. In the shocking pacifist condition, a warning always preceded a shock; thus, use of the warning light switch actually signalled a move instead of communicating intent. In the warning pacifist condition, the light signal was never followed by a shock. Although the naive subject might still expect a shock at any time, the credibility of an opponent who always threatens but never acts upon his threats must be extremely low. What is needed are studies of a communication warning system which periodically, but not always, reinforces threat with action.

A study with restrictions on the scope, content, time, and ambiguity of communication similar to those imposed by Todd, Hammond, and Wilkins and by Vincent and Tindell is reported by Tedeschi, Bonoma, and Novinson (1970). Tedeschi and his associates studied the effects of limited communication attempts at specific times during 150 trials of a modified PD game. Only one message was available to the subject, and he was given the option of sending or not sending it when the experimenter turned on a white light at fixed intervals. The message from the subject to his simulated target or opponent (ST) stated that if the ST did not make a cooperative choice on the next trial, the subject would take 10 points away from him, an action made possible by the modification of the PD game. The ST could respond with one of three messages but could never initiate communication, a restriction of which the subject was aware. The three possible ST replies were that he would comply, that he would not comply, or that he did not intend to disclose his intentions. The subject had 10 seconds to decide whether to send a message. If the message was sent and the ST did not comply, a red penalty option light went on, allowing the subject 10 seconds to decide whether to subtract 10 points from the ST's score. Each time the subjects used the penalty option, 5 points were subtracted from their scores, as a *fixed cost* of doing business. In the *retaliation* condition, subjects were informed that the ST had retaliatory power to subtract the 5 points if the subject subtracted 10 points from his score and that this power could be used at the ST's option. The ST complied with the subject's request for cooperation every third time and was always completely truthful in indicating compliance or noncompliance. The message indicating unwillingness to divulge intentions was never actually sent.

Tedeschi, Bonoma, and Novinson examined frequency of threat usage, frequency of use of the penalty option, and proportion of cooperative choices made by the subjects. Males sent more threats than females. In terms of number of threats, there were no differences between the fixed costs and retaliation conditions. A significant sex-by-condition interaction was observed for the threat message variable. In the fixed-costs conditions, males used about 29 of the 30 threats available to them while females averaged only 14. In the retaliation condition, males used an average of 27 threats and the average for females increased to 24.

Tedeschi et al. interpret this interaction in terms of the females' concern over presentation of self as contrasted with the males' concern for winning the game. It is more acceptable to threaten a retaliating opponent than an opponent who is apparently not at fault. An alternative explanation might be the general activity interpretation discussed earlier. If females are generally less active in PD-type games, they should use fewer threats than males, and this was true in the fixed-costs condition. In the retaliation condition, however, the apparent activity of one's opponent in taking 5 points away from one's score may be enough to jar the less active females into a more active role in the game, producing an increase in their threat usage.

Perhaps the most interesting result for students of communication is the significant sex-by-condition interaction for the proportion of cooperative responses made on trials where subjects chose not to exercise their option to send a threat. When threats were not sent, females made about 62 percent cooperative responses under the fixed-costs condition and about 69 percent cooperative responses under the retaliation condition. By contrast, males cooperated over 80 percent of the time in the fixed-costs condition but less than 20 percent of the time under conditions of retaliation. There were no significant differences in level of cooperation on trials where subjects did choose to exercise their threat options. Thus, the communication behavior of the subjects apparently had a rather complex effect on their level of cooperation. Females apparently expect that conciliatory gestures (failure to use an available threat) will produce cooperation by the opponent regardless of his capacity for retaliation, while males expect that conciliatory gestures will get them nothing if the opponent has retaliatory capacity.

Wallace and Rothaus (1969) also allowed written messages to be exchanged by all subjects, who played ten trials of a PD game. Using real money as rewards, they established a maximum payoff for any subject of 60 cents and a minimum loss of 30 cents; however, all subjects knew the worst they could do was break even over the ten trials. Subjects were 48 male volunteers from two open neuropsychiatric wards of a VA Hospital, with diagnoses ranging from anxiety reaction to schizophrenic reaction. This sample is in sharp contrast to the college subjects used in most gaming experiments; consequently, the findings of this study should not be combined with the results of other gaming studies without taking possible subject differences into account.

Both wards were using group therapy techniques to develop cohesive patient groups. Half of the subjects from each ward were told that the individual with the highest winnings would receive an additional $2.00 reward. The other half were told that everyone from the ward scoring the most points would be awarded $2.00. Half of the subjects played in intergroup and half in intragroup conditions. Intergroup subjects were strangers to their opponents. Before each trial of the game, subjects indicated their degree of trust in the other on a nine-point scale and were allowed to exchange written messages. Wallace and Rothaus content-analyzed these notes, but the procedures used for this analysis are questionable and the results are not reported here.

Wallace and Rothaus found that with written communication allowed, intragroup dyads displayed significantly higher cooperation over all conditions than did intergroup dyads. In addition, a significant reward condition by group condition interaction occurred for cooperative responses. Under individual reward, intragroup cooperation was 83 percent and intergroup cooperation a rather high 55 percent. In the group reward conditions, intragroup cooperation climbed to 93 percent while intergroup cooperation dropped to 23 percent. Trust ratings for intragroup conditions were significantly higher than for intergroup conditions, but this seemed to result from prior interaction history and game instructions rather than from game conflict. Because the possibility for communication was not independently manipulated, any conclusions concerning its effects on cooperative behavior must remain tentative.

Although the studies discussed thus far have dealt with communication in gaming studies of conflict, none has achieved a fully independent manipulation of communication as a variable after the start of play. The studies reported next employ at least one form of communication as an independent variable. In them, attempts at communication range from written messages with restricted content to full and open oral interchanges.

An early gaming experiment that used communication as an independent variable is reported by Scodel, Minas, Ratoosh, and Lipetz (1959). Their subjects played a PD game under two conditions: one group played fifty trials under the usual conditions of no communication, while the second played twenty-five trials with no communication, discussed the game in any way they pleased for two minutes, and then played twenty-five additional trials. When compared with the noncommunication group, the frequency of cooperative choices increased after the communication period but still remained below 50 percent. Although communication did lead to a slight increase in cooperation, the effect of the two-minute communication period was confounded with the experience of playing twenty-five trials with the same opponent under conditions of no communication. Future studies must separate these two effects if the results are to be interpreted unambiguously.

Using only a single trial, Deutsch (1957, 1958, 1960) varied the professed purpose of the PD game across two levels of communication. One group of subjects (the cooperative condition) was told that they should seek to maximize the welfare of both players. A second group (individualistic condition) was instructed to do as well as possible and to forget the other player (the standard instruction used in most PD games). A third group (competitive condition) was told to do well for themselves, and in addition, to be sure to do better than the other player. Some subjects in each of the three conditions were allowed to write notes to each other before playing the single trial, while the others were not. These notes, which could contain anything the subjects wanted to write, were the only communications allowed.

Deutsch found that the communication attempts produced increased cooperation in each of the three conditions. The differences were especially marked in the individualistic condition, with cooperation jumping from 36 to 71 percent, and in the competitive condition, with cooperation increasing from 13 to 29 percent. Subjects given the cooperative description of the game cooperated 80 percent of the time without communication and 97 percent of the time with it. In this condition, communication apparently eliminates any confusion the players may have as to which response the experimenter wishes them to make. In conditions using individualistic or competitive instructions, the response desired by the experimenter is not so obvious. Thus, these two conditions provide clearer evidence about the effect of communication on subsequent gaming behavior. In one group that played ten trials without communication, the percentage of cooperative responses was much closer to that typically reported: 71 percent in the cooperative condition, 36 percent in the individualistic condition, and 26 percent in the competitive condition. The high cooperative percentages reported by Deutsch on the first trial are sometimes known as *start effects*.

Loomis (1959), using a modified PD game, studied the effect of sending or receiving one of five messages on a subject's perception of his opponent's next play. If both players perceived that the other would make the cooperative choice, the situation was defined as one of *mutual trust*.

Loomis studied only the results for the first trial of a five-trial series. He found that as communication increased from no communication through a message stating exact expectations for both parties, the level of mutual trust increased significantly. The effect was principally observed for those subjects who received messages, though message senders were much higher in trust than the no-communication control. Both communication and no-communication subjects made an unusually high proportion (around 80 percent) of cooperative choices, probably because of the single trial used in the study.

On the whole, Loomis' results indicate that if someone sends a note promising to do something, persons will tend to believe him and also to believe that the sender thinks they will act in a trustworthy manner. Moreover, the act of sending the note seems to inspire trust in the other, as well as a belief that the receiver will trust the sender. The first finding says that people tend to trust other people who ask them to, at least initially. But asking someone mutual trust questions and observing a person's game behavior may be two entirely different things. Interestingly enough, Loomis found that none of the 18 subjects in the no-communication condition who perceived a condition of mutual trust made competitive responses, while 26 of the 180 subjects in the five communication conditions seized the opportunity to "double-cross" their partners when they perceived that mutual trust existed. Thus, while communication led to an increase in perceived mutual trust, its effect on the overall level of cooperation was mixed, with some subjects using the trusting information contained in the notes to sabotage their opponents. This tactic was especially true of subjects who received rather than sent notes.

Using 110 trials of a PD game, Gahagan and Tedeschi (1968) examined the effect of two random strategies of 50 percent and 75 percent cooperative responses by the opponent across three levels of source credibility. Subjects were told that on every tenth trial the opponent would have an opportunity to send a message and the subject would have a chance to respond. The subjects were shown five written messages purported to be of the kinds they might receive from the opponent. The messages stated an intent to (1) cooperate on this trial, (2) compete on this trial, (3) not disclose strategy on this trial, (4) play tit-for-tat on the next trial, or (5) cooperate on the next trial in exchange for the subject's cooperative response on this trial. The only message the subject actually received was the one stating intent to cooperate. The subject was allowed to return one of two messages indicating agreement to cooperate or refusal to disclose intentions. Because the subject always received the same message, the experimenter informed him on the fiftieth trial (fifth message trial) that he had reminded the opponent that any of the five messages could be sent, that the opponent understood his options, and that he still wished to send the cooperative message.

Credibility was operationalized as the degree to which the opponent's behaviors actually conform with his stated intent. Three credibility levels were employed, with the opponent behaving credibly on 30 percent, 60 percent, and 90 percent of the trials, respectively. The effects of the credibility and strategy factors and their interaction were analyzed on nine dependent variables. The credibility factor showed a significant difference on only one of the nine variables. Subjects in the 90 percent credibility condition cooperated more on the trial following the communication than did those in the 60 percent or 30 percent conditions. The latter two conditions did not differ from each other. The strategy manipulation produced no significant differences on any of the nine variables. Strategy by credibility interaction effects were significant for the proportion of cooperative choices over all 110 trials and the proportion of cooperative choices on the trial following communication. For students of communication, the findings demonstrate that behavioral credibility must be high if promises are to induce a significant increase in cooperation by opponents in gaming situations.

As indicated earlier, Shure, Meeker, and Hansford (1965) introduced a game requiring subjects to send a message of five units through a six-unit capacity channel. Meeker and Shure (1969) varied communication in fifteen trials of this SMH game. Communication condition subjects exchanged written messages with the pure pacifist after the fifth, sixth, and seventh trials, while subjects in the no-communication condition were not allowed to send between-trial messages. The messages from the pacifist stated his conciliatory intent, the fairness of his demands, his refusal to use shock, and his intent to force the subject to use shock if the subject intended to play the game unfairly.

Comparison of the two groups revealed a significant increase in cooperation by subjects in the communication condition. Although no messages were sent after the eighth trial, the increase in cooperative responses for communication subjects remained stable through the end of the fifteen trials. This increase in cooperation fails to occur in only one condition. For purposes of control, some subjects played in the presence of a silent observer, some with a cohort of the experimenter who urged them to dominate the pacifist, and some in a no-audience condition. Subjects in the observer condition made significantly more cooperative responses than subjects in the other two conditions; however, communication increased cooperation significantly in the cohort and no-audience conditions but not in the observer condition. Meeker and Shure believe the presence of the observer produced pressure for the subject to cooperate with his opponent, even when no communication was allowed. If so, there would be few uncommitted subjects in the observer condition to be influenced by communication. On the other hand, communication would serve the same function as the observer in the no-audience and cohort conditions.

Thus, messages from a pacifist stressing his intent to persist in his convictions and behavior can foster increased cooperation. Moreover, the mere presence of another person, who is apparently aware of what is occurring, also engenders increased cooperation. This effect can be interpreted as a communication phenomenon. Without doing or saying anything, the observer, by his mere presence, nonverbally communicates the fact that the subject's behavior is public. But in addition, the potential for a reporter effect must also be considered. Though one may behave morally because of concern for possible approbation by the observer, the observer's ability to relate these behaviors to others may constitute an even stronger moral force. It would be interesting to compare the effect of an observer capable of making moral judgments but incapable of reporting his observations to others with an observer who could both make judgments and communicate observations and with an observer who could not make moral judgments but could communicate observations, such as a tape recorder or TV camera.

Cheney, Harford, and Solomon (1972) used ten trials of the Deutsch and Krauss trucking game to investigate the effects of contingent and noncontingent threats and promises. Subjects were assigned to one of four experimental conditions: no communication, negative communication, positive communication, or positive plus negative communication. In the negative communication condition, both players were provided with four threatening messages, two containing contingent and two containing noncontingent threats. A contingent threat was dependent on an action of the other player, while a noncontingent threat was a statement of intent to act regardless of the other's behavior. In the positive communication condition, players were given four messages containing promises, two of which were contingent and two noncontingent. Positive plus negative communication condition subjects were allowed to use all eight messages. Subjects were given 60 cents to start the game with the possibility of earning as much as an additional $2.40.

Frequency of message usage was highest in the positive plus negative communication condition and lowest in the negative communication condition. Positive plus negative communication subjects used five times as many promises as they did threats. Unfortunately data were not collected on the order in which these subjects chose to send their messages. In addition, positive communication subjects sent twice as many messages as their negative communication counterparts. Finally, significantly more contingent messages were sent in the positive and in the negative communication conditions (about 75 percent contingent) than were sent in the positive plus negative communication condition (about 60 percent contingent). Thus, contingent messages are used more when communication is restricted to positive or to negative options than when both positive and negative messages can be sent.

Cheney, Harford, and Solomon emphasize the need to study the effects of contingent versus noncontingent threats and promises on subjects' perceptions of each other and of their game behavior. Three measures of cooperation were used in their study: number of moves to goal, alternate route usage, and gate usage. Both the positive and the positive plus negative communication conditions produced significantly more cooperation than the negative communication and no-communication conditions on all three measures. There were no significant differences on any of the three cooperation measures between the positive and the positive plus negative communication conditions. The only significant difference in cooperative behavior between the negative communication and no-communication conditions occurred for the gate usage measure, with the negative communication condition using the gate less frequently. Cheney et al. interpret this lowered gate usage in the negative communication condition as a sign that subjects used the threats, rather than the gates themselves, as a coordination device. Nordin (1967) has suggested that threats may be perceived as coordination devices when other communication options are not available. Nevertheless, threats used in this way have strong potential for ambiguity, because they may be perceived as attempts to intimidate as well as efforts to coordinate. But putting aside interpretive questions, the Cheney study does indicate that the availability and use of messages promising cooperation does increase cooperative behavior and that subjects apparently find promises of cooperation more useful devices than threats of competition when playing the trucking game.

Using twenty trials of the trucking game, Deutsch and Krauss (1962) investigated the effects of allowed and forced communication on the game-playing behavior of 152 female telephone company employees. Results indicated that subjects who were allowed, but not forced, to talk to each other often chose not to talk, apparently because they were in a strange situation and could not see the other player. In fact, Deutsch and Krauss found that the forced-communication condition, in which subjects were compelled to talk to each other, produced greater payoffs than either the allowed communication or the no-communication control conditions, though this advantage varied over conditions of threat. Because the three communication conditions were studied with independent groups of subjects at different times and places, the results for the three conditions may not be strictly comparable.

Krauss and Deutsch (1966) again used female telephone company employees to study the effects of communication between trials of the trucking game. All subjects were also allowed to communicate *during* each trial, so the results are properly interpreted as resulting from a combination of between-trial and during-trial communication. Several different sets of instructions were used to vary the emphasis placed upon communication. There were no significant differences between instructions stressing the use of pre-trial communication to cordinate behavior for future moves and instructions not containing this suggestion. A second variation of the instructions given was significant. Instructions to some subjects underscored the importance of communicating but did not discuss the content that might be communicated. Conversely, other subjects were told to focus their discussion on a fair solution to the bargaining problems. Subjects given content instructions accumulated significantly higher payoffs than subjects told only that communication was important. Though Krauss and Deutsch do not mention it, there is a fairly simple explanation for this effect. The content instructions emphasized the importance of being fair, reasonable, and considering the interests of both parties. As it so happens, this is precisely the best way to maximize trucking game payoffs for both players. Thus, Krauss and Deutsch found that subjects given a strong hint of how to play the game did better than subjects not receiving the hint, hardly a startling discovery.

A fairly consistent finding in the trucking game is that subjects become deadlocked by the seventh trial, with both using their gates to block the other. Krauss and Deutsch allowed one group of subjects to communicate between each of the first seven trials and a second group to communicate between trials 8–14. Interest was centered on the effects of communication introduced at the beginning of the game as opposed to communication introduced after playing several trials. This comparison is necessary to separate the effects of communication per se from its interactions with experience on previous trials. Unfortunately, the Krauss and Deutsch manipulation is contaminated by the fact that all subjects were allowed to talk during the trials, with the opportunity to communicate varied only during the between-trial periods.

The results indicated that post-deadlock communication (trials 8–14) was more effective than pre-deadlock communication (trials 1–7) in increasing the total joint payoff. Krauss and Deutsch suggest that communication opportunities occurring after a deadlock has been experienced will be used more effectively than opportunities occurring before the need to communicate is clearly established. In order to make this explanation convincing, a less ambiguous manipulation of communication opportunities is needed.

Swingle and Santi (1972) investigated the behavior of 180 female subjects who played 100 trials of one of three games: PD, Chicken, or a nonsymmetrical power game in which one player could, if he wished, guarantee himself a positive payoff of four units and his opponent a payoff of zero. Forced-, optional-, and no-communication conditions were employed in the study. In the forced-communication condition, subjects were required to exchange messages with their opponents after every fifteen trials. In the optional communication condition, subjects could use their discretion about exchanging messages.

The findings revealed that the addition of a single communication opportunity at the fifteenth trial yielded a sharp increase in cooperation for both forced and optional communication in the Chicken game, resulting in a significant communication by game interaction. Forced and optional communication was equally effective in the PD and power games, but optional communication produced a greater increase in cooperation than forced communication in the Chicken game.

Over all 100 trials, optional communication was significantly more effective than forced communication in producing cooperation in the PD and power games. Although Deutsch and Krauss (1962) found forced communication somewhat more effective than optional, it should be remembered that most of their subjects in the optional communication condition failed to use the option, which may account for the difference in findings. Also, Deutsch and Krauss used the trucking game, and Swingle and Santi's results suggest a possible interaction between game situation and forced versus optional communication.

A series of studies reported by Ackoff and his associates (1967) investigated the effects of written communication in various escalation games using real money as rewards. Each subject played in two game matrices at once, one matrix representing the development and the other the arms sector. In one experiment, subjects were preconditiond to the effects of escalatory behavior by being subjected to a simulated attack. In the no-communication condition, escalation occurred between all subject pairs save for one regardless of the preconditioning condition. When communication was allowed, the pre-attacked subject was able to communicate the consequences of the attack to the antagonist and a significantly higher degree of cooperation resulted. Even without preconditioning, the availability of communication decreased the probability of escalation. In games where annihilation of one or both parties was possible, mortality was so high in noncommunication conditions that the Ackoff team decided to keep communication channels permanently open to avoid loss of data from many of the subject pairs. This decision constitutes an interesting finding in itself.

In the experiments run under conditions of open communication, a random numbers table was used to select the last trial to avoid end effects. Players were given money to start the game, which they had to invest in the development and arms sectors. A limit of 20 percent of the amount of money available to the richest player was placed on investments in the arms sector. Some subjects were then allowed to spy on each other. There was a tendency for spying to decrease the probability of escalation, especially when used in combination with communication. The spying served as a check on the truthfulness of the communication before the move sequences were carried out. Results also indicated that the more open the communication, the greater the probability of the conflict's deescalation. Though lack of communication does not necessarily lead to open aggression, the findings suggested that aggression is encouraged by noncommunication. Conrath (1970) also used the Ackoff two-sector game, allowing three-minute written communication periods for all subjects. His results concerning communication are similar to those reported by the Ackoff team.

Bixenstine, Levitt, and Wilson (1966) examined the effects of open oral communication on game behavior using real money as a reward. These researchers transformed a PD matrix from a two-person to a six-person game by making the payoff for each person dependent on the choices of all the others. An individual achieved maximum reward when he chose competitively and all others chose cooperatively; conversely, minimum individual reward resulted when everyone chose competitively. A competitive choice by any individual guaranteed him a larger reward than anyone who chose cooperatively on that trial, but if any two persons chose competitively while all the others cooperated, the competitive reward was no larger than the size of the reward for all choosing cooperatively. If there were more than two competitive choices, the reward for each person was lower than it would have been if all had made cooperative choices. Maximum total reward for the group, comprised of the sum of the individual rewards, occurred with all cooperative choices and minimum total reward occurred with all competitive choices.

Two variables, anonymity of choice and opportunity for communication, were investigated. Half of the subjects were in the knowledge and half in the no-knowledge condition. Subjects in the knowledge condition were aware of the choice of each individual in the group, while subjects in the no-knowledge condition knew only the degree of group cooperation on a trial, but not who, if anyone, had defected. Half of the knowledge and half of the no-knowledge subjects were in the communication condition and half were in the no-communication condition.

The game lasted for forty trials. At the end of twenty trials, subjects in the no-communication condition took a 15-minute break while a tape recorder played Gershwin's *Rhapsody in Blue*. The experimenter remained in the room during this time, and subjects were instructed not to talk. Subjects in the communication condition also took a break after playing twenty trials, but in this condition, the experimenter covertly activated the record switch on the tape recorder and then left the room.

After the 15-minute break, all subjects played the remaining twenty trials.

The findings revealed that communication increased the proportion of cooperative choices in both the knowledge and no-knowledge conditions; however, the major effect occurred in the communication-knowledge condition. For all trials, every group was under 50 percent cooperation with the exception of the communication-knowledge condition, which achieved a level of 83.5 percent cooperative responses for the last twenty trials. Three of the four six-person groups in the communication-knowledge condition played almost 100 percent cooperatively on the last twenty trials, with some type of end effect reducing the level of cooperation in the fourth group. The tape recordings and post-game questionnaires revealed that the three near-100 percent groups negotiated a pact to cooperate during the communication period, as did the fourth communication-knowledge group. Unfortunately, this group arrived at a rather complex agreement and it collapsed near the end of the play. Still, all communication condition groups at least attempted to establish a cooperative agreement, even though the attempt failed in the communication–no-knowledge groups, apparently for lack of information about who was defecting.

When comparing their results with Scodel et al. (1959), who studied the effects of a two-minute communication period between groups of twenty-five trials in a two-person PD game, Bixenstine, Levitt, and Wilson suggest that with the increased number of players in a six-person game, the probability is greater that at least one person will grasp the need for cooperation and communicate his insight to the other players. This interpretation would explain the relatively small increase in cooperation found by Scodel et al. under conditions otherwise comparable to the communication-knowledge condition employed by Bixenstine et al. It should be noted, however, that in the Bixenstine study the effect of communication is once again confounded with the effect of playing twenty trials of the game before an attempt to communicate occurs. Thus, the communication effect actually represents an interaction between communication and the experience of playing twenty trials with a group.

Such persistent confounding points to a dilemma faced by a communication researcher wishing to study the effects of communication on behavior in game-type conflict situations. If the researcher concerns himself only with pre-game communication, he ignores the interesting possibilities inherent in within-play communication exchanges. Yet as we have indicated, those studies which have allowed communication during play confound its effects with prior game-playing experience. In the next section, we report a study that attempts to resolve this dilemma by clearly separating the two confounded components. In addition, we describe research based on a game which permits players to increase their payoffs by arriving at creative solutions not directly provided by the game matrix itself. Such a situation assigns a crucial role to communication not present in the studies discussed thus far.

COMMUNICATION, COOPERATION, AND THE DEVELOPMENT OF CREATIVE ALTERNATIVES

Experiment 1

As we have mentioned, most of the studies discussed earlier confound the effects of communication alone with its effects when combined with the experience of playing several trials of the game. The first experiment (Steinfatt, 1972) sought to separate these two effects.

Figure 3 summarizes the payoff matrix for the PD game employed. Subjects were eighteen pairs of undergraduate students enrolled in speech courses at the University of Michigan. All subjects were questioned concerning their prior knowledge of PD games and game matrices in general. Two subjects were discarded before play began because of their familiarity with the matrices. In all cases, subjects were paired with unfamiliar partners.

Previous studies (Gallo, 1963; Gallo and McClintock, 1965) have stressed the difference between real reward and imaginary reward in

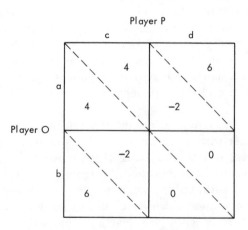

Figure 3 Payoff matrix for Experiment 1.

game situations. As mentioned earlier, these writers argue that when rewards have little perceived value, players may seek to maximize the difference between themselves and their opponents, rather than playing to maximize their own rewards. It could also be argued that knowledge of the form "my score is 50 points" is no knowledge at all: human knowledge requires a reference scale or a comparison point, because singular, isolated knowledge is not informative. If a reward has real value to a player then he can compare the reward to his real scale of values or utilities to determine its relative worth. If the reward is imaginary, however, as in the case where people play games for points, there is no valued reference scale. Thus, a comparison point must be found to determine the value and meaning of "50 points," which will be quite different when the other player has 1 point than when he has 80,000. This comparison point could be a prearranged scale such as an agreement that 15 points wins the game. Or there may be no prearranged reference scale, in which case the only meaningful reference point is determined by "How well is the other doing?" The PD game played under imaginary reward conditions is such a case.

If generalization from the gaming laboratory to nonlaboratory situations is desired, this type of situational difference imposed by the difference in reward conditions must be taken into account. Suppose I earn $10,000 a year and you earn $9,000. Our supervisor gives you two choices. Either you can reduce your salary to $8,000 and mine to $7,000 or you can increase both of our salaries by 10 percent of their current level. The choice seems obvious. You might like to earn more than I, but not at the expense of a cut in salary. But in laboratory studies using rewards of little or no real value to the person, the results do not reflect this choice. Thus, cooperative-competitive measures used in studies of game behavior employing imaginary rewards may not generalize directly to nonlaboratory settings unless such settings involve strong motivation to maximize payoff differences among participants. Although small amounts of money are occasionally used as rewards, it is often difficult to assess their perceived value to the players.

In order to enhance the likelihood that subjects would perceive the rewards as worthwhile, Steinfatt used class grade points in his study. After scoring the mid-term exam for three classes, 15 points were subtracted from the score of each student. The students had been informed that the mid-term would be quite difficult and would be graded harshly.

At the beginning of the term, all students were told they would be expected to act as subjects in an experiment sometime during the semester. A few days after the exams were returned, they were told that they would have a chance to both fulfill this requirement and to get back some points on the mid-term exam. Actually, after the study was completed, all students were apprised of the deception on the mid-term scores and assured that the 15 points would be added back on their scores no matter how they had fared in the game.

Subjects played the game in a large classroom, with the experimenter seated at one end and an assistant at the other. Three pairs were run at a time. The assistant explained to the subjects how to read a game matrix and then seated each pair side by side in front of a table but facing slightly away from each other. The game matrix was situated in the middle of the table, and each player had a pencil and a score sheet in front of him. The assistant was seated about fifteen feet away, facing the subjects. The tables were ten feet apart, facing the assistant. Six pairs of subjects were randomly assigned to each of three conditions: immediate communication, delayed communication, or no communication. Subjects in the delayed- and no-communication conditions were instructed not to talk with, or look at the other player. After twelve trials, delayed-communication subjects were told that they should now face the other player and that they could now talk freely about anything either during or between the trials. Subjects in the no-communication condition were not allowed to talk to or look at their partner during all fifty trials. After the twenty-fourth trial, delayed-communication subjects were asked to assume their original position facing away from each other and were told not to talk or communicate in any way. The assistant was close enough to enforce the no-communication periods, but far enough away that subjects could talk relatively privately if they kept their voices low. Subjects in the immediate-communication condition followed the same procedures except that they were allowed to talk for the first twelve trials and instructed to remain silent thereafter.

On each trial, each player made a mark on his move sheet which could not be changed. When all players indicated to the assistant that they had made their choice, he signalled them to reveal their moves to the other player. Six pairs were male, six female, and six were mixed, with one pair from each category participating in each of six experimental sessions and two pairs from each category being assigned to each experimental condition.

Subjects were told before beginning play that the experimenter was busy correcting papers at the far end of the room and that when they were finished with the game the assistant would tally the total score for each subject and give him or her one poker chip for every 20 game points. Each pair was then to walk to the experimenter's end of the room together where the experimenter added 1 point to each person's midterm grade for each poker chip the person handed him. After "cashing in" their chips, all subjects completed a brief post-experimental questionnaire before leaving.

These features of the experimental procedure were intended to create a situation in which each subject would be motivated to do as well as possible on every trial without regard for the gains or losses of the other. In addition, they provided the opportunity for side deals or kickbacks, since subjects could see from the setup that they would have ample opportunity to exchange poker chips while en route between assistant and experimenter. The possibility of such exchanges was never mentioned or hinted at by the assistant.

In any PD game, no advantage is gained by negotiating side payments, because by definition, no outcome cell in a PD game can have a larger total payoff than the cell involving cooperative choices by both players. Thus, in the present study, an agreement by Player O to choose cooperatively while Player P defects, in exchange for a "cut" of the 6 points P would gain, would not be a rational action, for the total gain for both players would be only 4 points as compared to the 8 points they receive if both cooperate. For this reason, few side payment deals were expected, and comparison of the scores obtained from the move sheets with the point totals recorded by the experimenter revealed that none materialized. The closest any pair came to a side payment was when one subject dropped a handful of chips, but responded with a firm "No, thank you!" to the other player's offer to help pick them up.

The findings revealed no major sex differences for the number of cooperative choices either across or within communication conditions, a result in accord with Rapoport's finding that sex differences do not emerge in runs of less than 100 trials. Data for the three sex pairings were combined for analysis of the various communication conditions. These data are summarized in Table 1.

Analysis of variance of the data in Table 1, treating the trials

Table 1   Percentage of Cooperative Responses Over Trials by Communication Condition [a]

		Trials				Average All Trials	Average for Trials 13-50
		1-12	13-24	25-36	37-50		
Communication	Immed. Comm.	84	88	83	81	84	84
Condition	Delay Comm.	31	70	64	56	55	63
	No Comm.	37	29	26	35	32	30

[a] All percentages based on $N = 600$.

factor as correlated and the communication conditions factor as independent, yielded a significant trials-by-communication interaction ($p <$ .01) and a significant main effect for communication ($p <$ .01). In the no-communication condition, the results do not differ substantially from prior PD studies using small or imaginary rewards. Because the present study did not include a no-communication condition using imaginary rewards, it is impossible to compare the results to Gallo's (1963) finding that cooperation increased under conditions of real reward.

The initial decline in cooperation followed by a recovery, observed so often in PD studies, is evident in the no-communication condition. As would be expected, the first twelve trials of the delayed-communication and the no-communication conditions yielded similar levels of cooperation. During trials 13–24, cooperative responses increased dramatically in the delayed-communication group as communication was allowed. The high level (70 percent) of cooperation achieved by the delayed-communication subjects began to drop after communication was cut off on trial 25 and continued to decline in the later trials, though remaining substantially above the level of cooperation achieved prior to communication. By contrast, subjects in the immediate-communication condition, who were allowed to communicate during the first twelve trials, made 84 percent cooperative responses on these initial trials and then actually increased their level of cooperation after communication was cut off. Even during the final trials of the game, cooperation among immediate-communication subjects dropped only slightly. Apparently, the delayed-communication subjects were influenced by the effects of the first twelve precommunication trials and, as a consequence, they never reached the level of cooperation achieved by the immediate-communication subjects. Moreover, after communication was cut off, cooperation continued in the immediate-communication condition while declining among delayed-communication subjects. Thus, the level of cooperation is higher and more stable when players do not experience a high percentage of noncooperative choices by the other player before the two are allowed to communicate.

Because the subjects knew the results of their opponent's choices, Steinfatt's delayed-communication condition resembles the communication-knowledge condition investigated by Bixenstine, Levitt, and Wilson (1966). As indicated earlier, these researchers obtained 83.5 percent cooperative responses for the twenty trials following a 15-minute communication interval between the twentieth and twenty-first trials of a six-person PD game. Such a magnitude of cooperation occurred in the Steinfatt study only under conditions of immediate communication. Perhaps the effect of the group's existence increased the level of cooperation in the Bixenstine et al. study.

Experiment 2

A second experiment (Steinfatt, 1972) employed a Creative Alternative game devised particularly for the study. The payoff matrix for this game is found in Figure 4.

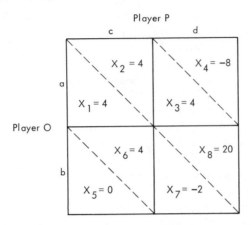

Figure 4 Payoff matrix for Steinfatt's Creative Alternative Game.

The CA game is an attempt to model the type of situation in which collusive crime may occur. Collusive crime (crime without a victim) is a situation in which two or more persons enter into a mutually beneficial agreement which increases the total payoff to the coalition in one of two ways: (1) if the situation is defined as constant sum with "the house" as a player, the gain to the coalition produces a loss of like amount to the house, and (2) if the situation is viewed as variable sum the increased payoff occurs at no one's expense, resulting instead from increased utilities to both parties. Examples of (1) might be the "spiff money" offered by some stereo and high fidelity equipment manufacturers to salesmen and retail outlets to push their products or to give them favorable display space, and other examples of bribes and kickbacks. Examples of (2), depending on one's point of view, might be the paying of a fee to a prostitute or buying a "nickel bag" of marijuana. The house is not usually represented in a CA matrix but is the source of the actual payoffs in the (1) situation.

An important feature of a CA simulation is that collusive crime must be self-generating. It must occur without any hint, suggestion, or encouragement by anyone other than the parties to the agreement. The value of the payoff to both parties should be such that at least one of the parties is able to see the possibility of such an arrangement without receiving outside information that such a solution exists and without encouragement that either party might wish to seek it. In such a situation, communication between the parties will be of maximum importance.

Six conditions may be specified for the solution of a CA game. The existence of the creative alternative solution must be (1) deduced from observation of the situation by at least one of the parties and (2) be communicated to the second party in such a way that (3) the second party is willing to admit the possibility of its existence and (4) perceives its increased benefits for him and (5) is willing to trust that the first party will not take advantage of the situation, to the extent that (6) the second party actually engages in the proscribed behaviors in conjunction with the first party.

A CA game may be defined as a matrix in which (1) there exists only one rational choice for one player (O) but a mixed motive situation for the other player (P); (2) the choice of his best move by O must result in only one rational choice remaining for P; (3) the payoff to both players from this semi-forced solution must be equal; (4) the total payoff to both players must be a maximum when both fail to choose their rational alternative (for P this means the alternative that is rational when O chooses rationally) and should be on the order of twice the total payoff available from the mutual rational choice cell; and (5) neither player has fate control over the other if the other chooses his rational alternative. Symbolically this may be expressed as:

$$X_1 = X_2 = X_3 = X_6; \ X_1 > X_5; \ X_1 > X_7; \ X_1 > X_4 ; (X_8 - X_7) > 2X_1.$$

The CA game is quite different from a PD game. First, it is non-symmetrical, since the payoffs are not the same for P and for O. Second, either player in the CA game can guarantee himself a payoff of four units, O by choosing a and P by choosing c. At first glance, it appears that P has an advantage over O, because P can conceivably get 20 units of reward for a single trial while O's maximum single trial payoff is four units. This advantage, however, is largely illusory, for O has no reason to choose b: if O chooses a, he guarantees himself four units of reward; while if he chooses b, he either gets nothing or loses two units. Thus, O is going to choose a. P may not grasp this fact before the first move. If P concentrates on his own rewards and fails to analyze the game from O's perspective, P may choose d as his first response, hoping that O will choose b.

As a pretest of the game revealed, O almost invariably chooses a on the first trial. As a consequence, subjects operating with P's payoff matrix permanently discarded the d response by no later than the game's third trial. About half of the P subjects made all c responses over the twenty-five trials used in the pretest. Only two of twenty subjects used the b response, and those two only used it once during the entire pre-test. One stated that he thought the game was silly and boring and wanted to break the monotony. The second, who indicated that she initially mis-understood the matrix, responded b on only the first trial. No communication was allowed during the pretest.

When played under these conditions, the CA game quickly becomes boring and uninteresting. Pretest subjects grow quite restless by the time they complete ten trials. But suppose the element of communication is added to the game. If subjects are allowed to communicate, perhaps one or both will see a creative alternative to the constant ac response pattern. For the third major difference between the CA and PD games is that one of the cells contains a joint total payoff greater than the sum of the payoffs for the obvious choice, the ac cell. When communication is not allowed, the existence of this cell (bd) has no bearing on the game be-havior of the subjects. Would it affect their choices if they could com-municate, particularly if they were playing for high rewards such as additional points on a mid-term?

It should be stressed that communication serves a somewhat dif-ferent function in the CA game than in the PD games discussed earlier in this chapter. In PD games, the matrix itself dictates the strategy that will yield the highest payoff for both players. Once the two players have determined this fact and have established their willingness to cooperate, further communication is unnecessary. But in the CA game, mere visual inspection of the matrix, followed by agreement on a move strategy, does not ensure the best result for the participants. To maximize rewards, they must also agree to a deal on side payoffs, an additional step which we have already indicated has no rational basis in PD situations. More-over, although players in a PD game may sometimes lock in on the best strategy without benefit of communication, it is next to impossible for such a resolution to occur in the CA game—i.e., it is inconceivable that O will accept -2 units of reward per trial so that P can obtain $+20$ units *unless* the two players have negotiated a split of the payoffs. Thus, com-munication is central to achieving an optimum, cooperative strategy in the CA game. In addition, we would argue that the role of communica-tion in the CA game more closely resembles its role in real-world con-flicts, where payoffs for the antagonists are seldom completely symmetrical and where a solution to the conflict usually hinges on negotiation of a compromise not clearly defined at the conflict's onset.

The dynamics of the CA game underscore an additional considera-tion that merits discussion. In some of its features, the CA game is reminiscent of the Denny Doodlebug problem, used by Rokeach (1960) to investigate the construct of Dogmatism. The Denny Doodlebug prob-lem deals with an imaginary insect, Joe Doodlebug, who can jump only

North, South, East, and West. Moreover, once he starts to move in a particular direction, he must continue in that direction four jumps before he can change direction (see Rokeach, 1960, for a complete description of the problem). The subject must determine why, given the rules governing Joe's movements, it will take Joe exactly four jumps to get to some food that has been placed in his vicinity. To solve the problem, the subject must examine the facts of Joe's existence and ignore certain assumptions normally made about the ways animals and objects move about. The problem cannot be solved until these assumptions and beliefs are replaced with new ones more relevant to Joe's situation.

Subjects who are allowed to communicate while playing the CA game are in a situation similar to that of subjects attempting to solve the Doodlebug problem. They must overcome specific beliefs about what is possible in the game situation and then develop new beliefs that permit a creative solution of the problem. Given delayed communication in the CA game, P develops a belief that O will always choose *a*, both from P's observation of the game matrix and from his observation of O's behavior. No matter what the conditions of communication, P also develops confidence in the belief that the reward structure of the game is irrevocably defined by the payoff matrix presented to him. This belief corresponds to the real-life assumption that things are as they obviously appear to be and cannot be changed. A third belief inherent in most gaming situations is that anything not specifically allowed by the rules is specifically forbidden; it is this belief that leads us to liken the CA game to a situation involving collusive crime. If P wishes to develop a creative solution to the problem, he must overcome all of these beliefs. The same thing holds true for O.

Because high Dogmatic persons take considerably longer than their low Dogmatic counterparts to solve the Doodlebug problem and because the CA game has been likened to the Doodlebug problem, it follows that high Dogmatic CA players should be less successful than low Dogmatic players in arriving at the creative solution yielding optimum payoffs for both players. This prediction is offered with some trepidation, particularly because several writers (e.g., Rapoport, 1969; Gillis and Woods, 1971) have been critical of gaming behavior studies that employ personality measures. These investigators argue that personality variables are of little use because they apparently account for only a small percentage of the variance in gaming behavior.

Although an exception or two can be noted (e.g., Druckman, 1967), we agree that prior gaming research dealing with personality variables has proved largely unprofitable. But we also believe this poor track record may be attributable to the frequent failure of researchers to specify clearly the relationship between the specific personality construct being investigated and relevant behavioral features of the particular gaming situation. Again, Druckman's study provides an exception to this generalization: he found that high Dogmatic subjects were less willing than low Dogmatics to compromise in a bargaining situation, a finding that fits nicely with Rokeach's conceptual distinctions between open and closed belief systems. Because a similar coordinate relationship between personality construct and gaming situation has been developed for Steinfatt's study, there are defensible grounds for expecting differences in the number of creative solutions reached by high and low Dogmatic CA players.

Thus, Experiment 2 was designed to test the effects of communication and Dogmatism on subjects' ability to achieve a creative solution to the CA game. All features of Experiment 2 were identical to Experiment 1 save for two exceptions: Experiment 2 used the CA matrix and subjects were paired by Dogmatism scores rather than by sex. Before the mid-term examination, subjects completed a short form Dogmatism test (Troldahl and Powell, 1965) under circumstances unrelated to the study. Subjects were assigned to one of four Dogmatism conditions on the basis of a median split of the test scores: two high Dogmatic players (HH), a high Dogmatic P and a Low Dogmatic O (HL), a low Dogmatic P and a high Dogmatic O (LH), and two low Dogmatic players (LL).

The immediate-, delayed-- and no-communication conditions used in Experiment 1 were also repeated, resulting in a four Dogmatism- by three communication-conditions design. Two pairs of subjects were assigned to each cell for a total of 48 subjects. Thus, eight pairs were assigned to each communication condition and six pairs to each Dogmatism condition. All pairs played forty trials of the CA game. The principal dependent measure was achievement of at least three consecutive *bd* responses, the response indicative of a joint creative solution to the game.

The findings relating to the effects of communication and Dogmatism on reaching a creative solution are summarized in Table 2. In the no-communication condition, no subject pair achieved three con-

Table 2 Number of Creative Solutions by Communication and Dogmatism Conditions

| | | Dogmatism Condition | | | |
		HH	HL	LH	LL
Communication Condition	Immed. Comm.	0	0	1	1
	Delay Comm.	0	0	1	2
	No Comm.	0	0	0	0

secutive *bd* responses. After the first few trials, no pair responded in any way except *ac,* save for one exception. The O player in one HL pair began to make an occasional *d* response after the twenty-fifth trial, and on the thirty-fourth trial, the two players responded *bd.* For the six remaining trials, they responded *ac.* Finally, no players in the no-communication condition made attempts at side payments. Thus, it seems safe to conclude that a creative solution to the CA game will not be realized if communication is not allowed.

Table 3 presents the percentage of *bd* responses for the immediate-

Table 3   Percentage of *bd* responses by Trial Block for Immediate- and Delayed-Communication Subjects [a]

		Trials		
		1–12	*13–24*	*25–40*
Communication	Immed. Comm.	22	25	25
Condition	Delay Comm.	0	35	38

[a] Percentages based on eight pairs over number of trials in each cell.

and delayed-communication conditions over all Dogmatism conditions by trial blocks. Again, no pairs achieved a single *bd* response before the onset of communication. In the delayed-communication condition, in which communication was allowed only on trials 13 through 24, three of the eight pairs began an unbroken pattern of *bd* responses on about the thirteenth trial, and this pattern continued through trial 40. The five remaining delayed-communication pairs made an occasional *b* or *d* response but were characterized by a continuous pattern of *ac* responses.

In the immediate-communication condition, two of the eight pairs established a continuous *bd* response pattern within the first five trials which continued through trial 40. The remaining six pairs fell into an *ac* pattern, although individual players presented an occasional *b* or *d* response.

In short, all pairs, with rare exceptions, locked into a highly consistent response pattern. When communication was not allowed, this pattern invariably took the form of an *ac* response. When communication was permitted, most pairs continued with the same *ac* pattern, but a few either switched to, or began with, an entirely new consistent pattern. This new pattern consisted of a continuous *bd* response instead of the *ac* response chosen by the majority of subject pairs. Thus, communication is a necessary but not a sufficient condition for achieving a creative solution. Once reached, this solution is quite stable and persists when communication is cut off.

The questionnaire responses suggest the following path for a creative solution. One player (in these five cases always P) suddenly realizes that both he and his partner could reap greater rewards by choosing the *bd* response. He suggests this possibility to his partner, specifying a proposed split of the twenty units of reward. In some cases, P's proposed a ten-ten split, and in others, they proposed nine for themselves and eleven for the O's, so that each player would gain nine reward units on each trial. In four of the five pairs reaching the creative solutions, the nine-eleven split was adopted.

Three subjects in the no-communication condition and five subjects in both the immediate- and the delayed-communication conditions said they considered ways of getting the twenty reward units but could not achieve this goal, either because they were unable to communicate at that juncture of the trials or because they could not convince the other player to go along with the plan. This latter barrier suggests a study of the kinds of communication strategies that are effective in this type of situation, for P must convince O that he is trustworthy and that he will actually divide the rewards after the game is completed.

Finally, the results on the Dogmatism variable are in line with theoretic expectations, but admittedly, more data are needed for a convincing test of the effects of this variable. Given the study's limited sample, low Dogmatic subjects were much more likely to achieve a creative solution as represented by three consecutive *bd* responses. In no case did a pair reach a creative solution when a high Dogmatic was in the P position. No HH or HL subjects arrived at a creative solution, while three of the four LL pairs did so (see Table 2). Thus, Dogmatism appears to be related to the achievement of a creative solution, but not as strongly as the presence or absence of communication. Still, the Dogmatism finding lends support to Rutheford's conclusions:

> If decision makers tend to possess paranoid personality systems, with attendant belief rigidity and suspicion, their ability to adopt creative and innovative perspectives may be curtailed. The ability of their organizations to enter into trustful relationships with other organizations may likewise be curtailed. (1966, p. 405.)

SUMMARY OF COMMUNICATION FINDINGS

After all of this research, even though it represents only the barest of starts, what do we know about the effects of communication behavior in game-theoretic conflict situations that we did not know before? In general, pre-game discussions of how to play the game and pre-game exchanges of commitment messages have produced increased cooperation in PD situations, but simply seeing one's opponent before the start of a PD game apparently has no significant effect on the level of cooperation. When a person receives a message before the start of play stating a pacifistic intent by the other, he has a greater probability of engaging in a sharing strategy in a SMH game than does someone who does not receive such a message. Yet reception of this pacifist message is no guarantee of sharing behavior by the receiver, because it is sometimes perceived as a trick, in which case the receiver feels even more justified in dominating the pacifist. These results also apply to a warning pacifist who signals his intent to shock the subject, but never carries through on his threat, perhaps giving his threat low credibility. A shocking pacifist, on the other hand, who both warns and shocks, is faced with even more aggressive behavior by the subject than either the "pure" or warning pacifist. When not in the presence of an observer, subjects in the SMH game cooperate significantly more often when they can communicate with their opponent than when they cannot. When an observer is present, cooperation is increased and the addition of communication to the observed situation apparently does *not* increase cooperation to an even higher level. It appears that the potential communication of information about the subject's behavior to unknown others acts as a spur to increased cooperation the same way actual communication does, although the two effects are not additive.

Some of the results from PD games seem to be quite straightforward, while others are quite complex. As an example of the latter, subjects who choose not to send a threatening message to their opponent are more likely to cooperate on the next response if they are males facing a fixed-expense situation than if they are females facing either a fixed-expense or a retaliation situation, but are much less likely to cooperate on the next move if they are males facing a retaliation situation. In the more straightforward category are the findings that a communication period between two sets of twenty-five trials produces increased cooperation, and that a behavioral credibility level of 90 percent in messages promising cooperation is more effective in producing cooperation than are credibility levels of 60 percent or 30 percent.

The situation or type of game seems to be related to the most effective type of communication. Optional communication between game opponents is generally more effective than forced communication, but this is especially true in dangerous games such as Chicken. In the trucking game, there is some evidence to suggest that communication periods allowed after a deadlock has occurred can be used more effectively than pre-deadlock periods if an increase in the joint total payoff is the criterion. Also, in the trucking game, promises tend to be used more than threats by independent groups to which only one or the other is available and by groups to which both threats and promises are available. When only threats or only promises are available, more contingent messages tend to be sent than if both threats and promises can be used. The availability of messages that promise cooperation, either contingent on the other's behavior or not, leads to an increase in sharing behavior.

Channel restrictions are also important predictors of behavior. The fewer the restrictions and the more open the communication allowed, the greater the probability of deescalation of a conflict. The addition of a channel which provides knowledge of the other's actual behaviors, such as a spy network, is quite important in producing even greater deescalation and an increased probability for cooperation. The addition of the opportunity for communication to a situation in which information concerning the moves of all players is known produces very high levels of cooperation. Intrateam consultation produces higher cooperation levels than is usually produced by individual players, who in turn cooperate more than teams where consultation is not allowed.

There is a strong tendency for communication to produce more cooperation whenever it is introduced, but the maximum effect occurs when communication is allowed from the beginning of the game interaction even if the opportunity to communicate is cut off at some point later in the trials. A delay in the start of communication until several interactions have occurred seems to depress the maximum level of cooperation and to require continued opportunities for communication to keep cooperation at even that level. In situations demanding creativity by the subjects, communication is a necessary but perhaps not a sufficient condition for the achievement of a creative solution. There is some evidence to suggest that even with communication opportunities, high Dogmatic persons in certain game roles may not be able to achieve a creative solution to the game.

The reader should be cautioned that this summary is too brief to contain all of the information relevant to the truth probability of the above statements. The summary *is* only a summary and the reader may better evaluate these statements by reviewing the whole section of this chapter on communication in gaming studies of conflict.

CONCLUSION

In this paper, we have explicated some of the basic terminology of game theory, discussed several ways of coming to know the strategies of other players in game-theoretic conflict situations, described previous research dealing with the role of communication in game-theoretic models of conflict, and presented the results of two recent studies which sought to delineate more precisely the effects of communication on game-playing behavior. To a large extent, then, our task has been descriptive; we have attempted to provide the relatively uninitiated reader with an overview of the current state of conceptual and empirical thinking relating to the study of communication effects in game-theoretic models of conflict.

Running through our remarks, however, sometimes implicitly and sometimes explicitly, is a tone of evaluation, and perhaps even an exhortation to the researcher concerned with the role of communication in the process of conflict. For at this date, we believe researchers have hardly commenced to probe the immense potential of communication in gaming-type conflict situations. In the majority of studies cited, communication has assumed only the most rudimentary forms—in some cases, we even question the utility of labeling the behaviors involved "communication"—and has satisfied the relatively mundane, albeit important, function of mutually reinforcing the choice of a strategy already dictated by the game's payoff matrix. In the daily political, economic, and social conflicts we all face, mutually advantageous solutions are seldom this sharply defined, and in seeking an acceptable solution, communication serves a myriad of cognitive and affective functions.

Nothing in our preceding comments is intended to detract from the value, or the quality, of previous game-theory research. What we do wish to underscore is captured by this caveat: if studies of the effects of communication in game-theoretic conflict situations are to have ecological validity—i.e., if findings are to be generalized to real-world conflict situations with at least modest confidence—richer conceptualizations of communication must be employed, and the variety of conflict situations investigated must be expanded. Moreover, a host of communication-centered questions merit concerted attention. Among a few of these are: How can persons already in conflict be induced to communicate? Does the use of various available channels of communication produce different effects in conflict situations? What are the side effects of communication? More specifically, are persons in conflict less likely to aggress when they are communicating with their antagonists, or are there circumstances in which communication heightens the instigation to aggression? And what about the work on threats and promises? How does the literature on communication and persuasion fit into a game-theoretic framework?

Even if communication researchers heed our preceding caveat, we are not naive enough to think the task of generalizing will be an easy one. As we noted earlier, the major advantage of game-theoretic paradigms lies in the situational control the investigator has at his disposal. Gains in control are usually offset by losses in generalizibility. Perhaps these words of Rapoport, Shubik, and Thrall (1965) best capture our present attitude about future research dealing with the effects of communication in game-theoretic models of conflict:

> It is not expected that the contributions of gaming to the understanding of conflict and conflict resolution will be made via facile generalization from laboratory experiments to real life. We can hope, however, that patient, systematic, cumulative investigations, guided by progressive interaction of theory and experiment, will eventually disclose patterns suggesting some broad features of typical mixed-motive conflicts. It is the mixed-motive conflict which is of greatest interest in the study of conflict resolution; for typically, games modeled after such conflicts (non-zero-sum and N-person coalition games) have no forced solutions. Their outcomes depend essentially on negotiated or tacit agreements among the participants, or on failure to achieve such agreements. (p. 66)

We would add only that success or failure in negotiations may be largely determined by the presence or absence, and the effective or ineffective use, of that instrumental process which many would argue distinguishes conflictful man from conflictful lower animal forms: the process of communication.

REFERENCES

ACKOFF, R. L., D. W. CONRATH, and N. HOWARD, *A Model Study of the Escalation and De-escalation of Conflict,* Vol. 1. Management Science Center, University of Pennsylvania, 1967.

AUBERT, V., "Competition and Dissensus: Two Types of Conflict and Conflict Resolution," *Journal of Conflict Resolution,* 7 (1963), 26–42.

BEISECKER, T., "Verbal Persuasive Strategies in Mixed-Motive Interactions," *Quarterly Journal of Speech,* 56 (1970), 149–60.

BERKOWITZ, L., *Aggression: A Social Psychological Analysis.* New York: McGraw-Hill, 1962.

BERNARD, J., "The Sociological Study of Conflict," in International Sociological Association, *The Nature of Conflict.* Paris: UNESCO, 1957.

BIXENSTINE, V. E., N. CHAMBERS, and K. V. WILSON, "Effect of Asymmetry in Payoff on Behavior in a Two-Person Non-Zero-Sum Game," *Journal of Conflict Resolution,* 8 (1964), 151–59.

BIXENSTINE, V. E., and J. W. GAEBELEIN, "Strategies of 'Real' Opponents in Eliciting Cooperative Choice in a Prisoner's Dilemma Game," *Journal of Conflict Resolution,* 15 (1971), 157–66.

BIXENSTINE, V. E., C. A. LEVITT, and K. V. WILSON, "Collaboration among Six Persons in a Prisoner's Dilemma Game," *Journal of Conflict Resolution,* 10 (1966), 488–96.

BIXENSTINE, V. E., and K. V. WILSON, "Effects of Level of Cooperative Choice by the Other Player on Choices in a Prisoner's Dilemma Game," Part II, *Journal of Abnormal and Social Psychology,* 67 (1963), 139–47.

72   PERSPECTIVES ON COMMUNICATION IN SOCIAL CONFLICT

BONACICH, P., "Putting the Dilemma Back into Prisoner's Dilemma," *Journal of Conflict Resolution*, 14 (1970), 379–87.

BORAH, L. A., JR., "The Effects of Threat in Bargaining: Critical and Experimental Analysis," *Journal of Abnormal and Social Psychology*, 66 (1963), 37–44.

BOSTROM, R. N., "Game Theory in Communication Research," *Journal of Communication*, 18 (1968), 369–88.

CHAMMAH, A. M., "Experiments," an unpublished paper. Cited by A. Rapoport in *Journal of Conflict Resolution*, 10 (1966), 209.

CHENEY, J., T. HARFORD, and L. SOLOMON, "The Effects of Communicating Threats and Promises upon the Bargaining Process," *Journal of Conflict Resolution*, 16 (1972), 99–107.

CONRATH, D. W., "Experience as a Factor in Experimental Gaming Behavior," *Journal of Conflict Resolution*, 14 (1970), 195–202.

COSER, L., *The Functions of Social Conflict*. New York: The Free Press, 1956.

DEUTSCH, M., "Conditions Affecting Cooperation." Final Technical Report, February 1957, Contract NONR-285 [10], Office of Naval Research.

———, "Trust and Suspicion," *Journal of Conflict Resolution*, 2 (1958), 265–79.

———, "The Effect of Motivational Orientation upon Trust and Suspicion," *Human Relations*, 13 (1960), 123–39.

———, "Socially Relevant Science: Reflections on some Studies of Inter-personal Conflict," *American Psychologist*, 24 (1969), 1076–92.

DEUTSCH, M., and R. M. KRAUSS, "The Effect of Threat upon Interpersonal Bargaining," *Journal of Abnormal and Social Psychology*, 61 (1960), 181–89.

———, "Studies of Interpersonal Bargaining," *Journal of Conflict Resolution*, 6 (1962), 52–76.

———, *Theories in Social Psychology*. New York: Basic Books, 1965.

DEUTSCH, M., and R. J. LEWICKI, "'Locking-in' Effects During a Game of Chicken," *Journal of Conflict Resolution*, 14 (1970), 367–78.

DRUCKMAN, D., "Dogmatism, Prenegotiation Experience, and Simulated Group Representation as Determinants of Dyadic Behavior in a Bargaining Situation," *Journal of Personality and Social Psychology*, 6 (1967), 279–90.

FINK, C. F., "Some Conceptual Difficulties in the Theory of Social Conflict," *Journal of Conflict Resolution*, 12 (1968), 412–60.

FLOOD, M. M., "Some Experimental Games," *Management Science*, 5 (1958), 5–26.

GAHAGAN, J. P., and J. T. TEDESCHI, "Strategy and the Credibility of Promises in the Prisoner's Dilemma Game," *Journal of Conflict Resolution*, 12 (1968) 224–34.

GALLO, P. S., "The Effects of Different Motivational Orientations in a Mixed-Motive Game." Unpublished doctoral dissertation, University of California at Los Angeles, 1963.

GALLO, P. S., and C. G. McCLINTOCK, "Cooperative and Competitive Behavior in Mixed-Motive Games," *Journal of Conflict Resolution*, 9 (1965), 68–78.

GILLIS, J. S., and G. T. WOODS, "The 16PF as an Indicator of Performance in the Prisoner's Dilemma Game," *Journal of Conflict Resolution*, 15 (1971) 393–402.

HORAI, J., and J. T. TEDESCHI, "The Effects of Credibility and Magnitude of Punishment upon Compliance to Threats," *Journal of Personality and Social Psychology*, 12 (1969), 164–69.

KELLEY, H. H., "The Consequences of Different Patterns of Interdependency in Small Groups." *Final report to National Science Foundation*, 1953.

————, "Threats in Interpersonal Negotiations." Unpublished paper presented at the Pittsburgh Seminar on Social Sciences of Organization, University of Pittsburgh, 1962.

————, "Experimental Studies of Threats in Interpersonal Negotiations," *Journal of Conflict Resolution*, 9 (1965) 79–105.

KRAUSS, R. M., and M. DEUTSCH, "Communication in Interpersonal Bargaining," *Journal of Personality and Social Psychology*, 4 (1966), 572–77.

LOOMIS, J. L., "Communication, the Development of Trust, and Cooperative Behavior," *Human Relations*, 12 (1959), 305–15.

LUCE, R. D., and H. RAIFFA, *Games and Decisions*. New York: Wiley & Sons, 1957.

MARTIN, M., "Some Effects of Communication on Group Behavior in Prisoner's Dilemma." Unpublished thesis, Case Institute of Technology, 1964.

MCCLINTOCK, C. G., and S. P. MCNEEL, "Reward Level and Game Playing Behavior," *Journal of Conflict Resolution*, 10 (1966), 98–102.

MEEKER, R. J., and G. H. SHURE, "Pacifist Bargaining Tactics: Some 'Outsider' Influences," *Journal of Conflict Resolution*, 13 (1969), 487–93.

MINTZ, A., "Nonadaptive Group Behavior," *Journal of Abnormal and Social Psychology*, 46 (1951), 150–59.

OSKAMP, S., "Effects of Programmed Strategies on Cooperation in the Prisoner's Dilemma and Other Mixed-Motive Games," *Journal of Conflict Resolution*, 15 (1971), 225–59.

OSKAMP, S., and D. PERLMAN, "Factors Affecting Cooperation in a Prisoner's Dilemma Game," *Journal of Conflict Resolution*, 9 (1965), 359–74.

PHILLIPS, J., "Alliance Structures in the Triad." Paper presented at a colloquium for the Department of Psychology, University of Miami, Coral Gables, Florida, December 1967.

PHILLIPS, J., and T. CONNER, "Studies of Conflict, Conflict Reduction, and Alliance Formation." Report 70-1, Cooperation/Conflict Research Group, Computer Institute for Social Science Research, Michigan State University, 1970.

PYLYSHYN, Z., N. AGNEW, and J. ILLINGSWORTH, "Comparison of Individuals and Pairs as Participants in a Mixed-Motive Game," *Journal of Conflict Resolution*, 10 (1966), 211–21.

RADLOW, R., "An Experimental Study of 'cooperation' in the Prisoner's Dilemma Game," *Journal of Conflict Resolution*, 9 (1965), 221–27.

RADLOW, R., and M. F. WEIDNER, "Unenforced Commitments in 'cooperative' and 'noncooperative' Non-Constant-Sum Games," *Journal of Conflict Resolution*, 10 (1966), 497–505.

RAPOPORT, A., *Fights, Games, and Debates*. Ann Arbor: University of Michigan Press, 1960.

————, Editorial Comment on Gaming, *Journal of Conflict Resolution*, 9 (1965), 211.

———, Editorial Comment on Gaming, *Journal of Conflict Resolution,* 10 (1966), 87, 209.

———, Editorial Comment on Gaming, *Journal of Conflict Resolution,* 13 (1969), 485–86.

———, Editorial Comment on Gaming, *Journal of Conflict Resolution,* 15 (1971), 487–88.

———, "Conflict Resolution in Light of Game Theory and Beyond," in *The Structure of Conflict,* P. Swingle, ed., pp. 1–44. New York: Academic Press, 1970.

RAPOPORT, A., and A. M. CHAMMAH, *Prisoner's Dilemma.* Ann Arbor: University of Michigan Press, 1965.

———, "Sex Differences in Factors Contributing to the Level of Cooperation in the Prisoner's Dilemma Game," *Journal of Personality and Social Psychology,* 2 (1965), 831–38.

RAPOPORT, A., M. SHUBIK, and R. THRALL, Editorial Introduction to Gaming Section, *Journal of Conflict Resolution,* 9 (1965), 66–67.

RAVEN, B. H., and A. W. KRUGLANSKI, "Conflict and Power," in *The Structure of Conflict,* P. Swingle, ed., pp. 69–109. New York: Academic Press, 1970.

ROKEACH, M., *The Open and Closed Mind.* New York: Basic Books, 1960.

———, *Beliefs, Attitudes, and Values.* San Francisco: Jossey-Bass, 1967.

RUTHEFORD, B., "Psychopathology, Decision Making, and Political Involvement," *Journal of Conflict Resolution,* 10 (1966), 387–407.

SCHELLING, T. C., *The Strategy of Conflict.* Cambridge: Harvard University Press, 1960. (Republished: New York, Oxford University Press, 1963.)

SCODEL, A., "Induced Collaboration in Some Non-Zero-Sum Games," *Journal of Conflict Resolution,* 6 (1962), 335–40.

———, "Effects of Group Discussion on Cooperation in a Prisoner's Dilemma Game." Paper presented at the meeting of the California State Psychological Association, December 1963.

SCODEL, A., J. S. MINAS, P. RATOOSH, and M. LIPETZ, "Some Descriptive Aspects of Two-Person Non-Zero-Sum Games," *Journal of Conflict Resolution,* 3 (1959), 114–19.

SHUBIK, M., "Game Theory, Behavior, and the Paradox of the Prisoner's Dilemma: Three Solutions," *Journal of Conflict Resolution,* 14 (1970), 181–93.

SHURE, G. H., R. J. MEEKER, and E. A. HANSFORD, "The Effectiveness of Pacifist Strategies in Bargaining Games," *Journal of Conflict Resolution,* 9, (1965), 106–17.

SOLOMON, L., "The Influence of Some Types of Power Relationships and Game Strategies upon the Development of Interpersonal Trust," *Journal of Abnormal and Social Psychology,* 61 (1960), 223–30.

SPEER, D. C., "Marital Dysfunctionality and Two-Person Non-Zero-Sum Game Behavior: Cumulative Monadic Measures," *Journal of Personality and Social Psychology,* 21 (1972), 18–24.

STEINFATT, T. M., "Communication in the Prisoner's Dilemma and in a Creative Alternative Game." *Proceedings of the National Gaming Council's Eleventh Annual Symposium,* pp. 212–24. Center for Social Organization of Schools, The Johns Hopkins University, Baltimore, 1972.

SWINGLE, P., "Dangerous Games," in *The Structure of Conflict*, P. Swingle, ed., pp. 235–76. New York: Academic Press, 1970.

SWINGLE, P., and A. SANTI, "Communication in Non-Zero-Sum Games," *Journal of Personality and Social Psychology*, 23 (1972), 54–63.

TEDESCHI, J. T., T. BONOMA, and N. NOVINSON, "Behavior of a Threatener: Retaliation vs. Fixed Opportunity Costs," *Journal of Conflict Resolution*, 14 (1970), 67–76.

TODD, F. J., K. R. HAMMOND, and M. M. WILKINS, "Differential Effects of Ambiguous and Exact Feedback on Two-Person Conflict and Compromise," *Journal of Conflict Resolution*, 10 (1966), 88–97.

TROLDAHL, V., and F. POWELL, "A Short Form Dogmatism Scale for Use in Field Studies," *Social Forces*, 44 (1965), 211–14.

TUBBS, S., "Two Person Game Behavior, Conformity-Inducing Messages, and Interpersonal Trust," *Journal of Communication*, 21 (1971), 326–41.

VINCENT, J. E., and E. W. SCHWERIN, "Ratios of Force and Escalation in a Game Situation," *Journal of Conflict Resolution*, 15 (1971), 489–98.

VINCENT, J. E., and J. O. TINDELL, "Alternative Cooperative Strategies in a Bargaining Game," *Journal of Conflict Resolution*, 13 (1969), 494–510.

VON NEUMANN, J., and O. MORGANSTERN, *The Theory of Games and Economic Behavior*. Princeton, N.J.: Princeton University Press, 1944.

WALLACE, D., and P. ROTHAUS, "Communication, Group Loyalty, and Trust in the PD Game," *Journal of Conflict Resolution*, 13 (1969), 370–80.

WATZLAWICK, P., J. H. BEAVIN, and D. D. JACKSON, *Pragmatics of Human Communication*. New York: Norton, 1967.

3

Communication
and
the Simulation of
Social Conflict

FRED E. JANDT

In their attempts to study social conflict, social scientists have themselves experienced intrapersonal conflict. On the one hand, they have sought to represent and to account for the complexity of conflict. On the other, they have sought to reduce that complexity to manageable research proportions. More than in most areas of the social sciences, the problem of coping with conflict's complexities evades tidy solutions.

Most investigators of conflict have preferred "simple-mindedness" to "muddle-headedness." As Steinfatt and Miller indicate in the preceding chapter, these researchers have studied social conflict through the vehicle of experimental games, knowing full well that games such as Prisoner's Dilemma greatly sacrifice external for internal validity. In "Prospects for Experimental Games," Rapoport (1968), a leading advocate of game research, has himself cautioned that extrapolation from laboratory results with games to real-life settings is *especially hazardous in the area of conflict* because of the lack of realism in games and the usually limited range of results obtained. The simplest two-by-two game with eight independent variables would require 6,561 experiments to obtain a body of data suitable for a comprehensive description of how the choices are influenced by the payoffs.[1]

One virtue of experimental games is that they help us to see more clearly what a more adequate design for the study of conflict ought to encompass. In Prisoner's Dilemma, for example, the alternatives are always well-defined and never change. In a sense, Prisoner's Dilemma freezes the conflict process at one point in the perception of alternatives and only permits the players to react repeatedly in that "frozen" time in only one of two ways. This situation itself reveals a second restriction. A player, in a very real sense, can communicate only with his responses to the game, because that is probably the communication of greatest consequence to the other player. This limitation seems unduly restrictive and unrealistic of human communicative as well as conflict behaviors, such as those behaviors which may precede a divorce. Finally, while the alternatives may be well-defined, games assume that the alternatives are relevant to the parties. The alternatives in a game translate to the *rewards* of the game, but just as the rewards are a function of the game so are the *losses,* which in games are only the failure to win. The loser brought nothing to the game he lost; the winner won only from the structure of the game. In real-life conflict a loser loses something that is relevant to him or else he would not be involved in the conflict.

Most important, as Rapoport (1968) and Raser (1969) are careful to point out, gaming is not a theory. Experimental gaming, according to Rapoport, should be "devoted to the simplest formats, which alone make possible a systematic build-up of *a* theory. The relevance of this theory to a general theory of conflict is a question which can be posed only after the theory has been constructed" (p. 470). Raser has emphasized the same point by describing gaming as "a laboratory for studying basic principles of human behavior and as an admittedly inadequate framework for conducting research leading to the improvement of the framework itself" (p. 29).

---

[1] Rapoport explains the figure 6,561 in a personal letter dated September 28, 1972, as follows: ". . . by an 'experiment' I meant a set of experimental runs involving a single iterated 2 × 2 game. To establish statistically stable results using some hundreds of iterations about 10–20 subject pairs would be required. Now any statistic of such a collection of protocols would be a function of eight independent variables, since each of the eight payoffs of a 2 × 2 game can be varied independently within the limits prescribed by the structure of the game (which is defined by the orders of inequality of each player's payoffs). If we assign just three values to each payoff (low, medium and high) independently, the number of experiments required to get complete information of the effects of payoffs in the statistics of interest would be $3^4 \times 3^4 = 6561$."

Is there a happy medium in the study of conflict between the "simple-mindedness" of gaming methods and the "muddle-headedness" of other procedures? In particular, are there ways of coming to grips with communication in social conflicts and with individual differences in attitudes that give rise to differences in communication behaviors and in conflict outcomes? Some investigators have looked to simulation techniques as a compromise solution to the "simple-mindedness–muddle-headedness" dilemma. This chapter presents an introduction to simulation techniques as methods for studying communication in social conflicts.

Before discussing simulation research, two definitions are in order. By "social conflict," I have in mind a clash of interests or values that is perceived as such by two or more parties to the dispute and that is manifested by communication between them. The definition thus focuses on manifest conflict but places the locus of conflict in the attitudes and perceptions of the conflicting parties. By "communication" I mean any verbal or nonverbal symbolic act to which others may attach meaning. This definition includes the types of moves found in experimental games but it also includes verbal interactions.

SIMULATION AS A RESEARCH DESIGN

In their first edition, Zuckerman and Horn (1970) catalogued 404 simulations and listed an additional 450 more; in their second edition, they catalogued 613 simulations and listed an additional 473 more discontinued, in development, or lacking complete information (Zuckerman and Horn, 1973). Even these listings probably represent only a third of the simulations presently in use. Students of speech communication, however, have not rushed to adopt simulation techniques. Tucker (1968) and Gorden (1969a, 1969b, 1971b) have described a few of the simulations available and have discussed their possible instructional uses in speech courses. Additionally, Gorden (1971a) has prepared an academic game simulation of Supreme Court decisions on free speech and free press. Recently, Ruben (1972) has described a few of the simulations available for human relations training.

Theoretical and research literature on simulation techniques is rapidly expanding. Useful bibliographies include those of Werner and Werner (1969) and Kidder (1971). In 1970, a new journal, *Simulation and Games: An International Journal of Theory, Design, and Research,* appeared. A tabloid, *Simulation/Gaming/News,* has also recently commenced publication. The National Gaming Council has been formed to include individuals interested in simulation techniques, especially in the fields of sociology, political science, urban and environmental studies, military and civil defense, business and economics, and education. The Center for Social Organization of Schools has had an active staff involved in simulation techniques.

A simulation is a representation of a *model* of some external reality through which the players interact in much the same way they would in reality. This feature of simulation techniques sets them apart from experimental gaming procedures. That a simulation is an *operating model* through which process and change may be observed is accepted by such scholars in the field as Dawson (1962) and Raser (1969). Verba (1964) elaborates on the defining characteristics of a simulation:

> A simulation is a model of a system. Other models . . . may attempt to represent a system through verbal means, mathematical means, or pictorial means. Like simulations, they involve the abstraction of certain aspects of the system one is studying and an attempt to replicate these aspects by other means, such as words or mathematical symbols. But the simulation model differs in that it is an *operating* model. Once the variables that have been selected are given values within the simulation and the relations among the variables are specified, the model is allowed to operate. It may operate through the interaction of people who play roles within the model; or it may operate on a computer. The rules given to the human participants in the simulation or the computer program represent the premises of the model. Its operation produces the implications. (p. 491)

Hermann (1967), in his monograph on validation problems in simulations, specifically develops the concept of a simulation as an operating model. He describes simulation techniques as being part of the generic class called models. As a model, a simulation is a partial representation of some independent system designed for the purpose of increasing understanding of the system the simulation is intended to represent. The distinctive property of a simulation that separates it from verbal, pictorial, or mathematical models is its ability to evolve through time as the related components interact with one another and assume different values. Thus, simulations as operating models are capable of producing events that could not readily be derived by an observer from the initial conditions of the simulation. This dynamic, over-time quality is an important defining characteristic of simulations.

The relation between human performance in a simulation and in role-playing must be specified at this point. As Hermann has pointed out, in a simulation participants are *not* to be given unfamiliar roles to enact because when a participant is assigned a role for which he has little or no information, the resulting behavior may result in major and systematic distortions. For example, North American college students cannot be reasonably expected to accurately "act like" Soviet military policy makers in an international simulation without severely distorting the relationship between the simulation model and reality. In a simulation, participants are assigned to positions with which they are familiar, or the simulation itself is so structured that certain constraints and responsibilities are imposed by the format of the model. In other words, in a simulation the participant is instructed to act as himself with role attributes indicated by specified requirements built into the model. Techniques for role-structuring include the use of rewards, definition of communication channels, and specification of the kind of information that can be transmitted.

The relationship between gaming and simulation has been specified in position papers published by Instructional Simulations, Inc. (1970). Games such as Prisoner's Dilemma are described as a class of generic models designed for explicit human factors analysis in a simplified manual or programmed version of a problem. Games "behavioralize" only the "least required" element of a process and system to depict a problem; they set aside questions of real world approximation. By contrast, simulations replicate the interactions of states, events, objects, variables, and factors to express the dynamic operation of systems.

As Emshoff and Sisson (1970) have put it, the operating model of reality should be as abstract as possible and still be predictive. Moreover, these behavioral models are especially needed in situations in which other kinds of experimentation are not physically or economically feasible, such as in conflict situations. Although the operating model must be an accurate representation of some external reality, it need not be a complete representation. The description of the model given to the participants must be complete enough so that each enters the simulation with perceptions of the situation that are consistent with the intent of the simulation. However, the description of the model should not be so complete that a player feels he has no real alternatives during the course of the simulation. This degree of entropy is the critical factor for successful experimental replications. A recent study (Philippatos and Moscato, 1969) seems to indicate, however, that even players operating under conditions of complete ignorance about the nature and rules of business games are able to decipher the most important characteristics of the games, along with the variables and the ranges of minimum and maximum performance.

The use of simulation techniques must always proceed on two courses: as an artificial reality and as an operating model of some external reality. Simulation use should include both the development of the model to predict behaviors in the simulation itself and the subsequent and repeated testing of the model in the real world. Research uses of simulations which include this necessary second step should have greater reliability. Druckman and Zechmeister (1970), for example, when using a simulation of the political decision-making process, recognized the need to check the simulation model's representativeness of the real world.

For research purposes, the most interesting use of simulation techniques centers on the assessment and evaluation of human performance. Simulation techniques offer a unique opportunity to assess human performance in lifelike settings that often cannot be tested by other means. It would appear, as the previous discussion would suggest, that the more closely the test situation approximates the real-life situation, the more powerful the prediction. Useful sources for using simulations for measurement are Frederiksen (1962), McGuire and Babbott (1967), and Schalock (1969). Additionally, simulations have been used in a number of research studies, such as those in international relations by Guetzkow (1959) and by Druckman and Ludwig (1969) and in industrial negotiations by Morley and Stephenson (1969) and by Smith (1969). In these cases, the use of simulation techniques provides an opportunity to evaluate behaviors in situations that would not otherwise be easily evaluated.

The use of simulation techniques for research need not be limited to reproducing situations that could not otherwise be easily evaluated. Simulations may be used to reproduce situations that are subject to evaluation in the real world, but the use of simulation techniques in such situations to reproduce the real world in the laboratory also permits the experimenter to manipulate variables more easily and to replicate more easily. For example, Stoll and McFarlane could study acquaintanceship and sex differences (1969) and Nagasawa could compress time to study success-striving behavior (1970).

The use of simulation techniques may be one of the most appropriate research designs for the study of social conflict. That social conflict should be studied by simulation techniques is advanced by the Proceedings of the Third Annual Symposium of the American Society for Cybernetics (1971). Man, man-machine, and machine interpersonal-ascendant simulations (as contrasted to media-ascendant simulations and nonsimulation games) can be devised to focus on social conflict.

Interpersonal-ascendant simulations are characterized by role-playing, participant interaction, and decision-making and are thus most likely to allow for social conflict. Media-ascendant simulations emphasize learning through the vicarious experiences permitted by films, machines, and the like. Cockpit and operational flight training as typical examples of media-ascendant simulations clearly indicate that this technique is not conducive to situations of social conflict. Nonsimulation games, such as WIFF'N PROOF and EQUATIONS, structure a competitive context for learning concepts and principles drawn from formal disciplines. Nonsimulation games, as their ancestor gaming, can be shown to be unduly restrictive in simulating the complex process of social conflict. Therefore, interpersonal-ascendant simulations, which include most management and social studies simulations, provide the most representative model to study social conflict.

The question that must be clearly answered concerns the relationship between the study of social conflict and simulation techniques. This relationship has been discussed by Burton (1969). As a scholar of international relations, he advocates the technique of "controlled communication" derived from the hypotheses that social conflict results from ineffective communication and that conflict resolution is a process of altering competitive and conflicting communication relationships into ones in which common values are being sought.

Ignoring Burton's conceptualization of social conflict and conflict resolution at this point, we see that his recommendations of methodologies for studying social conflict apply to any set of assumptions. Burton advances simulation techniques and content analysis as integral parts of an historical trend of the study of social conflict from the art of historical and philosophical approaches to an applied science.

That social conflict can be simulated is well demonstrated by the well-known "Robber's Cave" experiment conducted by Sherif et al. (1961) at the University of Oklahoma. As an experiment, it combined observation in a natural setting with manipulation of variables. Sherif and his colleagues structured conflict between two groups of eleven-year-old boys at a camp called "Robber's Cave." Sherif induced hostilities between the two groups by giving them different and conflicting goals. Through the infusion of what were called "superordinate" goals (goals that could not be achieved without both groups cooperating), the tension between the two groups was reduced and eliminated.

Jandt (1973) has devised a simulation which focuses on communication and conflict. The simulation is an attempt to structure a situation in which intense social conflict is likely to occur. Based upon a real-life situation described in the January 30, 1970, issue of *Life* magazine, the simulation requires the participants to interact as members of a major chemical company planning the construction of a new plant, highly skilled and professional people who share a common vacation area, activist students attending a state college, permanent residents of an off-shore island, and elected government officials and Chamber of Commerce members. The participants must deal with Chemical Company's plans to construct a chemical plant on Resort Island. This simulation is being used for instructional and research purposes.

This particular simulation of communication and conflict has been used instructionally in a community college setting in a class enrolling students from various backgrounds, including some students who had been involved in police work. In this particular use of the simulation, the island residents decided that the conflict could be resolved by "kidnapping" the mayor of the island's town. Before coming to class, the participant designated as the "kidnapper" stepped into a restroom, donned a stocking mask, and readied his toy pistol. Relating this incident and his feelings to the class later, the participant told in frightfully realistic language his own fear and trembling at preparing to commit an "illegal" act. At least this one participant and others through vicarious experience could begin to have some partial understanding of the law violator or some greater understanding of their own feelings toward violating laws.

As an example of a research use of this same simulation, it has been used in an unreported pilot study with various age groups to study the use of emotional language. After participating in the simulation, both high school student groups and adult groups were asked to write various statements about their experience. These written statements were examined for differences in the use of emotional language. Hilyard and Kivatisky (1972) and Wilcox and Jandt (1972) have reported various instructional and research uses of this simulation.

The use of simulation techniques requires some modification of standard research methodology. As has been previously discussed, the experimenter must be satisfied that his simulation's operating model produces outcomes under a certain set of circumstances corresponding to outcomes observed in external reality under a comparable set of circumstances. When a simulation has reached this stage of development, the experimenter may observe the outcomes produced under circumstances which for some reason do not, cannot, or should not occur in external reality. However, a carefully developed simulation also permits the experimenter to directly observe the ongoing process of his operating model without interrupting that process with test instruments. An experimenter using simulation techniques need not rely exclusively upon paper-and-pencil responses to the simulation collected *after* the experience but can now more directly evaluate the process through such procedures as collecting and evaluating verbal communicative message characteristics in time sequence, or recording and evaluating the use of physical space in time sequence as related to the development of the process being simulated. For example, a simple frequency count of interaction or average message length may be shown to be related to the degree of the intensity of social conflict. Furthermore, the relationship between passive and active use of the environment ("sitting" versus "movement") may be shown to be related to the degree of the intensity of social conflict. The process of a simulation need not be stopped for experimental evaluation. Simulation techniques do provide a procedure to suggest the effects in most experimental research of "stopping" a dynamic process for experimental evaluation.

Social conflict has been the subject of several studies using simulation techniques. The purpose of these researchers was to study conflict as such and not to use simulation techniques to evaluate behaviors in situations which could not otherwise be easily evaluated. Druckman (1967, 1968) investigated the relative contribution of personality and situational variables as determinants of orientation in a non-zero sum, simulated, labor-management bargaining game. In a later study, Druckman and Zechmeister (1970) utilized a simulation of the political decision-making process in order to evaluate the relationship between conflict of interest and "dissensus" by contrasting a conflict of interest derived from an ideological "dissensus" with a conflict in which value and belief differences remained implicit.

MAN-MACHINE AND
MACHINE SIMULATIONS

The beginnings of computer simulations (both man-machine and machine) can be traced to the RAND Corporation's war games developed almost two decades ago. Business and industry have long utilized computer simulations. The first were developed in 1956 for the American Management Association. By 1959, Pillsbury, General Electric, IBM, and others were using computer simulations in their management training programs. Based upon the Zuckerman and Horn (1973) cataloguing, at least fifty percent of general business simulations utilize a computer. Theoretical and research literature on man-machine and machine simulations is rapidly expanding (e.g., Feigenbaum and Feldman, 1963; Naylor et al., 1966; Evans, 1967; Martin, 1968).

Some speech communication researchers may object to the use of man-machine and machine simulations by contending that social conflict, much less human communication, is too complex a process to be adequately represented by a machine. Still, both current economic theory and existing mathematical models of human behavior suggest that a satisfactory computer simulation of social conflict can be developed. An operating model of social conflict, or human communication, adequate for a successful man simulation, can be developed into a man-machine or machine simulation. Simon (1957), for example, has translated postulates derived from Homans' *The Human Group* (1950) and from Festinger's "Informal Social Communication" (1950) into mathematical statements. Coleman (1960) and Rapoport (1963) have reviewed other mathematical models of human interaction. Computer simulations, however, need not be limited to arithmetic operations; means-ends analysis, for example, may simulate some of the main processes that human beings use in solving problems. As Frijda (1967) has indicated, the computer program for a simulation *represents* a theory; unambiguous theory formulation is the advantage of computer simulation.

Some developed man-machine and machine simulations do have applications in communication research. Several of the models developed for these simulations can be useful in developing an operation model of social conflict. Warr and Knapper (1968), for instance, have proposed a machine simulation of the process of person perception. Any operating model of the role of communication in social conflict will probably have to account for person perception.

In the area of small-group behavior, McWhinney (1964) has simulated network studies with the circle and the all-connected network patterns. Coleman (1965) has discussed interaction frequency in simulated triads. A. Paul Hare (1961, 1970) has presented a simulation of group decision-making. Admittedly still a simple program, the simulation predicted actual group decisions in over 75 percent of the trials. The task for each group was to predict a series of answers of an unknown subject on a value-orientation questionnaire after being given a sample of his typical responses. More specifically to the issues of conflict and conflict resolution, Gullahorn and Gullahorn (1963, 1965, 1970a, 1970b) have developed a computer simulation based on the social exchange theory of George Homans. The activity repertoire incorporates Bales' twelve-category system. The program can simulate groups up to three members in size and has been used to simulate the decision-making strategies of labor union members completing a questionnaire on role conflict resolution by successfully reproducing their responses.

Larger-group behavior has also been simulated. Pool and Abelson (1961) conducted a simulation during the presidential election campaign of 1960. Conducted for the Democratic party, it used poll data to predict voter behavior. The simulation of the social psychological influence process (attitude change or persuasion) is represented by the Abelson and Bernstein (1963) simulation of the diffusion of competing communications in a community referendum controversy. The model reflects a two-step flow of communication; individual opinion change is affected by exposure to mass media and particularized channels, such as town meetings, followed by reinforcement from others. The model incorporates some fifty interrelated propositions concerning social influence processes. Preliminary runs of the Abelson and Bernstein model with hypothetical data have produced plausible outputs.

Whatever simulation techniques a researcher uses—man, man-machine, or machine—the important consideration is the operating model upon which the simulation is based. Social conflict has been simulated, and through simulation techniques, relationships have been quantified and demonstrated. Communication researchers can utilize simulation techniques in a like manner to study social conflict if there is agreement upon a model of the process of social conflict. By using such techniques, both the oversimplicity of the gaming laboratory and the overcomplexity of unstructured field environments can be circumvented.

REFERENCES

ABELSON, R. P., and A. BERNSTEIN, "A Computer Simulation Model of Community Referendum Controversies," *Public Opinion Quarterly*, 27 (1963), 93–122.

BURTON, J. W., *Conflict and Communication: The Use of Controlled Communication in International Relations*. New York: Free Press, 1969.

COLEMAN, J. S., "The Mathematical Study of Small Groups," in *Mathematical Thinking in the Measurement of Behavior*, H. Solomon, ed., pp. 1–149. Glencoe, Ill.: Free Press, 1960.

———, "The Use of Electronic Computers in the Study of Social Interaction," *European Journal of Sociology*, 6 (1965), 89–107.

DAWSON, R. E., "Simulation in the Social Sciences," in *Simulation in Social Science: Readings*, H. Guetzkow, ed., pp. 1–15. Englewood Cliffs, N.J.: Prentice-Hall, Inc., 1962.

DRUCKMAN, D., "Dogmatism, Prenegotiation Experience, and Simulated Group Representation as Determinants of Dyadic Behavior in a Bargaining Situation," *Journal of Personality and Social Psychology*, 6 (1967), 279–90.

———, "Prenegotiation Experience and Dyadic Conflict Resolution in a Bargaining Situation," *Journal of Experimental Social Psychology*, 4 (1968), 367–83.

DRUCKMAN, D., and L. D. LUDWIG, "Consensus on Evaluative Descriptions of One's Own Nation, Its Allies, and Its Enemies," *Journal of Social Psychology*, 23 (1970), 431–38.

EMSHOFF, J. R., and R. L. SISSON, *Design and Use of Computer Simulation Models*. New York: Macmillan, 1970.

EVANS, G. W., II, *Simulation Using Digital Computers*. Englewood Cliffs, N.J.: Prentice-Hall, Inc., 1967.

FEIGENBAUM, E. A., and J. FELDMAN, eds. *Computers and Thought*. New York: McGraw-Hill, 1963.

FESTINGER, L., "Informal Social Communication," *Psychological Review*, 57 (1950), 271–82.

FREDERIKSEN, N. "Proficiency Tests for Training Evaluation," in *Training Research and Education*, R. Glaser, ed., pp. 323–46. Pittsburgh: University of Pittsburgh Press, 1962.

FRIJDA, N. H., "Problems of Computer Simulation,"*Behavioral Science,* 12 (1967), 59–67.

GORDEN, W. I., "Academic Games in the Speech Curriculum," *Central States Speech Journal,* 20 (1969a), 269–79.

———, "Recent Educational Games," *The Southern Speech Journal,* 34 (1969b) 235–36.

———, *Nine Men Plus.* Dubuque: Wm. C. Brown, 1971a.

———, "Rhetoric-Communication Concepts Illustrated by Several Academic Games: Metaphor and Mystique at Play," *Today's Speech,* 19 (1971b), 27–33.

GUETZKOW, H., "A Use of Simulation in the Study of Inter-Nation Relations," *Behavioral Science,* 4 (1959), 183–91.

GULLAHORN, J. T., and J. E. GULLAHORN, "A Computer Model of Elementary Social Behavior," *Behavioral Science,* 8 (1963), 354–62.

———, "Computer Simulation of Human Interaction in Small Groups," in *American Federation of Information Processing Societies Conference Proceedings,* 1965, pp. 103–13.

———, "A Nonrandom Walk in the Odyssey of a Computer Model," in *Social Science Simulations,* M. Inbar and C. S. Stoll, eds. New York: Free Press, 1970a.

———, "Simulation and Social System Theory: The State of the Union," *Simulation and Games,* 1 (1970b), 19–41.

HARE, A. P., "Computer Simulation of Interaction in Small Groups," *Behavioral Science,* 6 (1961), 261–65.

———, "Simulating Group Decisions," *Simulation and Games,* 1 (1970), 361–75.

HERMANN, C. F., "Validation Problems in Games and Simulations with Special Reference to Models of International Politics," *Behavioral Science,* 12 (1967), 216–31.

HILYARD, D. M., and R. J. KIVATISKY, "Simulating Established Group Communication Behavior," in *Proceedings of the National Gaming Council's 11th Annual Symposium,* S. J. Kidder and A. W. Nafziger, eds., pp. 231–36. Baltimore: Johns Hopkins University, 1972.

HOMANS, G. C., *The Human Group.* New York: Harper, 1950.

Instructional Simulations, Inc., Box 212, Newport, Minnesota 55055. See especially Position Paper 90, copyright 1970.

JANDT, F. E., "Interactive Synecology: A Simulation for the Study of Conflict and Communication," in *Conflict Resolution Through Communication,* F. E. Jandt, ed. New York: Harper & Row, 1973.

KIDDER, J., "Simulation Games: Practical References, Potential Use, Selected Bibliography." Report No. 112, Center for Social Organization of Schools, Johns Hopkins University, Baltimore, Maryland, 1971.

KNIGHT, D. E., H. W. CURTIS, L. FOGEL, *Cybernetics, Simulation, and Conflict Resolution.* New York: Spartan Books, 1971.

MARTIN, F., *Computer Modeling and Simulation.* New York: Wiley & Sons, 1968.

McGUIRE, C. H., and D. BABBOTT, "Simulation Technique in the Measurement of Problem-Solving Skills," *Journal of Educational Measurement,* 4 (1967), 1–10.

McWHINNEY, W. H., "Simulating the Communication Network Experiments," *Behavioral Science,* 9 (1964), 80–84.

MORLEY, I. E., and G. M. STEPHENSON, "Interpersonal and Inter-Party Exchange: A Laboratory Simulation of an Industrial Negotiation at the Plant Level," *British Journal of Psychology,* 60 (1969), 543–45.

NAGASAWA, R. H., "Research with Simulation Games: An Analysis of Success Striving Behavior," *Simulation and Games,* 1 (1970), 377–89.

NAYLOR, T. H., et al., *Computer Simulation Techniques,* first corrected printing. New York: Wiley & Sons, 1966.

PHILIPPATOS, G. C., and D. R. MOSCATO, "Experimental Learning Aspects of Business Game Playing with Incomplete Information About the Rules," *Psychological Reports,* 25 (1969), 479–86.

POOL, I. DE SOLA, and R. ABELSON, "The Simulation Project," *Public Opinion Quarterly,* 25 (1961), 167–83.

RAPOPORT, A., "Mathematical Models of Social Interaction," in *Handbook of Mathematical Psychology,* Vol. II, R. D. Luce et al., eds. New York: Wiley & Sons, 1963.

———, "Prospects for Experimental Games," *Journal of Conflict Resolution,* 12 (1968), 461–70.

RASER, J. R., *Simulation and Society: An Exploration of Scientific Gaming.* Boston: Allyn and Bacon, 1969.

RUBEN, B. D., "Games and Simulations: Materials Sources and Learning Concepts," in *The 1972 Annual Handbook for Group Facilitators,* J. W. Pfeiffer and J. E. Jones, eds., pp. 235–39. Iowa City, Ia.: University Associates, 1972.

SCHALOCK, H. D., "Situational Response Testing: An Application of Simulation Principles to Measurement," in *Instructional Simulation: A Research Development and Dissemination Activity,* P. A. Twelker, ed. Monmouth, Ore.: Teaching Research Division, Oregon State System of Higher Education, February 1969.

SHERIF, M., et al. *Intergroup Conflict and Cooperation: The Robber's Cave Experiment.* Norman: University of Oklahoma, 1961.

SIMON, H., *Models of Man: Social and Rational.* New York: Wiley & Sons, 1957.

SMITH, D. H., "Communication and Negotiation Outcome," *Journal of Communication,* 19 (1969), 248–56.

STOLL, C. S., and P. T. McFARLANE, "Player Characteristics and Interaction in a Parent-Child Simulation Game," *Sociometry,* 32 (1969), 259–72.

TUCKER, R. K., "Computer Simulations and Simulation Games: Their Place in the Speech Curriculum," *Speech Teacher,* 17 (1968), 128–33.

VERBA, S., "Simulation, Reality, and Theory in International Relations," *World Politics,* 16 (1964), 490–519.

WARR, P. B., and C. KNAPPER, *The Perception of People and Events.* London: Wiley & Sons, 1968.

WERNER, R., and J. T. WERNER, *Bibliography of Simulations: Social Systems and Education.* La Jolla, Cal.: Western Behavioral Sciences Institute, 1969.

WILCOX, J. R., and F. E. JANDT, "Uses of Simulations in Speech Communication

Instruction." Paper presented at the 58th annual Speech Communication Association convention, 1972.

ZUCKERMAN, D. W., and R. E. HORN, *The Guide to Simulation Games for Education and Training*. Cambridge, Mass.: Information Resources, Inc., 1970.

————, *The Guide to Simulation/Games for Education and Training*. Lexington, Mass.: Information Resources, Inc., 1973.

4

A
Transactional Paradigm
of
Verbalized Social
Conflict

C. DAVID MORTENSEN

If a history is ever written on the classic neologisms in social science, a special place must surely be reserved for the fate of "transactionalism." Since the idea of viewing social conduct as a transaction was advanced by Dewey and Bentley (1949), the term has gained currency among a growing cadre of adherents clustered mainly in psychiatry, in psychology, and recently in communication theory. The disparate literature on the subject evokes reactions ranging from curt dismissal as social science cliché to probing philosophical scrutiny and whimsical adulation. Typical of the adverse judgment is that advanced by Brecht (1959) who considers the term "one of the most unfortunate, least suggestive, and most misleading names ever given a needed concept," an iconoclastic substitute of a name in place of a problem. In contrast are testimonials from those who find in transactionalism the promise of a sweeping methodology for "analyzing and understanding behavior" and a corrective to mechanistic paradigms of social inquiry (Kilpatrich, 1961).

It can hardly be claimed that the original discussion of transactionalism was born of immodest aims. For the task undertaken in Dewey and Bentley's *Knowing and the Known* consisted of nothing less dramatic than a purge of scientific language from its most persistent forms of inconsistency and vagueness. The inquiry centered around a confrontation with time-honored dualisms: mind vs. matter, subject vs. object, self vs. nonself, subjectivity vs. objectivity. Dewey and Bentley saw in such dualisms the specter of false causality owing to the tendency of science to account for events as elements acting either under their own independent powers ("self-acting") or as a balance of particulars in causal relation ("interaction"). Seeking to dismiss any hint of hypodermic notions of causality, Dewey and Bentley conceived of transactionalism as the gestalt force of organism and environment so interposed that none of the particulars could be understood apart from other constituents of subject matter. Hence, a transaction was the "knowing-known as one process . . . the known and the named . . . taken as phases of a common process in cases in which they would otherwise have independence, and examined in the form of interactions" (p. 304).

Anyone who attempts to translate the logic of transactionalism into operational terms will not find ready models for imitation. This is due mainly to the gap that exists between the theory and the conditions required for its implementation. To account for the divergence, it must be remembered that Dewey and Bentley were grappling with an untidy range of terminological problems. Hence, they had no particular truck with the conventions necessary to translate their idealized conceptions into operational terms. Mere inattention to such transformational matters would not have proven so troublesome to future adherents had the underlying assumptions of their model corresponded more closely with the prevailing scientific practice of the time. But the dominant mode of social inquiry in their day, and to a lesser extent our own, was grounded in reductive and atomistic notions of causality that lend themselves to sharply delimited interests in segmented properties of subject matter. Hence, it is hardly surprising that no one school of scientific practice has been able to articulate the alternative rules and conventions required of transactional research. Still, those who conceive of transactionalism as a mere adjunct to conventional modes of experimentation are patently mistaken. The intent of *Knowing and the Known* was clearly subversive and the implementation of its vision requires more than incremental changes in commitment. The shift in logic approaches more of the magnitude of change suggested by Kuhn (1970) in his discussion of scientific development:

> New theory implies a change in the rules governing the prior practice of normal science. Inevitably, therefore, it reflects upon much scientific work . . . already successfully completed. That is why a new theory, however special its range of application, is seldom or never just an increment of what is already known. Its assimilation requires the reconstruction of prior theory and the reevaluation of prior fact, an intrinsically revolutionary process that is seldom completed by a single man and never overnight. (p. 7)

In the case of conflict research, there is a pressing need for preliminary attempts at reconstruction. The burgeoning literature on social conflict is excessively dependent on formalistic models which either abstract completely away from the goals of conflict agents, as in systems theory, or resort to "depsychologized" research strategies, as in game theory, which examine rules and logic and ignore behavior. And it is precisely what gets left out—namely, the communicative aspect of conflict behavior—that holds the greatest promise for a transactional approach to the study of social conflict. The issue, to borrow again from Kuhn, results from the tension between paradigm and anomaly, with formalistic schemata functioning as the prevailing paradigm and with transactionalism deserving no more the entitlement than that of potential anomaly. However, because there is reason to suppose that the anomaly could prove irksome (in a dialectical sense), this paper seeks to translate a transactional conception of conflict into paradigmatic terms.

PHENOMENOLOGICAL REQUIREMENTS

Conflict research is not infrequently judged to be deficient in fundamental matters of conceptualization (Smith, 1971). Such vulnerability is hardly surprising, given the amorphous nature of the subject, the vastness of the literature, and the multiplicity of interests and methods which it serves. Still, it is just such entanglements for which transactionalism, with its concern for passage from loose to firm meanings, seems ideally suited.

Of central import are referents that are implicit in the *knowing-known* distinction. For Dewey and Bentley, the notion of *knowing* literally translates as the act or process of constructing personal reality, conceived not in a narrow mentalistic sense but rather in the emergent and phenomenological sense of whatever forces are required to transform sensory activity into reflective, conscious experience. Moreover, the construct of the *known* refers to the sources or targets of the act of knowing—that is, the objects of orientation themselves. The hyphen between the two god terms signifies an interest in obviating any dichotomy between organism-environment. Hence, social inquiry is concerned with the complex transactions that involve the act of knowing and their known objects, never "as *of* the organism alone, any more than *of* the environment alone, but always as of the organic-environmental situation, with organisms and environmental objects taken as equally its aspects" (Dewey and Bentley, p. 290). Finally, transactionalism considers in a most inclusive way all of "man's behavings, including his most advanced knowings, as activities not of himself alone, nor even as primarily his, but as processes of the full situation of organism-environment; and to take this full situation as one which is before us within the knowings, as well as being the situation in which the knowings themselves arise" (p. 104).

If social conflicts would be more fully approached in a transactional manner, the results would differ strikingly from the formalistic efforts to study social conflict as a phenomenon sui generis, independent of origin, content, context, and personality. Transactionalism augurs for methodology that renders a nonelementalistic account of the origin, structure, and taxonomy of actions that link parties to conflict. Translated into a definition of conflict, this entails an interest in the gestalt force of whatever "knowing-knowns" are involved in expressed struggles over incompatible interests in the distribution of limited resources. Note that the emphasis is placed on the *expressive* nature of social conflict. This is not to imply, of course, that all conflict must be viewed in expressive or social terms. If the necessary and sufficient condition for conflict is the *existence* of a struggle over some scarce resource, then any given instance may or may not be dependent on communication, at least in the overt deliberative sense. To illustrate, a conflict can conceivably involve much overt communication (e.g., student-police confrontation at a picket line), little overt communication (e.g., two men competing for the attentions of a woman), or only slight overt rancor (e.g., Macy's and Gimbel's department stores fighting over business). It is mainly the first class of events—manifestly expressed social conflict —that is the object of transactional inquiry and the concern of this chapter.

It has already been suggested that the interplay among the "knowing-knowns" requires an interest in the phenomenology of social conflict. This, of course, greatly complicates matters. Nonetheless, there is no way around it, despite the inconveniences that are caused. One, after all, either attempts to impose a sense of conflict or allows it to unfold. Either way, there comes a point where it is necessary to determine if the respective parties actually perceive their entanglement as a conflict *between* them. Hence, the only real question is how the necessary data are to be garnered. A number of questions come to mind. Why do the parties perceive what they are doing as a conflict? What are the constituents of their respective perceptions? What leads to the perception of conflict in the first place? To what degree are the parties conflict-prone? To what extent are their mutual orientations a function of previous association, predispositional factors, and immediate social context? Although these and related questions have been posed before, the resultant discoveries have been overshadowed by investigative overkill in matters bearing, as they say, on the logic of the game.

Inattention to the perceptual bases of conflict is, in a sense, understandable. After all, phenomenological issues do not lend themselves to a marriage of convenience between transactionalism and the many formal models that are designed to examine only abstracted and "depsychologized" brands of conflict which are governed by rules imposed solely by an outside agent. In game theory, for example, it is a third party who wields exclusive control over the definition of conflict. At no time are the protagonists permitted to shape salient aspects of their assigned task; nor do they have any say in the definition of rules, options, equity principles, utilities, and degrees of coorientation. Such procedures are justified on grounds that the object of inquiry is the logic of the game, not the players themselves. Within such limited aims, no problem arises. The rub comes only when the model is appropriated as a test of social reality. And here, despite stock disclaimers about the limited objectives of game theory, the temptation can be quite acute, as evidenced by the following comments by Rapoport (1970):

> Game theory must abstract entirely from all the psychological or sociological factors of conflicts, thus sacrificing the immediate relevance for logical precision. This does not mean, however, that the relevance of the theory to the understanding of "real" conflicts is excluded. On the contrary, such understanding makes itself felt as the purely logical relations of conflict situations are uncovered and "factored" out, as it were. For then what has been left out is revealed all the more clearly. (p. 39)

Yet once the "purely logical" matters are factored out, the student of social conflict is left either in a state of silence (over what has been ignored) or he must confront the interminable task of interpreting the link between formal and personal utilities; a decision which necessarily leads back to phenomenological considerations. To illustrate, consider all that is taken for granted about the players of formal conflict games. At once there is the assumption that the players will adhere to a predetermined concept of rational choice. Unfortunately, the mere existence of an abstract notion of rationality in no way assures that the players will actually work through the consequences of each respective move nor that they will act in accordance with the assumptions imposed by an agent who is both external and incidental to the process. Even if the right moves are made, there is no way of knowing that the agents will define their task as a conflict *between* themselves. Such a situation requires an argument for the construct validity of the manipulation. Otherwise, only presumption is left to augur for consistency between imposed utilities and personal ones.

In light of the stir among dissonance theorists over the motivational significance of monetary utilities, it is worth noting that constant-sum games are at the mercy of an economically grounded payoff where the values are merely taken for granted. Yet contrary to reassurances about the supposed "washout" effect of organismic variables in such highly structured social activities, there is reason to believe that psychological and social factors do not operate in a tidy and predictable manner. Even the value associated with winning or losing is presumed to be uniform, despite evidence that cognitive style, motivation, goal orientation, biases toward the task and related factors have a marked bearing on the logic of the players' choices (Coleman, 1957; Marlowe, 1967; Terhune, 1970). These findings are consistent with larger evidence of cognitive bias in far more rudimentary tasks such as trained judgments of the validity of syllogisms (Miller, 1969). It is doubtful whether inattention to personal utilities can be justified out of an interest in the logic of the game if it is true, as one reviewer concludes, that "the utility functions themselves . . . are a function of the subjects' personalities" (Terhune, 1970).

It is not enough, of course, to say that the existence of logical incompatibility does not assure social conflict. Nor, on the other hand, is it sufficient to claim that conflict exists simply because someone declares it so. What is crucial is the interplay between that which goes on in the eye of the beholder and the expressions given to the act of beholding. Hence, social conflicts may be taken as "transactions of knowing and known jointly, they themselves as knowings occupy stretches of time and space as much as do the knowns . . . and they include the knower as himself developed within the known cosmos of his knowledge" (Dewey and Bentley, 1949, pp. 136–37). For the aims of communication research, "knowing" translates as "conflict state" and "known" translates as "social acts" that follow or accompany those states.

This brings us to a major task for transactionalism, namely the need to account for the conditions that give rise to the expression (the "knowings") of social conflict. Here much can be gained by not attempting to conceive of the cognitive antecedents of conflict states in highly individuated and segmented terms. As an alternative to a futile search for "all of the relevant variables," it may be more useful to couch the problem in more inclusive and generalized form. By abandoning any claim to account for all of the salient particulars, we may focus on the underlying dimensions which give shape and substance to the particulars. These dimensions may be conceived as the leading indicants or underlying expressors through which any combination of variables become salient. Said another way, it is not necessary to know all the particulars which give rise to perceived conflict so long as an account is given of the general dimensions of their variability. It will now be argued that conflict states differ along dimensions of *disposition, orientation, time, frequency,* and *salience.*

Disposition. Cognitive states differ in the degree to which they arise out of a general set of conflict expectancy. At one extreme are persons who have the pervasive sense that they are always about to encounter a conflict situation. These are persons who are most sensitive to the existence of incompatible tendencies in their internal thought processes. We might think of them as conflict-prone in that they are disposed to order and interpret internal cues as conflict-laden. The stronger the disposition, the greater becomes the likelihood that the state will evolve into a generalized cognitive trait, perhaps even to the point where the person associates conflict with the very act of communicating with others. Symptomatic of such a trait would be the tendency to affirm statements such as "I avoid arguments at all costs," "I dislike competitive social activity," or "Everybody manages to distort what I say."

At the other extreme are persons who lack any generalized conflict set. These are persons who typically begin to anticipate conflict only when they are alerted to specific social possibilities. Their experience of social conflict is situation-specific and situation-bound. Hence, there may be a parallel between the notion of conflict dispositions and traits of persuasibility, dogmatism, and the like. However, any generalized sense of impending conflict could presumably still be altered by situational cues. Two persons could score equally high on a measure of conflict expectancy and still differ markedly in their response to social cues; i.e., one decodes Cue X as a sign of impending conflict and the other does not.

Generalized (situation-free) and individuated (situation-bound) dispositions also differ in matters of conflict avoidance. Generally, one would expect the more undifferentiated conflict states to evoke the strongest avoidance tendencies; that is, persons who are most disposed to define given social settings as threatening are also the most apt to seek out ways of avoiding them. Hence, the stronger the association between communication and social conflict, the more intensive should be the tendency to try to avoid communication with others. The link between disposition and avoidance suggests something further about conditions under which inner conflicts are likely to be verbalized to others. Because avoidance tendencies lead to social resistance, we can expect that communication about inner conflicts will more likely occur in the absence of a generalized conflict state.

Orientation.   Cognitive states differ also in object of orientation. Following Newcomb (1953), the construct "orientation" refers to a constellation of attitudes which a (conflict) agent has about himself (A), another party (B), and their coorientations (X). A given attitude may operate at the level of "A" ("I never know which side of an issue to take," or "The whole issue seems contradictory to me"), at the level of "B" ("She provokes arguments," or "He haggles over everything") or at the level of "X" ("You say yes and I say no," or "One of us has to be wrong here"). At first glance the distinctions among A, B, and X may appear to entail the very dualisms that transactionalism seeks to avoid. Yet in truth there is no difficulty, so long as the *objects* of orientation are not conceived in a segmented or self-acting way. The notion of object is designed simply to identify sources of knowing. Yet the distinctions it permits are important. Two persons may have comparable dispositions in all respects except that one is defined as an object of social experience while the other is conceived in more personal terms.

There is little point in being able to describe a given orientation merely for its own sake. However, as an aid in prediction, such information can be useful, particularly in determining whether a conflict will ever be expressed overtly. Because the act of anticipating communication with another necessarily entails a shift away from personal and private objects of orientation (A) to more social and reciprocal ones (B and X), one might hypothesize that pressures for communication will increase to the degree that objects of orientation shift from A to B or X. To illustrate, take the case where two men independently and simultaneously begin to covet an adjoining piece of property. So long as each man defines the problem solely in personal terms ("Do I really want to lay out so much money?"), the conditions necessary for social conflict remain unsatisfied. At such a point all we really have is the essential requirement necessary for what might be termed the cognitive precursor of social conflict; i.e., the activation of A in the absence of transactions with B about X. So long as it is only the internal conflict that escalates ("Now I am REALLY torn about that land!"), the pressure for social communication still remains unaffected. Because conflict states may be resolved in any number of ways, many of which do not involve overt encoding of any kind, the pressure for communication builds only at the point where one of the agents begins to define their conflict in relation to B and X ("What! That miserly neighbor of mine wants the property too?").

In effect, then, by focusing on shifts in the *ratio* of the salient objects, we obviate any need for a dichotomy between intrapersonal and social conflict. Thus, we may posit simply that the greater the proportion of B and X objects to the total, the greater becomes the probability that the conflict state will be expressed socially.

Time, Frequency, and Salience. Because sheer probability of occurrence tells us nothing about magnitude of effect, it is necessary also to specify the strength or intensity of conflict. In the case of a rift over property, one may become only minimally involved in the thought of his neighbor's intentions ("So he wants the land too."+[1]) while the other rages over the same idea ("SO HE WANTS THE LAND TOO!"+++++). What accounts for such differences? Obviously one is more salient than the other. The problem is knowing what units of information will provide the most accurate barometer of salience or intensity. Because the problem of intensity is so central to subsequent discussion of manifest social conflict, all that is required here is the working assumption that salience may be conceived as an indicant *derived* from the *frequency* and *temporal* dimensions of conflict states. In operational terms, salience may be taken to be a function of the product of B × X over a given time interval. This is, of course, the most parsimonious of assumptions. The more frequently a conflict agent thinks of the potential actions of a protagonist, the more intense becomes the anticipation of conflict. Conversely, the greater the separation of conflict cues over time, the less salient the conflict state may be said to be. This is not to imply that all particulars (X and O) must be conceived of as equal in import but it is to insist that the gestalt force of conflict states will be reflected in the frequency and distribution of salient cues over time.

The assumed link between frequency and salience gains support from the logic implicit in additive conceptions of attitude change. Among representative findings are those gained in a word association test (Mortensen, 1972) investigating the theory that frequency and duration of overt verbal response vary in proportion to the salience of discussed items. Subjects were instructed to arrange a deck of ten cards according to the strength of their initial reaction to such concepts (words such as *parents, stereos, hangnails, acid, guns*). An interviewer then examined the deck and asked the person to indicate "What is it about item no. —— that accounts for the strength of your reaction to it?" Findings indicated that the amount of verbalized response—duration, rate, number of words —varied with the ranked salience of items; i.e., the higher the salience,

---

[1] Crosses indicate units of intensity.

the greater the level of verbalization. Such a finding has important implications, as we will discover shortly, for an assessment of the intensity dimension of social conflict.

Before the discussion turns to the role of communication in verbalized conflicts it may be useful to formalize what has been advanced so far. Conflict states arise, it has been claimed, from incompatible modes of thought. However, the mere existence of inconsistent cognitions should be taken as a necessary but insufficient condition for communication. The key, as far as pressures for communication are concerned, is the nature of certain transactional shifts in cognitive orientation. The changes are: (1) from generalized (situation-free) to individuated (situation-bound) states; (2) from intrapersonal (A) to social (B and X) objects of orientation; and (3) from low-salient to high-salient conflict cues. In short, it is not principally the *number* but shifts in the *ratio* of given cues over time that engender pressures to verbalize latent conflict. However, even when cognitive pressure does increase, there is no assurance that any verbal combat will take place, since actual communication depends upon so many social forces, the accessibility of another party, and so on.

BEHAVIORAL REQUIREMENTS

In assessing various approaches to conflict behavior, there can be little doubt that transactionalism offers a clear and unequivocal alternative to prevailing formalistic paradigms. On grounds of its astonishing popularity and elegance alone, game theory would seem ideally suited for comparative and illustrative purposes. In the matter of key assumptions, for instance, game theory seeks to impose predetermined, formally derived assumptions about the activity of the players together with a host of notions about their adherence to an idealized conception of rationality, their conformity to prescribed rules, and the values they supposedly attach to their respective moves and to the equity principles imposed by the experimenter. Transactionalism, in contrast, assumes "no pre-knowledge of either organism or environment alone as adequate" (Dewey and Bentley, 1949, p. 123). If game theory may be likened to interactional activity, that is, the "inquiry of a type into which events enter under the presumption that they have been adequately described prior to the formulations of inquiry into their connections," then transactionalism "is inquiry of a type in which existing descriptions of events are accepted only as tentative and preliminary, so that new descriptions of the aspects and phases of events, whether in widened or narrowed form, may freely be made at any and all stages of the inquiry" (p. 122).

In addition, game theory relies on purely formal, imposed modes of structuring a conflict situation whereas transactionalism rejects all predetermined, obtrusive modes of structure in favor of emergent and developmental ones. Moreover, the logic of game theory is autonomical; that is, it seeks always to factor out, to isolate "formal" components, to identify the supposedly "depsychologized" and individuated particulars, thereby bypassing the problem of psychological variability. Until the formal elements have been properly factored, so the argument goes, all untidy matters must wait. Transactionalism, by comparison, is far more integrative and wholistic with its emphasis on shifts over time in the larger constituents of a single system of subject matter. Closely related is the tendency of game theorists to conceive of the moves of the game in a linear, dichotomous fashion. One example is the construct of a constant-sum game where each incremental gain by A is assumed to represent an automatic and exactingly corresponding loss by B. (It is doubtful that social situations ever approximate constant sum; individuals can be notoriously uncooperative in such matters, as indicated by the lengths to which some go to impose idiosyncratic meaning to even the simplest of social contingencies, say the significance of losing a coin flip.) As a further consequence, the moves in conflict games are purely static; aside from the possibility of their sheer repetition, they have little durational or extensional significance. Rather they occur in click-clack fashion, one at a time, usually for brief periods in a social vacuum that makes no provision for revision or adaptation in rules of play. Transactionalism, on the other hand, posits no such linearity between the moves of conflict agents. In fact, it shifts the loci of behavior away from discrete moves altogether in favor of an interest in the unfolding stream of cues and symbols that link organism and organism (as against organism and idealized object.) Dewey and Bentley (1949) assert that

> *Transaction* is the procedure which observes men talking and writing, with their word behaviors and other representational activities connected with their thing-perceivings and manipulations, and which permits a full treatment, descriptive and functional, of the whole process, inclusive of all its "content," whether called "inners" or "outers" in whatever way the advancing techniques of inquiry require. (p. 123)

Finally, by precluding opportunity for negotiation or coordination between the players along the way, the game paradigm tends to discourage interaction in any but the most primitive and constrained forms of verbal interchange.

Mindful of these paradigmatic constraints, game-theoretic research has recently moved away from the original mathematical logic which sought formal solutions to zero sum games. In the development of non-zero sum games such as Prisoner's Dilemma, numerous modifications have been made to insure better correspondence between the model and requirements of social inquiry. The resultant gains prompt some to conclude that only in its most idealized, formal sense does game theory prevent concern with the psychological aspects of conflict and with the role of communication in conflict situations. There is, of course, nothing unique to this rejoinder, particularly because it can be offered in defense of any line of research. In the case of game theory, it is true to an extent. Yet it is also the case that there is usually something symptomatic about a shift in the ground of appeal from formal considerations to pragmatic ones. At the least, it is a sign that the workability of the paradigm requires substantial tinkering. Moreover, it tends to call attention away from concern with potentially troublesome assumptions. Independent of subsequent application, it seems fair game to ask whether the formal enunciated theory is itself valid; that is, whether it provides an accurate formalized approximation of what happens when lovers, businessmen, salesmen, employees, and families engage in what they define as conflict-laden social activity. And even when due allowances are made for the malleability of theory, it is still the case that formal considerations have a way of imposing their assumptions on the logic and objects of behavioral investigation. So while the game paradigm may not automatically exclude communication variables, it does, in actuality, leave them out, or diminish them, in lieu of concern over moves and payoffs. By and large, the central concern with "communication" in non-zero sum games among experimenters is simply whether or not to permit the participants to talk along the way.

The stock justification for such severe reductionism—namely, the need for logical precision in isolating strategic aspects of the moves themselves while holding other considerations in abeyance—delays but does not resolve the problem of interpretation, particularly in phenomenological matters. Of what significance are discoveries gained from a "formal strategy" that ignores problems of decoding and attribution of intent, to say nothing of motives, values, predispositional factors, and social forces? And if the effects that may be attributed to the logic of a game are not generalizable beyond the involvements required of many laboratory tasks—scoring hypothetical points or judging the number of beans in a bottle—it seems doubtful that the lawfulness of such game strategies counts for much. Research on matters of ego-involvement, interpersonal attraction, communication networks, and a mélange of related topics indicates that the best predictors of communicative behavior are the unfolding and contingent aspects of the activity itself. Hence, severely limit the degree of volitional control between parties to conflict and you will evoke dramatic and disruptive changes in their intentions and actions. The debilitating effects associated with severe restrictions in communication networks offer a case in point (Shaw, 1964). Another is the discovery that persons tend to judge their communicative behavior against the standard of volitional control; generally satisfaction is related to the feeling that individuals can express their ideas freely and openly in the absence of a sense of social constraint. In fact, the need for a sense of spontaneity turns out to be more important than the variables used as post-test measures of much communication research, particularly source credibility, cohesion, and perceived influence (Mortensen, 1972).

Although transactionalism does not bypass the problem of psychological variability, it unfortunately offers only scant assistance in specifying a logic for any given mode of social inquiry. And given the rather cosmic tenor of the *Knowing and the Known,* the usefulness of its logic is for our purposes best served as an aid in identifying leading communicative indicants of social conflict.

The schemata advanced in the remainder of this paper are intended to be applicable in any face-to-face conflict setting which meets the following conditions: (1) the respective parties define their communication as a conflict between themselves; (2) the structure of conflict evolves naturally out of the deliberation itself; (3) the participants maintain a substantial degree of freedom in the definition of the rules of their conduct; (4) the inquiry employs nonobtrusive methodology. It further assumes that the units of measure will center on conjoint aspects of behavior which will be interpreted in a manner consistent with transactional assumptions. Finally, it assumes that any particular constituent of conflict will be manifestly expressed along dimensions of *intensity, affect,* or *orientation-related behavior.* Before the interplay among these three indicants is considered in detail, it will be useful to indicate the grounds for their inclusion.

There are a number of reasons for conceiving of the structure of social conflict along lines of intensity, affect, and orientation. All three rank among the most central indicants in numerous taxonomies of interpersonal behavior (see Carson, 1969, pp. 93–121 for a review of literature). Variations of affect underlie constructs of solidarity (Brown, 1965), sociability (Carter, 1954; Borgatta, Cottrell, and Mann, 1958; Borgatta, 1960, 1964), love-hate (Schaefer, 1959, 1961; Becker and Krug, 1964), dominance-submission (Leary, 1957; Schutz, 1958; Lorr and McNair, 1964; Carson, 1969). Also, the construct of orientation dovetails nicely with assumptions implicit in notions of interpersonal attraction, person perception (see review by Taguiri, 1969); and ego-involvement (Sherif and Sherif, 1967). Moreover, the three indicants are all amenable to a language-centered inquiry that focuses on the interplay among verbal, nonverbal, and referential indices of social conflict. Hence, the framework is inclusive of the fundamental constituents of language and yet it is also sufficiently differentiated to permit precise, fine-grained forms of analysis.

Intensity

The concept of intensity is implicit in the notion of conflict escalation. As a social conflict becomes stronger, we tend to think of it as having escalated or intensified. Conflict escalation, then, designates the potency or strength of activation necessary to express a given conflict state. So the question is one of ascertaining what qualifies as the primary expressors of the intensity or potency of communicative acts. Because the notion of potency is purely formalistic, devoid of substantive reference, the notion of communicative intensity should also ideally correspond in a formalistic way. This assumes, of course, the efficacy of viewing communicative acts as a subset of behavioral intensity generally, and it also presupposes the legitimacy of more specialized notions of intensity, such as attitudinal intensity or language intensity, so long as they also are consistent with a larger, potency-based conception of behavioral intensity. Here the work of activation theorists (see Bandura and Walters, 1963; Berkowitz, 1964, pp. 103–108; Cofer and Appley, 1964, pp. 390–98; Walters and Parke, 1964) is most relevant, particularly their assumption that all social motivation is indicative of some specifiable state of internal arousal; consequently, the intensity of verbal behavior must be equal to whatever strength of activation was necessary to perform the act. It is not clear whether such a notion of activation involves a disposition of heightened responsiveness to stimuli or rather some mobilized energy source. Nonetheless, the idea of verbal intensity bypasses this conceptual problem. Verbal acts are by definition expressive states. Hence, any verbal behavior can be ordered along some underlying dimension of intensity (and without recourse to external manipulation or obtrusive measures). Elsewhere I have argued that verbal intensity is conveyed by the very potency of activation required to sustain verbal interaction among a given number of persons (Mortensen, 1972). Specifically, the primary expressors of potency include the frequency, duration, rate, amplitude, and fluency of verbalization. Thus, a person who speaks the most frequently, for the longest periods of time, at the fastest rate, and with the greatest amplitude and fluency may be said to have expressed the most verbal intensity.

There is reason to believe that social conflicts escalate in line with predictable changes in frequency and distribution of talk between conflict agents. In one study, volunteer subjects agreed to discuss a controversial social topic with a person who had endorsed a position diametrically opposed to their own (Cardwell, 1972). Each was instructed to persuade the other of the soundness of their respective positions with an aim of reaching consensus on the topic. Pairs were assigned randomly to either a high-conflict or a low-conflict condition as induced by instructions which emphasized competitive or cooperative modes of negotiation. Results showed marked differences in both the frequency and duration of verbal acts; generally, more frequent and shorter comments occurred under high conflict. Figures 1 and 2 show the pattern of verbalization during one representative 25-minute segment. Note that low conflict is characterized by extensive pauses, few interruptions, long comments, and low proportion of talk relative to total interaction time. In the absence of a control group or sufficiently large cell sizes ($n = 12$), the findings must be interpreted tentatively, in the spirit of a case study, though hopefully a revealing one.

The link between intensity and activation raises important issues. One has to do with the problem of personal awareness. It is not certain that persons have any pervasive sense that their speech patterns correspond in any meaningful way with the intensity of their expressed feelings. Such a link could exist, after all, but only beyond consciousness. Fortunately, on this point, substantial evidence does exist. In a test of Predispositions toward Verbal Intensity, subjects were instructed to rank the degree to which they participated verbally in social situations generally (Mortensen, 1972). The test consisted of twenty-five Likert-type items all dealing with the frequency, duration, rate, amplitude, and fluency of verbal behavior. The following are representative: "I have a tendency to dominate informal conversations with other people"; "I prefer to keep my comments brief"; "I tend to react quickly to what others say"; "I tend to hesitate when I speak." Subjects reacted to each item along a continuum bounded by "very strong agreement with the statement" to "very strong disagreement with the statement." A middle position used a question mark to designate uncertain or neutral feelings about the statement.

Now if people tend to be unaware or uncertain of how much they tend to participate verbally in social situations generally, one would expect their responses to cluster around the center position. Yet quite the opposite pattern occurred. On every item except one, less than 20 percent of the subjects checked the middle position and the average percent of uncertain or neutral responses for all items was 13 percent. This finding is consistent with the notion that persons do tend to have reasonably clear impressions of the overall intensity of their verbal activity, though the finding indicates little about the degree of accuracy of those perceptions. Also relevant is evidence cited earlier suggesting

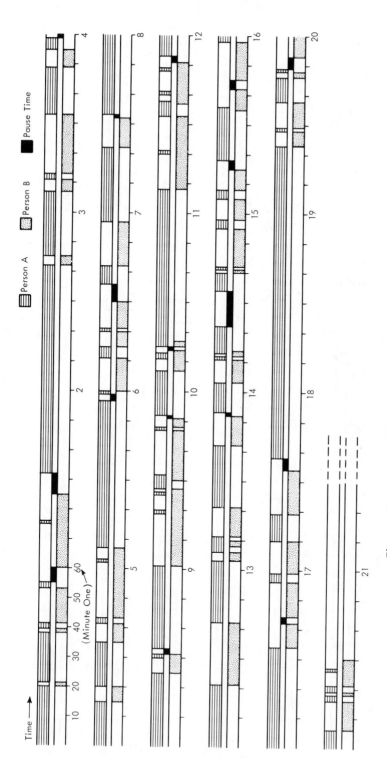

Figure 1 A transactional view of the low-conflict situation.

105

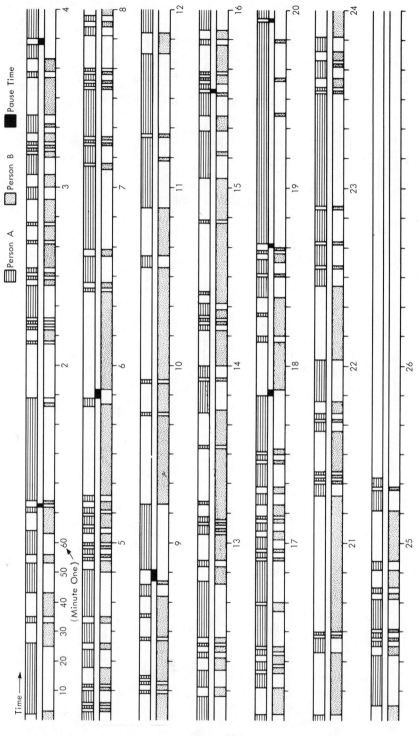

Figure 2 A transactional view of the high-conflict situation.

that the salience of word items tends to correlate positively with amount of verbalization. Moreover, the same study found that the persons who talked the most, independent of salience, viewed themselves as having expressed more intensity than did those who were not so verbal. It remains to be known whether this link between self-reports and actual verbal behavior holds as well for the perceptions individuals have of other people. However, there is evidence to suggest that observers tend to be highly conscious of the speech patterns of other people and that such awareness is a major determinant of their social perceptions (Mortensen, 1970).

Closely related are issues bearing on the problem of escalation in social conflict. Again, the different patterns shown in Figures 1 and 2 afford dramatic testimony to the cyclical, rhythmic qualities of verbal intensity. In both conditions conflict seems to escalate in line with the intensity of struggle over the right to talk. Under high conflict, particularly, the parties interrupt, cut off statements, jump into the conversation, and clip off the ends of sentences. Consequently, the battle over who talks when helps to create and then to accentuate the sense of volatility in the verbal combat. Yet it is also clear that conflicts cannot escalate without limit (unless each party engages in the impulse to shout one another down, unmindful of the claims of periodic silence). Soon a point is reached where further incremental gains in the potency of conflict fail to bring about corresponding changes in the intensity of verbal interchange. Parties to conflict, after all, are always engaged in a struggle to modify the rhythm and cadence of the business at hand. Typically, the conflict first escalates, then reaches an initial peak in intensity, then drops back, then surges to a new level of escalation before backing off to begin a new rhythmical pattern.

The unfolding nature of social conflict offers additional cues to the way in which conflict agents seek to establish equilibrium in their activities. Note again the differences shown in Figures 1 and 2. How quickly the low-conflict condition reaches a point of stability or equilibrium in the distribution of verbal acts. In contrast, high conflict is both more variable and less synchronous; so much so in fact, that it is difficult to detect a stage of activity where one can assuredly judge that a steady state of conflict has been reached. Perhaps one underlying characteristic of high conflict is this very heightened degree of dissynchronization that exists in the flow of talk. Here the temptation is to look solely at who talks when. However, the real key seems to lie rather in transactional units of measurement. One indicant might be the change in the ratio of time spent in talk by the respective parties. Another could be changes in *variability* of speech acts. Still another is the change in *differences* of reaction times. One would suspect that periods of greatest verbal intensity would be characterized by the following measures of disequilibrium: (1) high variability in distribution of speech acts (increased variance in frequency, duration, rate, amplitude, and fluency of verbal behavior); (2) asymmetricality in reaction times; and (3) verbal dysfunctionality (as measured by smoothness in the crossover between speaking and listening, increased frequency of interruptions, and points where two speak at once). What is particularly striking about these measures is that the notion of variance is integral to all of them (in contrast to conventional logic of teasing out variability of variables of interest). Yet if variability is itself a distinguishing feature of verbal conflict, then the conventional strategy may only serve to obscure what one is supposedly attempting to understand in the first place. Moreover, such measures shift the emphasis away from concern with the mere frequency of X to an interest in changes in the frequency levels or distributions or ratios of X either over time or in relation to Y and Z. To illustrate, if one focuses solely on a comparison of the number of "moves" that occur in conditions of high and low conflict, intrasubject variability might well be so great as to obscure evidence of lawfulness and prevent the sort of discovery that can be detected even when between-group variances do not differ appreciably, as in the shifts and patterns located by trend or pathway analysis or other tests of pattern, as against frequency recognition. In the final analysis, then, what is needed is sustained research that focuses on the formal synchrony of verbal interaction and its corresponding effects on other constituents of conflict behavior. It may well be the case that the reason why research on speech duration has lacked a distinguished history is because of inattention to the syntactical rules that govern the struggle of interactants to achieve a sense of synchrony in the expressions that flow between them. Said another way, if the key to grammar lies in syntax, and if the formal constituents of speech function as the syntactical equivalent of order and organization in written language, then it is conceivable that future research on speech patterning may shed new light on the old problem of the interplay between form and content, a matter that heretofore has been conceived almost solely in linguistic rather than behavioral terms. In this regard, it is my hunch that the formal properties of verbal behavior have a way of imposing their assumptions on both substantive and perceptual domains of virtually all verbal interchange. In the matter of social conflict, for example, we might expect to find correspondence between levels of verbal intensity and certain regularities in opinionated language, egocentric references, and linguistic intensity, and to see an inverse relationship between intensity and the inclusion of modifiers, qualifiers, and reservations. Other possibilities come to mind that can

be fruitfully examined only insofar as the substantive features of conflict
are linked to the formal syntax of verbal behavior itself.

Affect

There are strong empirical and logical grounds for including the
construct of affect as an indicant of social conflict. The notion of affect
is integral to some of the most fundamental constructs in social science,
including, among others, semantic space (Osgood, Suci, and Tannenbaum, 1957), social motivation (Berkowitz, 1964), activation (Cofer and
Appley, 1964, pp. 367–411), nonverbal influence (Mehrabian, 1973), and
the expressive import of emotional meaning (Davitz, 1964). Yet inex-
plicably, the literature on conflict bypasses the strong emotional base
of much social conflict. Such an omission can hardly be explained for
want of a solid conceptual base in research on the social effects of affect
display. After several decades of inconclusive testing of the ability of
persons to identify given emotions, more recent research suggests that
certain primary affects can be recognized with reasonable accuracy
(Schachter and Singer, 1962; Tomkins and McCarter, 1964; Boucher and
Ekman, 1965; Osgood, 1966). Also pertinent is support for the notion
that certain primary affects can be recognized even across diverse cultures (Izard, 1968; Ekman et al., 1969; Ekman and Friesen, 1971).

The link between affect and communication has also been the
subject of fruitful investigation. Particularly promising is research by
Tomkins (1962) and by Tomkins and McCarter (1963) based on the following two assumptions: (1) the primary human motives are affective in
nature; and, (2) the primary indicants of affect are facial behavior and
secondarily outer skeletal and inner visceral behavior. Hence, awareness
of facial response is tantamount to awareness of affect. Moreover, they
assert, though human beings experience affect through feedback of facial
response, they learn to retrieve affective experience through memory,
thereby minimizing the need for direct awareness of facial response. To
those who assert that affect consists primarily of inner bodily responses,
Tomkins and McCarter offer the following rejoinder:

> Important as these inner bodily responses undoubtedly are, we regard
> them as of secondary importance to the expression of emotion through
> the face. We regard the relationship between the face and the viscera as
> analogous to that between the fingers, forearm, upper arm, shoulders, and
> body. The finger does not "express" what is in the forearm, or shoulder,
> or trunk. It rather leads than follows the movements in these organs to
> which it is an extension. Just as the fingers respond more rapidly, with
> both more precision and complexity than the grosser and slower moving

arm to which they are attached, so the face expresses affect, both to others and to the self via feedback, which is more rapid and more complex than any stimulation of which the slower moving visceral organs are capable. (p. 120)

In addition, the authors offer support for the following conception of primary affective states: (1) interest-excitement; (2) enjoyment-joy; (3) surprise-startle; (4) distress-anguish; (5) fear-terror; (6) shame-humiliation; (7) contempt-disgust; and (8) anger-rage.

In sum, the cited findings support the theoretic utility of affect in a transactional conception of social conflict, the centrality of affect in messages that are decoded under conditions cited on page 102, and the salience of facial display as the primary expressor of affective states. Again, there is no apparent reason to view social conflict as an exception to the lawfulness that is generally manifest in interpersonal behavior. The central need is rather one of identifying the effective cues that are most salient in verbalized conflict. Here an important clue is found in Schlosberg's (1954) notion that emotive states may be ordered along dimensions of *pleasantness to unpleasantness, attention to rejection,* and *level of activation or arousal* (Figure 3).

The dimension of activation or arousal is important for our purposes because it permits us to anchor the constructs of intensity and affect in identical assumptions of activation theory cited earlier. Moreover, the dimensions of pleasantness-unpleasantness and attention-rejection are useful in specifying the shifts that should accompany changes in the intensity of verbal conflict. Hence, as conflict becomes more intense, affect should shift from displays of pleasantness and rejection to unpleasantness and attention. Particularly, we should expect more frequent displays of anger, determination, surprise, and fear during periods of escalation. Moreover, as the verbal struggle intensifies, the conflict agents should also have stronger dispositions to read each other's facial displays along the same predicted lines just stated. Fortunately, there is strong evidence to suggest that persons can recognize surprise, happiness, sadness, fear, anger, disgust, and interest as primary affective states (Schlosberg, 1941, 1954; Plutchik, 1962; Frijda and Philipszoom, 1963; Boucher and Ekman, 1965; Osgood, 1966; Ekman and Friesen, 1967, 1969). Also, by assuming consistency between intensity and affect, there should also be greater variability in the types of affect that are conveyed during periods of conflict escalation.

The same logic may also be extended to the hazardous business of theorizing about lawfulness in looking behavior. Because eye contact becomes more lengthy and intensive as personal involvement deepens, we might expect mutual eye contact to increase during more volatile periods of social conflict. However, the matter is complicated by the

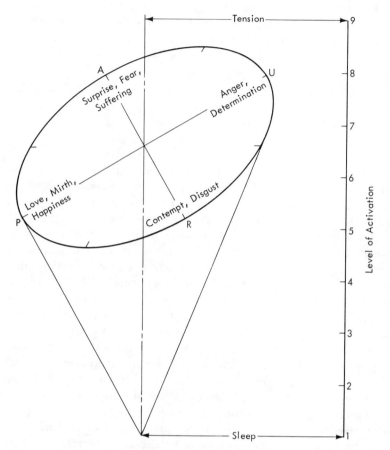

Figure 3   Schlosberg's dimensions of emotive states.

finding that eye contact tends to decrease during moments of negative feedback (Ellsworth and Carlsmith, 1968) or during mention of personal matters (Exline et al., 1965). Hence, the act of intensifying a conflict could lead to changes in either direction, depending on the state of balance or equilibrium between the respective parties. Still, because verbal synchrony is associated with less intense stages of social conflict, we might expect to find a similar pattern of dysfunctionality in looking behavior. Also, in the problem of decoding looking behavior, we would again expect to find some equivalent for what was earlier discussed as sensitivity to verbal intensity. Recall the evidence suggesting that persons have a fairly clear sense of the level at which they participate verbally and that these impressions are a reasonably accurate indicant of their actual behavior. Now if the same logic holds for looking behavior, we would expect that conflict agents will become increasingly sensitive to visual cues during periods of escalation and that they will use such information in their various attributions of the intensity of the other person.

Orientation

It was earlier suggested (see page 97) that pressures for communication evolve out of shifts in orientation from A to B and X. Taken a step further, the pressure may be said to increase to the degree that the overt conflict becomes anchored in specific social comparisons. The nature of this process of social differentiation may take many forms. In one, Party A may come to view Party B as an obstacle to the attainment of X. In another, the struggle may center on a discrepant social judgment where A and B strive to reach consensus on a matter that divides them deeply. From a communicative standpoint, it is not enough for the respective parties merely to be aware of their incompatibilities; of greater import is the point where they begin to state their respective positions to one another in the form of disjunctive social comparisons. Stated more formally, conflict orientation may be said to begin with the expression of divergent social comparisons and to escalate with increased frequency of occurrence of such acts. In short, the primary indicants of conflict orientation are to be found in the language of social comparison.

The exercise of social comparison further implies a choice between two or more alternatives. Likewise, the very notion of an "orientation" implies an evaluative and judgmental process of categorization. A given choice may be expressed as anything ranging from flat rejection (maximum discrepancy) to unqualified acceptance (consensus). On this matter, Sherif and his associates (Sherif and Hovland, 1961; Sherif, Sherif, and Nebergall, 1965; Sherif and Sherif, 1967) advanced a conception of social judgment based upon alignment of latitudes of acceptance, rejection, and noncommitment. It may be tempting, therefore, to seek to appropriate the work on social judgment *en masse* in matters bearing on conflict orientation. However promising such a prospect, there are a number of complications. Sherif's conception, for one thing, is not consistent with additive models and there are many problems associated with the determination of various latitudes. Nonetheless, the underlying logic of social judgment is generally consistent with the idea that the comparative orientations in conflicting behavior are manifested in expressors of acceptance, rejection, and noncommitment. To illustrate the possibilities, it may be useful to examine excerpts of conflict negotiations taken from a pilot study patterned after the research design used by

Sereno and Mortensen (1969) and Mortensen and Sereno (1970). The first segment is representative of high conflict and begins at about the 5-minute mark of the discussion. The second segment typifies low conflict and begins after four minutes of negotiation.

HIGH CONFLICT

Topic: The Calley Verdict

A: So what I'm saying—the reason I think Calley was even brought to trial was so that the American public would swallow all the guff and all the baloney— Oh, wow! We're really getting smart. We're really feeling pity for the dear old Vietnamese.

A advances strong evaluative claim which implies unqualified opposition to the position previously endorsed by B.

B: Is that so bad?

B rejoins with question which confirms state of mutual opposition.

A: Um, not when no one really does. No. Not when you're being, um brainwashed into believing that the conviction of Calley really did anything to anybody. How—

A engages in "back and fill" momentarily before reasserting opposition to claim of B.

B: (interrupts) I've been brainwashed into believing that another human being's life is important, that it is worth something. I don't see how you can be brainwashed into that. I mean, is that what you're saying, that—

B reinterprets conflict to fit his position and then offers another rejoinder.

A: (interrupts) Oh, I'm saying that—

B: (interrupts)—that you really don't believe that. And by bringing Calley to trial that, that we're being brainwashed into believing that—

B interrupts A in a manner which further solidifies sense of mutual opposition.

A: (interrupts)—By bringing Calley to trial, um, the United States government got a brownie point. Because people started to say, "Well, the United States is good. They're bringing this man to trial. He killed civilians."

A ignores B's change and continues his offensive by advancing another categorical, evaluative claim.

B: Don't you think our country needs a few brownie points? You think our country's okay? Huh?

B offers another confrontative question.

A: I think our country is full of shit.

A counters with another claim which is disjunctive with position of B.

B: You're contradicting yourself.

B responds with an accusation.

A: No I'm not. I'm saying that the United States government is looking for brownie points.

A continues pattern of claim-rejection.

B: We need 'em.

B again rejoins in a way that perpetuates sense of diametrical opposition.

A: Not false ones, we don't. And that was a false one. He was— It's just the whole thing was so absurd. Because, he because, he was not, he was not, he should not have been convicted for following orders. When you are told to follow orders, when you are just, practically coerced into following orders and if you are so afraid of the consequences of not following orders, why would somebody give you an order to kill somebody unless—I mean this is the whole thing. He probably believed exactly the way you did. Well, another human being's life is very important.

A divides issues, repeats accusation and continues pattern of uncompromised refutation.

B: (interrupts) No, he couldn't have because he wouldn't have shot 22 civilians if he believed the way I did. He wouldn't, he wouldn't have even come close to it. He would have turned to the commanding officer and said, "Fuck you buddy." And that's—

B confronts A with direct negation followed by counterclaim.

A: (interrupts) Why do you say that?

B: Because, I'm repeating myself, because if he had any respect for a human life he wouldn't have shot 22 civilians.

B retorts with restatement.

A: What about the respect he had for his job—which comes into it? For the things that he was told to do?

B: There are a lot of people in the service that haven't shot one person and they're still in there. But that doesn't, of course, that doesn't mean that they respect their job. I don't know, can you respect being in the Army?

A: No. But they're there.

B: So why should he?

A: *They're* there.

B: So he should respect it?

A: So if every person did that—

B: —did what?

A: If every person stood up to their commanding officer and said, "Fuck you," it'd be really great because we'd all go home.

B: That's right. So why shouldn't Calley have done it?

A: Um, because he probably wasn't willing to suffer the consequences of saying that.

B: Right! Which is right back to my point saying that that's why he's guilty. That's why we brought that man back to this country and tried him because he didn't have the guts to say "Fuck you."

A: In other words, following your string of logic, um, we ought to bring every serviceman home and put him on trial for carrying a gun over there and killing somebody.

B: Well, like I said, you can't, you can't do that. You have to start somewhere and we're starting with Calley.

A and B fall into question-response sequence which continues to punctuate in a pattern of disjunctive, opposing claims that only serve to reduce alternatives and lock combatants into confrontative, diametrical opposition to their respective claims.

A few moments later, when they were told their time was up, the respective parties concluded as follows:

B: That's absurd. That's really absurd. You know, calling over to Vietnam isn't like calling Chicago, or anything like that. President—

A: (interrupts)—Not for you, no.

B: But for Nixon, it might be, huh? I don't think we've reached any agreement.

A: I don't think we have either.

LOW CONFLICT

Topic: The Legalization of Marijuana

B: The only thing I can see about the trying to legalize marijuana would be the fact that if all of a sudden they can have all they want without having to sneak behind the door to buy it, because if they have all they want possibly it'll lose its fascination

B advances a claim that permits him to disassociate himself (I-they) from certain aspects of the general issue while still acknowledging tacit support for the principle on pragmatic grounds.

A: I think so too. I think that's very important. I think that, uh, when people are saying, are, are so much involved in, in legalizing marijuana, are, that, uh, it's it's, society is really as, as a lot of people say. Alienating us a lot by making something that a lot of people consider not harmful, not bad, illegal, but yet they, they say something like alcohol which is certainly as bad I think we both agree, um, and makes that legal. You, it's very hypocritical to do that.

A agrees with B but restates the claim in stronger terms.

B: I'm not for it one hundred percent, but I do think that it's worth a try. And that's to make it legal for a period of time and see what happens.

B seems to sense the greater force of A's position and quickly moves to attach qualifications to his claim.

A: I think so too. I think that if you make it legal that, um—

B: And I think it's harmful. I mean, marijuana itself. The constant use of it has really begun to prove that it has permanent effects on the mind.

A: I didn't ever hear of that study or remember it. Um, do you know what they said about it?

B: Well, I can't even tell ya which magazine I read it in. It's been within the last month. I don't think it's been proven conclusively; I think they're still working on it, but— I can't even remember the area of the brain that it's supposed to—

A: (interrupts) But you see, I mean, there are basic things that I think would get a lot better if you legalize marijuana. Things like, um, like people wouldn't feel, who use marijuana and their stand against the government or whatever. And, um, they, there'd be a lot—people wouldn't resent the government for that—which a lot of people do.

B: And a lot of people are gonna resent the government for a thousand and one reasons and using marijuana might be the handiest one for them at that particular time.

A: But things like, um, right now our courts are very overloaded. A lot of crime is going on. People are afraid to walk on the street if there are no people. In the city, say, well, I can't walk on the street at night; it's dangerous. And yet all this, all this money, all this time is spent dealing with, with minor cases in marijuana—people getting busted for, for, um, a joint or something and

A again agrees without showing any recognition of the differences implicit in their respective positions.

B now shifts the discussion back to his personal objection cited earlier.

A now responds cautiously, asking merely for additional information.

B hedges, attaches additional qualifiers before admitting to the uncertainty of his exact position on the issue in question.

A shifts discussion back to pragmatic considerations.

A again offers tacit agreement on a point where consensus was acknowledged from the outset.

A attempts to shore up his position by citing additional "safe" reasons for supporting the general notion.

it's taking up so much energy, so much money of this country and at the same time giving people police records that I really don't feel should have them. They're really gonna handicap them for a long time. People that are really important in the, in the future for this country.

B: Then why, if they if they are so important for the future of this country do they have to resort to using marijuana? For a false crutch?

B now calls A into question by offering a thinly disguised rejoinder, one that attributes negative and evaluative overtones to A's position.

A: But it's not—but its— I really don't think it's a false crutch. I think that, um, marijuana is like alcohol, that, um, that it's better, um, that young people instead of, you know, for instance, you know, take a drink, smoke a joint. And you find that, that many respected members of our society smoke marijuana, um, lots of respected members. And, I, I don't think that, um people use it any more as a crutch than people that drink use drinking as a crutch.

A avoids direct confrontation, content instead to neutralize unfavorable connotations implied by B.

B: I think that they use it for a crutch—the same way that they use liquor. They have some idea that it's going to make me—

B's comment is significant because it is the first instance of direct confrontation that leaves the two parties at a point of total polarized disjunction. Note, however, that this conflict is defined as one subset of the general proposition in which substantial areas of agreement already have been tacitly reached.

A: (interrupts) Yeah, but every—

A starts to object but is interrupted for the first time.

B: (interrupts) —more brilliant in my speech, more brilliant in my thinking and yet when you talk to them well they are—

B presses his point.

A: (interrupts) yeah, but—

A again attempts to talk but is cut off.

B: (interrupts)—as rattled as somebody who's drunk.	B is content merely to finish his sentence.
A: Oh, agreed, agreed. It's all relative to the person. People are getting used to it for different reasons.	A avoids further direct confrontation by redefining issue at a level that creates a sense of agreement, however superficial.

The two excerpts reveal strikingly different patterns of orientation. In high conflict, we see how readily the parties get themselves locked into a cycle of intractable and unyielding social comparisons. What is important is not simply that they should find themselves so completely at odds. It is rather the way they attempt to interrupt and then maintain those odds. Note how they both tend to express the conflict in the form of personal address; each one addresses or confronts the other with his respective claims. Most of the claims are comparative, evaluative, accusatory, disjunctive, and polarized. Note also the absence of any attached qualifiers or contingencies in the claims. Equally striking is the willingness of the conflict agents first to escalate and then to sustain a particular point of contention. Neither seems disposed to change the subject or resolve it. One advances a claim, the other rejoins; the first stands his ground; the other then offers a further rejoinder, all of which bear directly and specifically on the business at hand. Unlike low conflict, neither party gives ground, engages in back-and-fill, or any other disarming tactic. As a consequence, the conflict tends to become self-fulfilling. One disjunction provokes another, and still another, until a pattern is established where all further communication only serves to validate the prevailing climate of disjunction. In the end, the parties literally talk their way into a state of incompatibility which closes off options and intensifies a sense of divergent "knowings" which locate the trouble "out there" in the conduct of an opposing "known."

In sharp contrast is the pattern revealed in the low-conflict condition. Unfortunately, many outstanding differences in rhythm and synchrony can only be noted by watching a video tape of the negotiation. In contrast to high conflict, the parties talk more deliberately, for longer periods, and with fewer interruptions. There is also little sense of confrontation registered either in nonverbal or paralinguistic cues. However, the transcript is at least indicative of a prevailing social orientation that is more expressive than comparative in tone and substance. It is interesting that the respective parties do not so much confront or address one another as they simply express their respective positions. Transitions tend to be associative rather than discriminative, as evidenced by phrases such as "I think so too"; "I think we both agree"; "I think that's very important"; and "I think so too." Later, when differences become more apparent, there is a notable drop in expressions of agreement and an increase in expressions of noncommitment and rejection. Evidence of noncommitment exists in the frequent use of qualifiers and reservations ("I'm not for it one hundred percent, but—"; "I can't tell ya"; "I can't even remember—"). When the conflict does escalate toward the end, there is a certain unevenness in the pattern. Instead of mutual confrontation, in which both parties are equally involved in creating conflict and also equally disposed to avoid the dilution of it, we see evidence of a more dominant-submissive sequence. B states his position; A equivocates; B presses the matter and A then either backs off and changes the subject or fills the air with subterfuge. Correspondingly, the rejoinders tend to be more diluted and less polarized than in what typifies high conflict.

Although it is not certain that all of the cited patterns and regularities are generalizable beyond the social behavior discussed in this paper, the range of application would seem to be rather extensive. After all, the indicants of interest are grounded in mainstream assumptions that have been validated in various additive models, activation theory, and transactional logic. Furthermore, the central constructs meet the requirements associated with tests of operationalization, confirmability, and the requisites of formal language. To indicate some possibilities, the central tenets of the transactional paradigm are advanced below in propositional form.

A TRANSACTIONAL PARADIGM OF SOCIAL CONFLICT

Methodological Assumptions

1. Transactional inquiry renders a nonelementalistic account of the origin, structure, and taxonomy of communicative behaviors that link conflict agents in whatever "knowing-knowns" are involved in their expressed struggles over incompatible interests in the distribution of limited resources.
2. Conflict behavior is to be conceived transactionally as the gestalt force of the organic-environmental situation, "with organism and environmental objects taken as equally its aspects."
3. Transactional inquiry is applicable in any face-to-face conflict setting where (a) the conflict agents define their communication as a conflict *between* them, (b) the structure of conflict emerges naturally out of the course of deliberation, and (c) the parties maintain substantial freedom over the definition of rules of conduct.

Substantive Assumptions

1. Conflict is known through the attribution or naming of conflict-laden cues by organisms who are themselves among the phases of a developmental, emergent, and conjoint form of activity which has full durational and extensional significance.

2. The constituents of conflict states are manifest in the strength of dispositions, object of orientation, temporal extension, frequency of occurrence, and salience.

3. The constituents of verbalized conflict are manifest in the interplay among indices of intensity, affect, and orientation-related behavior.

   a. The primary expressors of verbal intensity are the frequency, duration, rate, amplitude, and fluency of verbalization.

   b. The primary expressors of affect are certain primary facial displays which can be recognized with reasonable accuracy by conflict agents.

   c. The primary expressors of orientation are grounded in discriminative social comparisons which vary principally in the frequency of expressions of agreement, rejection, and noncommitment.

Propositions

1. Pressures to verbalize inner conflict increase with shifts from (a) generalized to highly differentiated conflict-laden cues, (b) from intrapersonal to social objects of orientation, and (c) from low-salient to high-salient conflict-laden cues.

2. The higher the level of verbal conflict, the greater the frequency of verbalization, the shorter the duration, the greater the amplitude and rate, and the less the level of fluency.

3. The higher the level of verbal conflict, the more variable and less synchronized the distribution of verbal acts become.

4. The higher the level of verbal conflict, the greater the degree of verbal disequilibrium (as measured by the variability of speech acts, the asymmetricality of reaction times, and the dysfunctionality of overt changes between decoding and encoding).

5. Changes in verbal intensity lead to corresponding shifts in perceptual and substantive indicants of social conflict as manifested by characteristic levels of language intensity and the structure of the claims expressed by the conflict agents.

6. The higher the level of verbal conflict, the more affect display will shift from shows of pleasantness, rejection, and low activation to those of unpleasantness, attention, and high activation.

7. The higher the level of verbal conflict, the greater will be the variability in primary affects, looking behavior, and dissynchronization between shows of affect and intensity.

8. The higher the level of verbal conflict, the more frequent become the (a) shows of social comparison, (b) polarized social disjunctions, and (c) mentions of rejection and noncommitment (with corresponding decreases in expressions of agreement).

REFERENCES

BANDURA, A., and R. H. WALTERS, *Social Learning and Personality Development.* New York: Holt, Rinehart and Winston, 1963.

BECKER, W. C., and R. S. KRUG, "A Circumplex Model for Social Behavior in Children," *Child Development,* 35 (1964), 371–96.

BERKOWITZ, L., "Social Motivation," in *Advances in Experimental Social Psychology,* Vol. 3. L. Berkowitz, ed., pp. 50–135. New York: Academic Press, 1964.

BORGATTA, E. F., "Rankings and Self-Assessments: Some Behavioral Characteristics of Replication Studies," *Journal of Social Psychology,* 52 (1960), 297–307.

———, "The Structure of Personality Characteristics," *Behavioral Science,* 9 (1964), 8–17.

BORGATTA, E. F., L. S. COTTRELL, JR., and J. M. MANN, "The Spectrum of Individual Interaction Characteristics: An Interdimensional Analysis," *Psychological Reports,* 4 (1958), 279–319.

BOUCHER, J., and P. EKMAN, "A Replication of Schlosberg's Evaluation of Woodworth's Scale of Emotion." Paper presented at the Western Psychological Association Convention, 1965.

BROWN, R., *Social Psychology.* New York: Free Press, 1965.

CARDWELL, J., "A Transactional Study of Social Conflict." Unpublished manuscript, Department of Communication Arts, University of Wisconsin, 1972.

CARSON, R. C., *Interaction Concepts of Personality.* Chicago: Aldine Publishing Co., 1969.

CARTER, L. F., "Evaluating the Performance of Individuals as Members of Small Groups," *Personnel Psychology,* 7 (1954), 477–84.

COFER, C. N., and M. H. APPLEY, *Motivation: Theory and Research.* New York: Wiley & Sons, 1964.

COLEMAN, J. S., *Community Conflict.* Glencoe, Ill.: Free Press, 1957.

DAVITZ, J., *The Communication of Emotional Meaning.* New York: McGraw-Hill, 1964.

DEWEY, J., and A. F. BENTLEY, *Knowing and the Known.* Boston: The Beacon Press, 1949.

EKMAN, P., and W. V. FRIESEN, "Constants Across Cultures in the Face and Emotion." Unpublished manuscript.

———, "Head and Body Cues in the Judgment of Emotion," *Perceptual and Motor Skills,* 24 (1967), 711–24.

———, "The Repertoire of Non-Verbal Behavior: Categories, Origins, Usage, and Coding," *Semiotica,* 1 (1969), 49–98.

EKMAN, P., E. P. SORENSON, and W. V. FRIESEN, "Pan-Cultural Elements in Facial Displays of Emotion," *Science,* 164 (1969), 86–88.

ELLSWORTH, P. C., and J. M. CARLSMITH, "Effects of Eye Contact and Verbal Content on Affective Response to a Dyadic Interaction," *Journal of Personality and Social Psychology,* 10 (1968), 15–20.

EXLINE, R., D. GRAY, and D. SCHUETTE, "Visual Behavior in a Dyad as Affected by Interview Content and Sex of Respondent," *Journal of Personality and Social Psychology,* 1 (1965), 201–209.

FRIJDA, N. H., and E. PHILIPSZOOM, "Dimensions of Recognition of Expression," *Journal of Abnormal and Social Psychology*, 66 (1963), 45–51.

IZARD, C. E., "Cross-Cultural Research Findings on Development in Recognition of Facial Behavior," *Proceedings, American Psychological Association Convention*, 3 (1968), 727.

KILPATRICH, P. F., ed., *Explorations in Transactional Psychology*. New York: University Press, 1961.

KUHN, T. S., *The Structure of Scientific Revolutions*. Chicago: University of Chicago Press, 1970.

LEARY, T., *Interpersonal Diagnosis of Personality*. New York: Ronald Press, 1957.

LORR, M., and D. M. MCNAIR, "Methods Relating to Evaluation of Therapeutic Outcome," in *Methods of Research in Psychotherapy*, L. A. Gottschalk and A. H. Auerbach, eds., pp. 573–94. New York: Appleton-Century-Crofts, 1966.

MARLOWE, D., "Psychological Needs and Cooperation: Competition in a Two-Person Game," *Psychological Reports*, 13 (1963), 364.

MEHRABIAN, A., "A Semantic Space for Nonverbal Behavior," in *Advances in Communication Research*, C. D. Mortensen and K. K. Sereno, eds., pp. 277–87. New York: Harper & Row, 1973.

MILLER, G. R., "Some Factors Influencing Judgments of the Logical Validity of Arguments: A Research Review," *Quarterly Journal of Speech*, 55 (1969), 276–86.

MORTENSEN, C. D., "The Status of Small Group Research," *Quarterly Journal of Speech*, 56 (1970), 304–309.

————, "A Test of Predispositions toward Verbal Intensity." Paper presented at the Speech Communication Association Convention, 1972.

MORTENSEN, C. D., and K. K. SERENO, "The Influence of Ego-Involvement and Discrepancy on Perceptions of Communication," *Speech Monographs*, 27 (1970), 127–34.

NEWCOMB, T. M., "An Approach to the Study of Communicative Acts," *Psychological Review*, 60 (1953), 393–404.

OSGOOD, C. E., "Dimensionality of the Semantic Space for Communication Via Facial Expressions," *The Scandinavian Journal of Psychology*, 7 (1966), 1–30.

OSGOOD, C. E., G. J. SUCI, and P. H. TANNENBAUM, *The Measurement of Meaning*. Urbana, Ill.: University of Illinois Press, 1957.

PLUTCHIK, R., *The Emotions: Facts, Theories, and a New Model*. New York: Random House, 1962.

RAPOPORT, A., "Conflict Resolution in the Light of Game Theory and Beyond," in *The Structure of Conflict*, P. Swingle, ed., pp. 1–43. New York: Academic Press, 1970.

SCHACHTER, S., and J. SINGER, "Cognitive, Social and Physiological Determinants of Emotional State," *Psychological Review*, 69 (1962), 379–99.

SCHAEFER, E. S., "A Circumplex Model for Maternal Behavior," *Journal of Abnormal and Social Psychology*, 59 (1959), 226–35.

————, "Converging Conceptual Models for Maternal Behavior and for Child Behavior," in *Parental Attitudes and Child Behavior*, J. C. Glidewell, ed., pp. 124–46. Springfield, Ill.: Charles C. Thomas, 1961.

SCHLOSBERG, H. A., "A Scale for the Judgment of Facial Expressions," *Journal of Experimental Psychology*, 29 (1941), 497–510.

———, "Three Dimensions of Emotion," *Psychological Review*, 61 (1954), 81–88.

SCHUTZ, W. C., *Firo: A Three-Dimensional Theory of Interpersonal Behavior.* New York: Holt, Rinehart and Winston, 1958.

SERENO, K. K., and C. D. MORTENSEN, "The Effects of Ego-Involved Attitudes on Conflict Negotiation in Dyads," *Speech Monographs*, 26 (1969), 8–12.

SHERIF, C. W., and M. SHERIF, *Attitude, Ego-Involvement and Change.* New York: Wiley & Sons, 1967.

SHERIF, C. W., M. SHERIF, and R. E. NEBERGALL, *Attitude and Attitude Change: The Social Judgment-Involvement Approach.* Philadelphia: Saunders, 1965.

SHERIF, M., and C. I. HOVLAND, *Social Judgment: Assimilation and Contrast Effects and Attitude Change.* New Haven, Conn.: Yale University Press, 1961.

SHAW, M. E., "Communication Networks," in *Advances in Experimental Social Psychology*, Vol. 1, L. Berkowitz, ed., pp. 111–47. New York: Academic Press, 1964.

SMITH, C. G., ed., *Conflict Resolution: Contributions of the Behavioral Sciences.* Notre Dame, Ind.: University of Notre Dame Press, 1971.

TAGIURI, R., "Person Perception," in *Handbook of Social Psychology*, Vol. 3, G. Lindzey and E. Aronson, eds., pp. 395–449. Reading, Mass.: Addison-Wesley, 1969.

TERHUNE, K. W., "The Effects of Personality in Cooperation and Conflict," in *The Structure of Conflict*, P. Swingle, ed., pp. 193–234. New York: Academic Press, 1970.

TOMKINS, S. S., and R. McCARTER, "What and Where are the Primary Affects? Some Evidence for a Theory," *Perceptual and Motor Skills*, 18 (1964), 119–58.

WALTERS, R. H., and R. D. PARKE, "Social Motivation, Dependency, and Susceptibility to Social Influence," in *Advances in Experimental Social Psychology*, Vol. 1, L. Berkowitz, ed., pp. 231–76. New York: Academic Press, 1964.

5

Communication Strategies in Conflicts Between Institutions and Their Clients

JOHN WAITE BOWERS

Research on trust and suspicion, and more generally on the process of negotiation, has begun to shed light on the role of communication in conflicts between equals and near-equals. It seems clear, for example, that communication prior to bargaining can serve to establish a cooperative or a competitive atmosphere by bringing about agreement on the rules of the game, the quid pro quo; that once bargaining has begun in a cooperative atmosphere, a shift of either party to a competitive frame of reference forces the other party to shift also, or else fail to obtain his fair share of the rewards; that in a competitive frame of reference it is to the advantage of both parties to withhold information about their respective bargaining ranges; that the most likely response to a threat in bargaining among equals is a counterthreat; and that the threat of coercion is father to the act of coercion as the need to save face progressively takes precedence over the need to bring the bargaining to an equitable conclusion (Deutsch, 1949; Archibald, 1966).

Whether these previously unearthed generalizations also apply to asymmetrical relationships is not as clear, however—and, unfortunately, conflict theorists have expended considerably less energy on conflicts between the relatively powerful and the relatively powerless. The bargaining models which conflict theorists apply to symmetrical, mixed-motive conflicts generally assume that each side has tangible power to bargain *with*. This is not necessarily true of the disgruntled citizen who learns that it is not easy to "Go fight City Hall." And it may be even less true of those who feel impelled to confront private corporations.

It is precisely this last category of asymmetrical conflicts—those involving the large, profit-making organization and its relatively powerless clients—that is the central concern of this chapter. Short of expensive legal remedies, what can the disgruntled customer (or group of customers) do to achieve his (their) ends? What, in turn, are the social control mechanisms available to the institution? And how, in manifest conflicts, are these strategies of influence likely to function in interaction between the institution and the client?

THE FRAMEWORK

I will employ as the basic paradigm a two-dimensional matrix of communication strategies for two entities: an institution and a discontented individual or small group. The vertical axis displays options open to the individual, the horizontal axis, those open to the institution. Within each cell of the matrix are three items of information for each entity: (1) the probability for the occurrence of that cell as perceived by the entity (p); (2) a hypothetical cost to the entity of that occurrence (c); and (3) a hypothetical reward to the entity of that occurrence (r). This information for the individual appears in the lower left of each cell, for the institution, in the upper right half.

It should be noted that throughout this chapter I shall be assigning subjective estimates of probabilities, costs, and rewards (although I believe they are reasonable). Because the case studies to be considered will be used for heuristic purposes, it matters less what the actual values of variables are than that the reader can see how these variables might operate in interaction to determine strategies and counterstrategies. I recognize the possibility of calculating an expected value for each entity in each cell by summing the reward and cost and multiplying by the probability. I have not taken this step for two reasons: (1) the hypothetical nature of the data would make such calculations gratuitously pedantic; (2) I suspect that potential costs (risk) are not psychologically additive with potential rewards (opportunity).

For the individual, the system involves the following communication options, listed roughly in the normal order of their increasing costliness:

Oral petition.   Face-to-face or telephone communication of a request and, optionally, the rationale for the request.

Written petition.   Written communication of a request and its rationale. A petition "for the record."

Appeal to a superinstitution.   Normal petitioning procedures having failed, the individual may take his case to an institution having power over the unresponsive institution. An example would be a motorist who, receiving unsatisfactory service from his dealer, writes to the manufacturer of his automobile.

Promulgation.   Publicizing a petition and its rationale, often with the aid of the mass media.

Collectivization, organization.   Identifying, soliciting the aid of, and organizing those who may be expected to join in the petition. Usually followed by renewed petition with the added clout of the organization.

Nonviolent resistance.   Nonaggressively interfering with the normal operations of the institution in question by such means as boycotts, sit-ins, etc.

Escalation/confrontation.   Interfering with the operations of the institution in question in a violent or aggressive manner. Includes such tactics as trashings, bombings, highjacking, terrorism.

For the institution, the system provides the following options, again listed roughly in the normal order of increasing costliness when the transaction is an extraordinary one of the type to be considered:

Avoidance.   Ignoring the petition or acknowledging the petition but ignoring its substance by such means as form letters, passing the buck, recorded messages, etc.

Procedural counterpersuasion.   An attempt to defuse the petition by referring to a decision-making and implementing process resulting in a book of rules and limited responsibilities for the institutional official involved. The "I'm just followng orders—I don't make the rules" response.

Substantive counterpersuasion.   Denial of the petition with a principled rationale.

Adjustment. Granting all or part of the petitioner's request(s). Adjustment is the least costly response in a normal trading situation where it is in the institution's interest to strike a bargain with the individual.

Nonviolent suppression. Attempting to limit the activities of the individual without using physical force. Might involve blackmail or other forms of harassment such as wiretapping, tailing, entrapment in "immoral" activities. Gathering and using or threatening to use information designed to discredit the petitioner.

Violent suppression. Limiting the activities of the individual with physical force. This option is usually open only to political agencies and then only in severely circumscribed situations.

The basic paradigm is displayed in Figure 1. For each of the two cases to be considered, a series of such figures will be analytically used. The series should be imagined as a third dimension—time. Each exchange of moves (each two-dimensional matrix) makes up an interaction. The series of exchanges (the three-dimensional matrix) makes up a transaction.

The analytic system might be clarified by consideration of an example. In a normal business transaction, a consumer might enter a supermarket for the purpose of buying a loaf of bread. Assume that the price of the bread is 36 cents. On the basis of previous experience, the consumer fully expects to make his or her selection and to offer the full asking price for the bread. Given such a combination of events, the institution fully expects its agent to accept the offer. In terms of Figure 1, this transaction would comprise only one interaction: oral petition/adjustment. Both entities on the basis of reward and cost analysis as well as previous experience would have a perfect (for practical purposes) expectation of that cell being selected, so $p = 1.0$ in the consumer's half (lower left) of the cell and also in the institution's half (upper right). The cost to the consumer would be 36 cents ($c = .36$ in lower left half of cell), assuming that he or she was not required to travel a long distance to the supermarket, has no morbid fear of supermarkets, etc. The supermarket's costs include the cost to it of the bread (say 24 cents) plus whatever overhead must be assigned to this transaction (say six cents). Hence, $c = .30$ in the upper right half of the cell. Presumably, the bread has a value of at least 36 cents ($r = .36+$ in lower left half of cell) to the consumer, and for the supermarket $r = .36$ in the upper right half of the cell meaning a net of six cents for the institution. Both entities realize greater rewards than costs from the transaction, and we can verify by a common-sense examination of the other cells

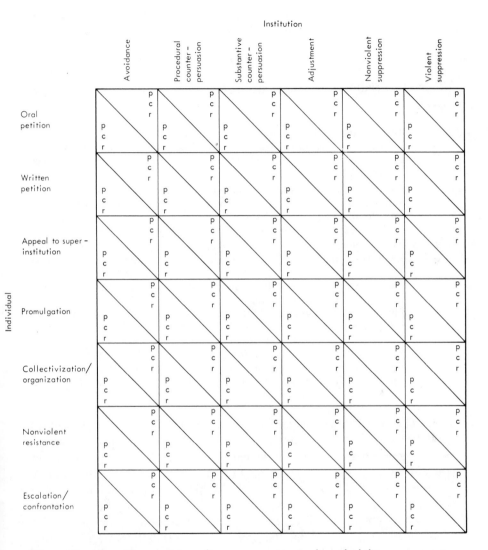

Figure 1 Interaction matrix, where p = perceived probability, c = cost, r = reward.

that neither entity could do better elsewhere in the matrix. The bargain is easily struck in one interaction. The situation has involved coordination rather than conflict.

As will become apparent, this paper is concerned with another kind of situation, one involving conflict. The basic elements of the cases to be considered are these:

1. The individual must initiate the transaction, normally with oral petition.
2. Adjustment is *not* the response yielding the highest profit to the institution in the initial interaction. Hence, the transaction analyzed will comprise more than one interaction.

The relationships analyzed are asymmetrical in at least three respects:

1. Because the individual must initiate each interaction, he must experience some uncertainty about the outcome ($p < 1.0$ in each cell of the row he chooses); the institution can complete the interaction with certainty ($p = 1.0$).
2. The institution has had much more experience with extraordinary transactions than has the individual. Therefore, it can estimate contingencies and decide on courses of action with considerably more expertise and a higher expectation of maximizing rewards while minimizing costs.
3. Most important, because of its impersonal nature, the institution (qua institution) does not experience emotional, intangible rewards and costs. For the institution, costs and rewards can be calculated in terms of time and money. For the individual, they must be calculated in terms of time and money plus stresses and satisfactions. An institution does not experience frustration and ego-satisfaction, while an individual cannot help but be subject to these additional pressures. Hence, if we were to calculate an expected value for each relevant cell by multiplying its net reward by its perceived probability (a step we will not take), cost and reward entries as well as perceived probability entries for the individual would require different criteria than would the same entries for the institution.

The analytic system employed makes it possible to represent in a different form some important aspects of each entity's cognitive/ motivational system. (I am indebted to Marr (1971) for pointing out these possibilities.) Figure 2, for example, represents an individual's cognitive/motivational system. The solid line shows a situation in which the individual could be expected to have a considerably narrower latitude of acceptance and a wider latitude of rejection (higher ego involvement) than would be the case if the dotted line were the representation. It would be simple to represent differing attitudes, strengths of belief, etc., using the same kind of representation, though I will not exploit those possibilities in this paper.

The situation is one involving conflict only where rewards for the individual are to some extent costly for the institution, and vice versa. This does not imply necessarily a zero sum situation. The magnitude of rewards for the individual in one cell or across all cells need not equal the magnitude of costs for the institution, or vice versa. We must remember, of course, that a mutually rewarding cell may exist in the matrix but that because of perceptual deficiencies the entities involved do not find it. We must also remember that to a great extent the de-

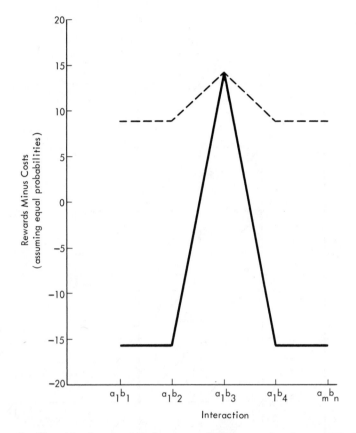

Figure 2   Cognitive/motivational system of high ego involvement (solid line) and low ego involvement (broken line).

sirability of an outcome depends on value systems intrinsic to the entities involved. For an individual who has as part of his value system a strongly anti-bureaucratic element, for example, a long and involved series of interactions with an institution may in itself be rewarding as reinforcement of his existential position. A long series of interactions might also be rewarding for a lonely individual. At any rate, Figure 3 shows a conflict matrix; Figure 4, a cooperative matrix.

TWO INDIVIDUAL/ INSTITUTIONAL TRANSACTIONS

The two cases to be considered are, from the point of view of most individuals, extraordinary transactions, though the growth of insti-

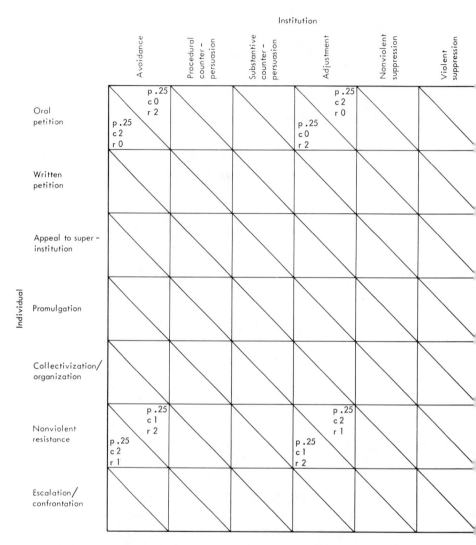

Figure 3 Matrix involving conflict.

tutions both in size and in number makes such transactions more common than they once were. The transactions under discussion do not include routine matters, such as buying food in a chain store or paying taxes to the government.

It will be apparent that my bias is anti-institutional. This bias has a basis in fact and logic. People working in institutions, I think, tend to value institutional maintenance and personal security above task performance. They also tend to feel little personal responsibility

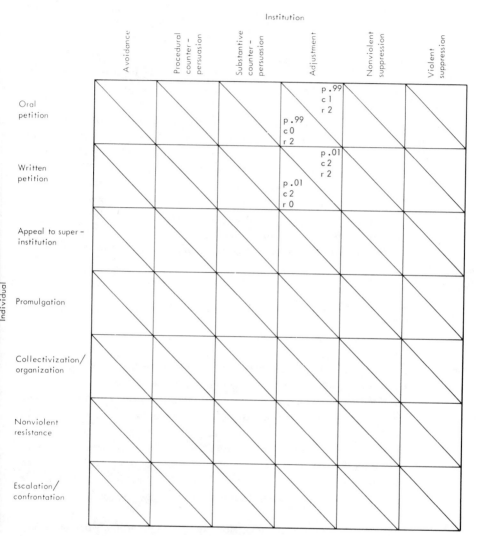

Figure 4 Matrix involving cooperation.

for their official acts because those who make decisions are seldom those who implement decisions. In addition, institutions tend to band together with other institutions of the same type in an often successful attempt to influence their own governing institutions in ways that assure institutional maintenance and growth with little regard to task performance.

John Crowe Ransom (1936) analyzed some of these problems as they are exemplified in business institutions. He makes an analogy between the internal organization of a big business and that of an army, where "responsibility . . . is limited, except at the top, and there are certainly many men in the world who like to reduce their responsibility, who like to carry out orders if they suppose that the orders are intelligent" (p. 303). This separation of decision making from decision implementation obviously carries with it dangers to accountability: those who make decisions can plead ignorance of consequences; those who implement decisions can plead that they were only following orders. In business institutions, as Ransom notes, even ownership entails no accountability for institutional behavior. Small owners "concur cheerfully" with executive decisions as long as "earnings are high"; when the value of a large owner's investment is endangered, his "Napoleonic decision . . . consists in ordering his broker to sell" (p. 303).

The temptation to extend Ransom's analysis of nonresponsibility and irresponsibility in big business to big government, big education, and big religion is difficult to resist. But perhaps a more specific analysis of some cases will make the possibility of such an extension more readily apparent.

Case 1

December 30, 1971, I returned from San Francisco to Cedar Rapids, Iowa, by air. Although I had made my reservation in October, United Airlines informed me that all coach class seats were taken on the Denver–Cedar Rapids leg of the flight and that I would have to fly first class. (A paradox is involved in that kind of transaction: first class is third class for those who want to fly coach class.) Because United is the only major airline serving Cedar Rapids, my choice was to fly first class or not to fly at all. Hence, at Denver I was occupying a seat in the first-class cabin and was in a position to witness a brief transactional drama, the account of which follows.

The scene was a hectic one. Holiday passenger traffic was heavy, and our flight was, in addition, blessed with a group of about forty people, traveling together, who were to transfer to our plane for Cedar Rapids after spending a few days in Las Vegas. Their tickets were in coach class, and personnel at the Denver airport had told me that their bloc of seats was what prevented me from being able to travel in coach.

I was among the first to board the plane, and I took my seat in first class. The tour group had not yet been seated, but they were backed up in the umbilical tube connecting plane to port.

A middle-aged man and woman (I inferred that they were husband and wife) entered, and the man showed their tickets to the stewardess (oral petition). She inspected the tickets and told the man that he and his wife would have to return to the airport (avoidance). The Denver facility has adopted a system where one check-in counter serves several gates, and the couple had failed to stop at the counter to have their tickets pulled.

The man persisted. He had paid for tickets in coach class; the tickets were on our flight; he was presently inside the airplane, and he did not intend to leave. He insisted that his petition be honored. The stewardess explained politely but firmly that with his tickets in their pristine condition she was powerless to permit them to board (procedural counterpersuasion).

The eyes of many impatient travelers were upon the exchange from both front and rear, and the man's demeanor indicated that he was experiencing some discomfort. His wife was even more distressed, and she began urging him to do as the stewardess asked. He quickly stifled that and continued to make it clear to the stewardess, addressing her as "Young woman," that he intended to stay in the airplane. He did not intend to leave under his own volition (nonviolent resistance).

The flight was now definitely being delayed. Passengers already on board felt some sympathy for the couple but also some frustration-induced aggression directed both toward the couple and the airline. Potential passengers in the tube were being prevented from boarding, and this inconvenience was made more unpleasant by uncertainty about whether they would be permitted to board. It was a tense scene for all of us.

Finally, the stewardess called the United desk inside the airport. Within seconds, a neatly dressed airline official appeared, courteously seated the couple in the first-class cabin, and left. Boarding continued. As far as I could tell, all the people on the tour were seated, some in the first-class cabin. Every seat in the airplane was occupied. I have no way of knowing whether any ticketholders with confirmed reservations were left behind.

I have tried to chart the progress of the transaction in Figures 5, 6, and 7, with a reward of 20 arbitrarily representing the couple's best possible outcome. Figure 5 shows the oral petition/avoidance interaction, and that cell has been shaded in. The relevant hypothetical data has also been provided in other relevant cells. Note that from the customer's point of view the oral petition/adjustment cell is the expected one with a perceived probability of .80. (I have assumed that the couple was unaware of the necessity to have the tickets pulled inside the airport. If that assumption was wrong, they probably had more substantial doubts about the success of their petition.) From the airline's point of view, the petition/adjustment cell in this case requires a slight cost. It would involve deviation from normal operating procedures, deviation for which the stewardess obviously was not authorized. Therefore, the institution attempts to avoid the petition, a strategy which, if successful

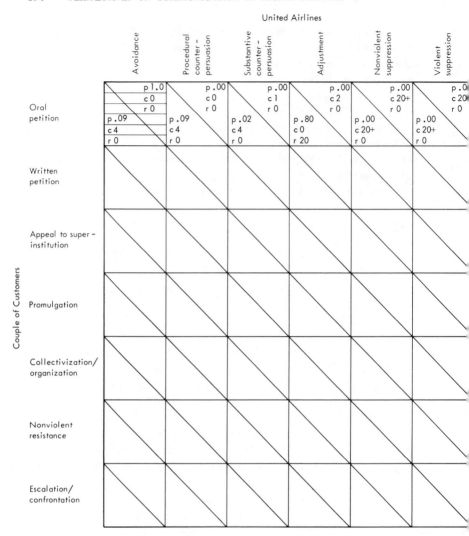

Figure 5 Case 1: First interaction.

(and the institution on the basis of past experience expects that it will be successful), involves costs for the airline only if the couple later resort to their more costly options. The couple can be shuttled back into the airport, another official, as part of his routine duties, can either further avoid the petition or adjust to it, and the aircraft can meanwhile be loaded, all this without inconvenience to the institution. This interaction, however, involves some costs, in this case apparently substantial, for the couple. If they leave the aircraft, they may be required to pay the difference between coach class and first class fare ($28), or they may have to wait for a later flight. True, if the couple were forced to wait they could collect a penalty from the airline, but they may not be aware of it, or the delay may be very costly for them, or they may be unwilling to follow through on the transaction that would result in the payment of the penalty.

Whatever his reasons, the man decides to cope with the crisis. The first interaction causes him to change his perception of the probabilities in the matrix (Figure 6). He sees that oral petition might not result in

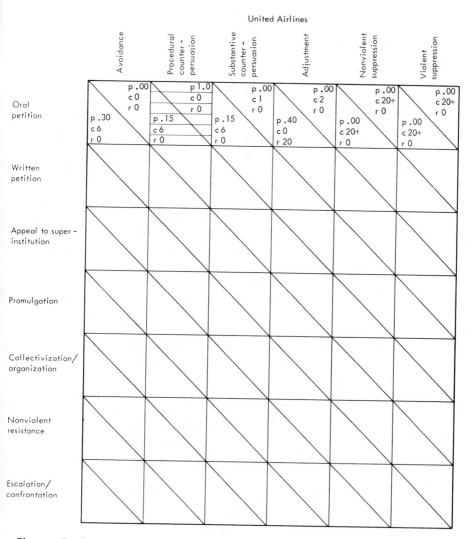

Figure 6 Case 1: Second interaction.

adjustment ($p = .40$) but he tries it again, possibly to gain time. This petition is not part of a routine transaction, and it is more costly to him than the first in terms of communicative effort and resistance to social pressures. The stewardess responds with procedural counterpersuasion. *The move involves some cost for her but, so long as the couple does not resort to more costly strategies and the flight is not delayed, none at all for the institution.* This is so because procedural counterpersuasion is part of the stewardess' duties. The airline must pay her the same amount whether or not she engages in the strategy.

This second interaction in the transaction, petition/procedural counterpersuasion, slides into nonviolent resistance by the couple (Figure 7). The flight is now definitely being delayed by the unauthorized presence of the couple. This makes the avoidance and counterpersuasion strategies more costly to the airline than adjustment would be, and the institution capitulates, seating the couple in the first-class cabin.

Some further comments about Figures 5, 6, and 7 are in order. First, the couple's expectations are initially unrealistic, for they must build up their fund of experience with institutions. The institution's much wider experience with individuals, however, gives it more accurate expectations and a ready mode of response to any strategy of the individual.

Second, the cost of suppression for this institution, as for most institutions in our culture, is very high. Suppose that the airline had carried the couple bodily from the plane. I assume that this response might have stimulated a lawsuit or an investigation by a regulatory agency or both. The cost of the suit and/or investigation, however, would be minor compared with the institution's loss of public esteem, or referent power (Bowers and Ochs, 1971). We power invulnerables (Simons, 1967) on the flight, to say nothing of others reached by the media, would have been much more likely to identify with the couple than with the airline. United, like most business institutions, recognized this cost. Not all institutions—notably political and educational ones—do consistently recognize it.

Third, the outcome is unusual in that the man refused to be intimidated either by the institution or by the open and embarrassing attention of the other passengers. A much more normal sequence, as the airline knew, would have been petition/avoidance, petition/avoidance, and eventually, petition/adjustment of the kind most convenient to the airline.

Finally, the transaction, in a sense, increased the cost of the couple's trip with each interaction, though it did not increase appreciably the costs for the institution. Individuals within the institution were required

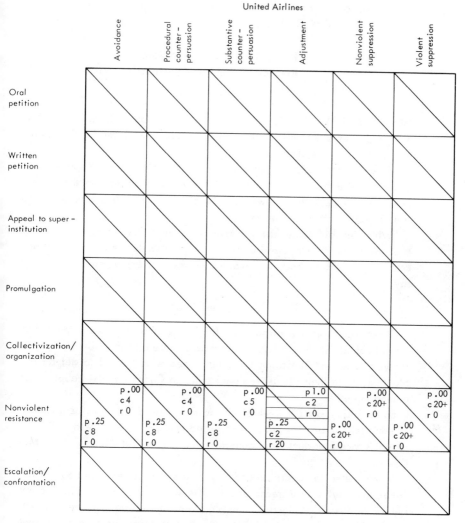

Figure 7 Case 1: Final interaction.

to put forth some effort, but they would have been paid the same amount by the airline with or without that effort.

Case 2

The second case is of the type with which all of us are familiar if we have ever tried to carry out an extraordinary transaction with a large, monopolistic institution. The case is reported below in full as it appeared in the *Des Moines Register* (February 13, 1972):

Town Angry at Phone Rate
Rise on Fire-Alarm System

By a staff writer

MOUNT VERNON, IA.—The mayor of this Linn County town of 3,000 is outraged over a 500 per cent increase in telephone rates for the town's private fire-alarm system.

Nicholas Berry, 35, says Northwestern Bell Telephone Company's decision to raise from $5.63 to $29.25 the monthly charge on the system linking five telephones in town with the phone at the fire station effective Jan. 1 "really hit a raw nerve with me.

"When the bill came last week, it came at a time when we're going over every item in our town budget to try to cut costs. Here was a 500 per cent increase that nobody had warned us about or explained to us," Berry says.

Got "Thank You"

"Taxpayers hold me responsible for the costs of city government, but when I called the local telephone company office all I got was 'Thank you for your concern.' The same thing happened when I tried to get an explanation from their (Bell's) regional office in Cedar Rapids—people kept putting me off."

So on Friday, after a week of talking to "customer-relations people who couldn't tell me anything and to recorded messages," Berry wrote directly to Bell's vice-president and general manager in Des Moines, Jack McCallister.

In his letter to McCallister, Berry asked for an explanation of the "extraordinary" rate increase and threatened to take the phone company before the Iowa Commerce Commission to have the rate increase nullified.

McCallister acknowledged Saturday that the rate increase for Mount Vernon "sounds awfully high to me."

"We are restructuring our tariffs on private lines, and across the state the rate increase averages about 6 per cent," McCallister explained.

He said he has instructed Bell's regional manager in Cedar Rapids, Roger Schraeder, to go to Mount Vernon Monday afternoon to meet with Berry. "Maybe they can work out some kind of accommodation," McCallister said.

Filed for Boost

He said Northwestern Bell first filed for permission for the rate increase last July 1, but that the Commerce Commission has not issued a ruling in the matter. "The new rates are in effect now, but we will refund any excess charges to our customers if the commission disallows the increase," Mc-Callister said Saturday. A hearing on the rate increase is scheduled before the Commerce Commission March 6.

McCallister said the private-line rate increase resulted from a change in the company's billing system.

"Under the old system, we charged on the basis of 'mileage.' So many dollars for so many miles of lines from the outlying phones to the terminal at the fire station.

"Now we have converted to charging a flat sum for the terminal. In the cases of larger cities where they had a lot of miles to private phone lines, our new way of billing actually means lower costs.

"But in smaller communities with short distances, the rates may have increased."

McCallister said he did not know how many communities in the state are now paying higher bills for their private-line, fire-protection system.

This case presents our analytic scheme with something of a problem in punctuation. The first move in the transaction was the increased bill sent from the telephone company to Mayor Berry. This could appropriately be called "petition," but the paradigm has no strategy of institutional petition.

"Petition" may not be the best word for the move anyway. The telephone company to a degree has behavior control over the town in a monopolistic situation. Flat refusal to pay could result in a loss of service, a contingency that would be unthinkable in this age of electronic communication. Therefore, the bill is not really a request; it is a demand backed by coercive power.

The problem for the paradigm can be avoided (and I will avoid it) by expediently punctuating the transaction differently, regarding as the first move Mayor Berry's first attempt to have the bill reduced.

The case presents another problem. Mayor Berry speaks for the town of Mount Vernon, which is, of course, an institution. Still, the essential elements of individual/institutional conflict seem to be fulfilled. A relatively powerless entity, represented by one person, is in conflict with a relatively powerful one, represented by a hierarchical bureaucracy. Mayor Berry may be more tenacious as an institutional spokesman than he would be acting individually, and he may have better access to the media in his institutional role. Thus qualified, the interactions in the transaction are familiar ones.

I have represented the transaction in Figures 8 to 15, using the difference between the old rate ($5.63) and the new rate ($29.25), or

$23.62 as the maximum possible reward to the town. I realize that this is an unrealistic assessment, for the telephone company obviously contemplates continuing at the higher rate, thus greatly increasing its own rewards and the town's costs over a period of time. Nevertheless, the $23.62 figure will serve to illustrate hypothetically the principles involved, all of which are relative. Any number would serve as well.

The first interaction is represented in Figure 8. Mayor Berry's first telephone call to the local phone company is assigned intrinsic

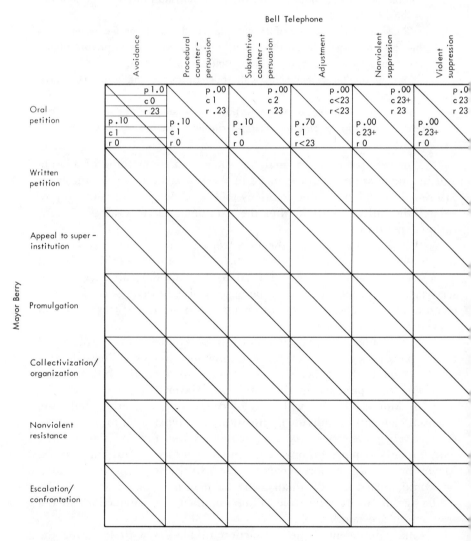

Figure 8   Case 2: First interaction.

and extrinsic costs (Mayor Berry must use his time and mental and emotional energy to make the call) of $1.00. He receives an avoidance response—"Thank you for your concern." As in Case 1, avoidance costs the institution nothing so long as the mayor employs the petition strategies.

The mayor's second response is to call the Cedar Rapids Bell Telephone office (Figure 9). This interaction is more costly to him, for he must get through to a higher level of the institution. The emotional costs are also higher, for his first experience increases his perception of

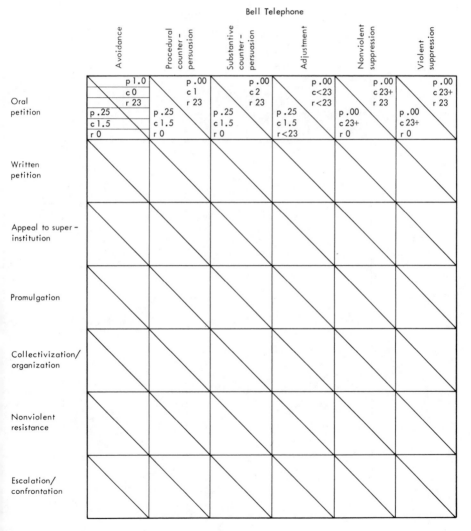

Figure 9 Case 2: Second interaction.

the probability of failure. I have made those costs $1.50. Added to the costs of the first interaction, Mayor Berry's total costs are now $2.50, compared with a possible reward of $23.62. Again, the avoidance response of the company involves no cost.

There follows a series (Figures 10, 11, and 12) of talks with "customer-relations people who couldn't tell me anything and to recorded messages." Each of these interactions, involving petition and sometimes electronic avoidance, costs Mayor Berry $1.50, assuming that

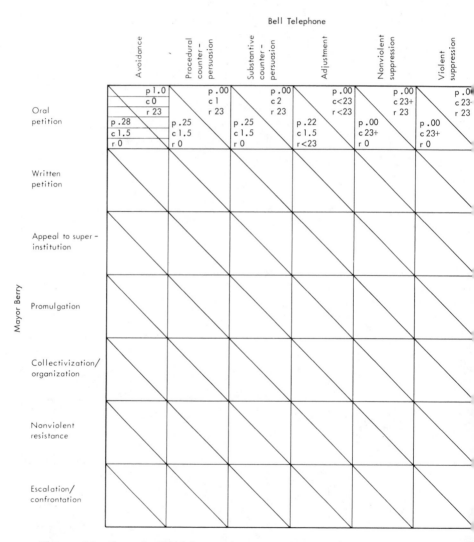

Figure 10 Case 2: Third interaction.

his costs are not sequentially increased by increased frustration, while the telephone company gets off free. The mayor's total costs are now $7.00.

At this point, Mayor Berry decides that oral communication will get him nowhere, and he writes a petitioning letter (I have conservatively estimated the cost at $4.00) to Jack McCallister in Des Moines (Figure 13). In the letter, Berry also threatens to appeal the new rate to a super-

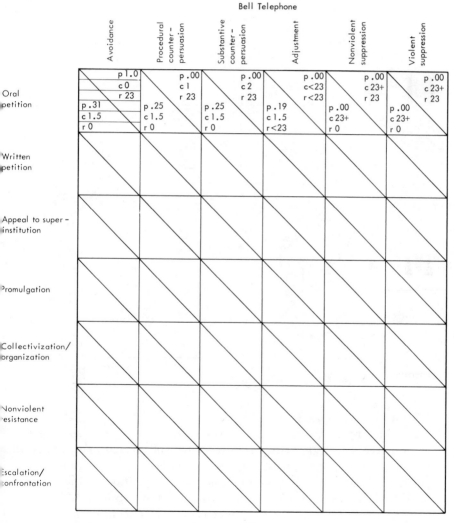

Figure 11 Case 2: Fourth interaction.

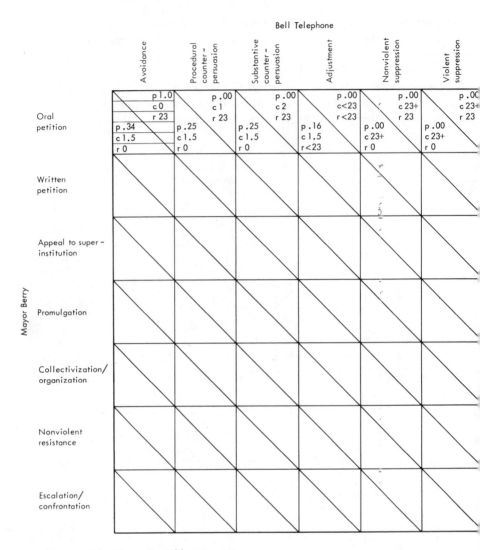

Figure 12   Case 2: Fifth interaction.

institution, the Iowa Commerce Commission. The mayor has not yet made that move, but if he did it could prove costly to the company, because the new rate structure would be endangered. For unknown reasons, McCallister apparently has no excessive worries about that possibility, and he continues to avoid Berry's petition by passing the buck back to Cedar Rapids. Berry's costs are now up to $11.00, almost half the possible payoff; the telephone company has continued to handle the matter routinely at no cost to itself. However, the possibility of high

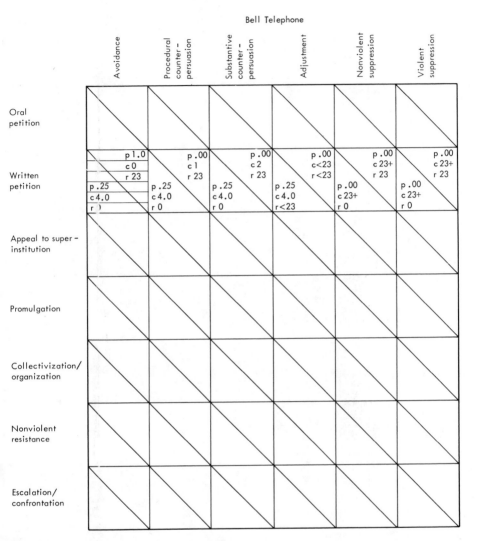

Figure 13 Case 2: Sixth interaction.

costs for the company has emerged with Berry's threat to enlist the ICC.

In the next move, Berry gains the full, fair, and favorable attention of the *Des Moines Register,* which carries the story prominently on the front page of its Sunday Iowa News section. I have estimated his costs in time and energy at $6.00 (Figure 14). This successful promulgation requires from the company a response other than avoidance, both because McCallister has to encode something other than a routine response for the *Register* and because publicity might result in public pressure

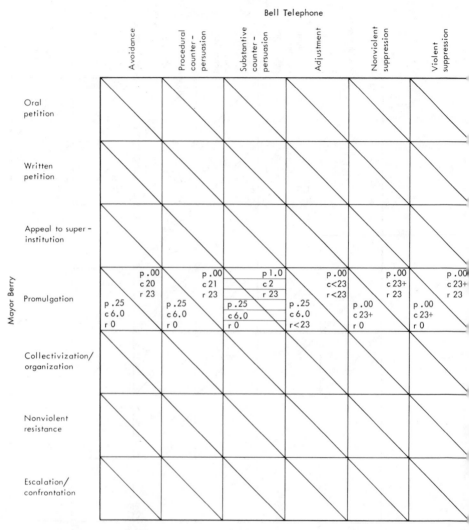

Figure 14 Case 2: Seventh interaction.

which would endanger ICC ratification of the new rate structure. The company therefore elects, under considerable duress, the substantive counterpersuasion strategy.

And there the matter stands as I write this. Mayor Berry, with the indirect help of the Iowa Commerce Commission and the direct help of the *Des Moines Register,* has managed to put a very large institution in a position in which adjustment is probably the least costly of its strategies. The series of interactions, however, has cost the mayor $17.00, conservatively estimated, in an effort to gain a possible payoff of $23.62.

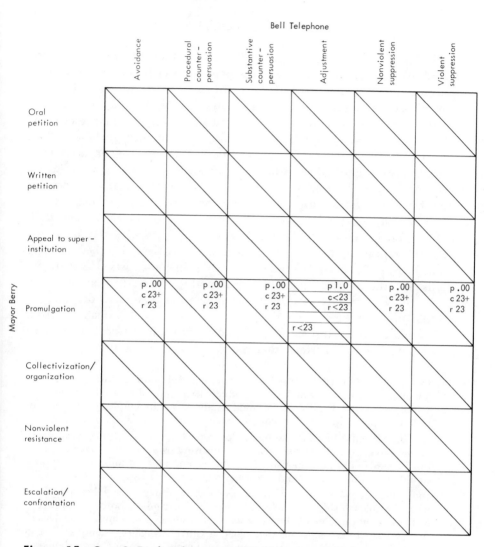

Figure 15   Case 2: Predicted outcome following seventh interaction.

My prediction (Figure 15) is that regardless of further action by Berry the telephone company will make a quiet settlement (adjustment).[1]

[1] I talked with Mayor Berry (by telephone, ironically) on August 22, 1972, approximately six months after I had written this paper. He told me that my prediction of adjustment had been correct to a degree: the telephone company had reduced the monthly charge after this series of interactions, but only by $3.50. The mayor was not satisfied with this adjustment, and he has filed a brief with the Iowa Commerce Commission, the superinstitution which is still considering the case as of this date (September 26, 1972). Hence, the transaction is not yet completed.

DISCUSSION

As mentioned earlier, my value system leads me to consider the kinds of transactions analyzed in the paper—especially interactions where institutions initially respond to petitions almost automatically with avoidance—to be inimical to the good life. I think that such transactions produce in most individuals an apathetic, unhealthy acceptance of many low-level frustrations, an attitude that results in such clichés as "You can't fight City Hall." [2] The state of affairs, given the present social/legal climate, is inevitable. Institutions will use avoidance so long as avoidance is their least costly response unless they are in an unusually competitive market. Institutions with a virtual monoply use the avoidance strategy so commonly that they have programmed it electronically. The individual, on the other hand, soon learns that his costs quickly mount as he tries repeatedly to get past the avoidance barriers. The best possible outcome just isn't worth the effort for him in most cases. He therefore falls into the habit of apathetically accepting the status quo.

If society wants to change the system, its best hope of doing so would probably be to alter the cost/reward/perceived probability paradigm under which institutions operate. This might be done in various ways, and I do not pretend that the list below is exhaustive.

1. If the institution itself wanted to change, it could adopt a system of rewards for employees who respond to individual needs, punishments for those who avoid them. In other words, it could establish for its employees a norm of instant responsibility to alleviate customer or client or public frustrations.
2. Individuals could be educated to employ appeals to superinstitutions as a very early strategy in their transactions with institutions. Assuming that the super-institutions would be responsive (and the assumption is dubious), institutions would soon learn that avoidance can frequently be costly.
3. Individuals could be educated to use as an early strategy nonviolent resistance when feasible, to subtly behave in such a way that mild disorder is produced in the institution. One of the students in my course, "Communication Theory in Everyday Life," tells me that when a university office attempts to send her to another office she politely requests permission to use the telephone. She then ties up the line until either she personally has received satisfaction or the avoiding official decides to act as her agent in solving the problem. If behavior like hers became the norm, bureaucrats would learn that avoidance is more costly than adjustment.
4. Legislation could prohibit the use of electronic avoidance devices, form letters designed for avoidance, and customer relations departments used solely as buffers between individuals and responsible officials of institutions;

---

[2] This generalization requires some qualification. Once an individual invests substantial effort in a controversy with an institution, he is likely to continue even though his costs mount far beyond any reasonable expectation of tangible rewards (see, for example, Gurr, 1970, pp. 71–73).

such legislation also could force institutions to pay the reasonable costs, or even double or triple those costs, of well-founded petitions directed to themselves. The effect of the legislation might be to provide an incentive for institutions to treat individuals as individuals, for the least costly institutional response would at least change from avoidance to procedural counterpersuasion.

5. Public servants might be hired to assist individuals with their communication strategies in conflicts with institutions. At one time, I thought that this was the best answer. Then after an exceptionally frustrating vacation I spent with my family in New York during the summer of 1971, I wrote a letter complaining about our hotel, detailing its inadequacies and the redress I desired, to the New York Consumer Protection Agency. A month or two later, I received a reply from that agency telling me that my complaint had been referred to the New York Hotel Association, an organization of hotel owners. I have received no further word.

RESEARCH IMPLICATIONS

Probably the most important inference to be drawn from this analysis is that generalization from individual/individual conflict to individual/institutional conflict is exceedingly hazardous. Institutions in general have more experience with conflict than individuals have, and it follows that institutions can be more exact in their predictions. More significantly, individuals experience emotional rewards and costs which cannot realistically be ignored. Institutions, on the other hand, insofar as their agents are interchangeable and replaceable, can safely consider individual frustrations and the like irrelevant to institutional calculations. This characteristic of institutions is amplified by the fact that those who make institutional decisions leading to emotional costs and rewards for the agents of the institution normally do not themselves experience the emotional consequences of those decisions. The bank's board of directors decides to require all customers to present an identification card for all transactions. The bank's tellers take the heat.

A laboratory approach to the kinds of cases considered in this paper would be difficult but probably not impossible. The experimenter would require considerable resources in tangible assets to be manipulated, for institutional decision makers must be able to realize profits and losses and institutional agents must be paid for their services. Given these resources, manipulation of the crucial variables should be feasible. Some interesting questions for such research might be:

1. What possible communication strategies for individuals and institutions has the analysis proposed here failed to consider? With what consequences for theory?
2. What happens when the institution must petition the individual? Do

the dynamics of such a transaction differ from those analyzed in this paper?

3. How does competition among institutions for the individual's attention and business as opposed to the monopolistic systems considered in this chapter affect the course of individual/institutional transactions? More generally, how are transactions affected when either or both entities have the option of withdrawing?

4. Does an entity behave differently under conditions of maximizing reward than it does under conditions of minimizing cost? That is, does increasing possible rewards have an effect different from that of decreasing possible costs? Do these effects act differentially on individuals and institutions?

SUMMARY

This paper has explored some theoretical possibilities for the analysis of communication in the process of conflict between individuals and institutions where the individual initiates the transaction by petitioning the institution. A matrix employing a set of strategies for each entity was devised for the purpose of describing and ultimately predicting the process of such transactions, and three variables—perceived probability, reward, and cost—were entered in the matrix for each entity in each relevant cell or intersection of strategies. This system was used to analyze two actual individual/institutional conflicts. Finally, possible applications of social engineering to the system were proposed and research implications were explored.

REFERENCES

ARCHIBALD, K., ed., *Strategic Interaction and Conflict.* Berkeley, Cal.: Institute of International Studies, 1966.

BOWERS, J. W., and D. OCHS, *The Rhetoric of Agitation and Control.* Reading, Mass.: Addison-Wesley, 1971.

Des Moines Register, February 13, 1972, p. 1B.

DEUTSCH, M., "A Theory of Cooperation and Competition," *Human Relations,* 2 (1949), 129–52.

GURR, T. R., *Why Men Rebel.* Princeton, N.J.: Princeton University Press, 1970.

MARR, T. J., "Verbal Behavior as Related to Conciliatory Behavior in a Consensus Achieving Context." Unpublished paper, Department of Speech and Dramatic Art, University of Iowa, 1971.

RANSOM, J. C., "The South is a Bulwark," *Scribner's Magazine,* 99 (1936), 303.

SIMONS, H. W., "Patterns of Persuasion in the Civil Rights Struggle," *Today's Speech,* 15 (1967), 25–27.

6

Conflict and
Communication within
the University

PHILLIP K. TOMPKINS
JEANNE Y. FISHER
DOMINIC A. INFANTE
ELAINE V. TOMPKINS

Because the university is a kind of organization, this paper will approach the topic of conflict from the general models of organizational conflict. It will proceed from those considerations to a brief review of conflict within the university. The paper will then consider data gathered in a recent study of a northeastern state university bearing on attitudes toward conflict and conflict aftermath. The relationships between conflict and communication will be considered throughout the paper.

MODELS OF ORGANIZATIONAL CONFLICT

After sifting the large body of literature on the subject of organizational conflict, Pondy (1967) offers a synthesis of concepts and models. He defines conflict as a dynamic process, a sequence of events in a conflict

153

episode. The first is *latent conflict;* i.e., there must be preconditions to conflict. Pondy condenses the underlying sources of organizational conflict into three: competition for scarce resources, drives for autonomy, and divergence of subunit goals. One or more of these sources of latent conflict may be present at the same time.

The second sequence in a conflict episode is *perceived conflict.* According to Pondy, conflict may be perceived when no conditions of latent conflict exist; latent conflict conditions may be present in an organization without being perceived. "The case in which conflict is perceived when no latent conflict exists," writes Pondy (1962), "can be handled by the so-called 'semantic model' of conflict" (p. 301). That is, such conflict can be resolved by full and open communication between and among the parties perceiving the conflict. Pondy correctly observes that this model (which the speech communication field was probably more responsible for promoting in the past than was any other field) can lead to *exacerbation* of conflict if the parties enter into open communication about their true positions—only to discover that the positions *are* in opposition. The case of latent conflict which fails to reach the level of awareness is explained by Pondy by means of such psychological mechanisms as suppression. Pondy does not consider the role of communication (and its absence) in such a case, but it seems to us that latent conflict could not often blossom into perceived conflict without open communication. It may therefore be useful to conceive of communication as a facilitator of *perceived* conflict in certain situations.

The third sequence in a conflict episode is *felt conflict.* This, as opposed to the cognitive character of the second sequence, is an affective condition involving the *personalization* of conflict. The personalization of conflict, writes Pondy (1967), "is the mechanism which causes most students of organization to be concerned with the dysfunction of conflict" (p. 302). The anxieties within the individual must be vented, according to the "tension model," if the individual is to maintain internal equilibrium.

The fourth sequence is *manifest conflict.* Pondy would define a behavior as conflictful (1) only when some or all of the participants perceive it to be conflictful and (2) only when a participant *knowingly* frustrates the goals of another participant. Can communication contribute to the resolution of manifest conflict? Tedeschi (1970), apparently echoing Schelling (1960), argues that "most conflicts can be viewed as bargaining situations in which there is opportunity for one party to influence the others" (p. 155). Small-group and attitude-change research, as well as common sense and experience, would suggest that communication among parties often contributes to conflict resolution. It is worth noting that the courts and legislatures, in their pragmatic wisdom, have promoted collective bargaining between management and labor. Unwillingness to engage in communication and to practice bargaining "in good faith" is considered to be an unfair labor practice (Gregory, 1958). Raven and Kruglanski (1970) observe that "under reward power, communications are likely to consist of promises and exchanges of information regarding the positive outcomes each side has in store for the other, thus increasing the likelihood of a mutually satisfactory agreement" (p. 91). However, they continue in the next sentence to say, "Equipped with punitive capacities, the sides are likely to communicate threats which (by virtue of their offensive nature) might intensify *underlying interpersonal* conflict."

The nature of the communication medium employed may well make a difference. In the case of the Vietnamese conflict, one would have thought (apparently correctly) that secret negotiations offered a better chance of achieving a settlement than public negotiations. Tedeschi (1970) hazards the guess that "the more personal and private the threat, the less resistance target would give to the source, all other things being equal" (p. 182). In short, the answer to whether communication plays a functional or dysfunctional role in conflict and conflict resolution appears to be—both. Communication can, if our analysis is correct, facilitate the perception of conflict. It can resolve manifest conflict when there is no corresponding latent conflict. Finally, depending on the nature of the source, message, medium, and character of the relationship between source and receiver, communication can achieve resolution of the conflict as well as its exacerbation and escalation.

The fifth sequence in a conflict episode is *conflict aftermath*. If the conflict is resolved to the satisfaction of all participants, writes Pondy, the basis for a more cooperative relationship may have been laid. If the conflict has not been resolved, he continues, the sources of latent conflict may be aggravated, taking on the potential of an even more explosive conflict.

Pondy (1967) also considers three conceptual models of conflict within the organization. They can also be viewed as types or kinds of conflict: "(1) bargaining conflict takes place among the parties to an interest-group relationship; (2) bureaucratic conflict between the parties to a superior-subordinate relationship; and (3) systems conflict among parties to a lateral or working relationship" (p. 296).

The question of whether conflict is functional or dysfunctional for the organization is discussed by Pondy at some length. The charge of "harmony bias" has been leveled at such theorists as Mayo, Boulding, and March and Simon. The anti-conflict bias seems to originate in two areas. (1) concern for the deleterious effects of conflict on the health of the individual; and (2) concern for the organization's disequilibrium, which is assumed to be created by conflict among its members. It would seem to us, as in our conclusion about the relationship between communication and conflict, that conflict is *both* functional and dysfunctional for an organization. The social sciences in recent years have extrapolated the biological model of homeostasis to a variety of behavioral phenomena. The resultant models are often presented in such a way as to suggest that homeostasis (whether in an individual or an organization) is a static, passive condition. The original biological model, however, posits an equilibrium achieved by the coordination of opposing forces or vectors. This suggests another way of viewing conflict within an organization; i.e., that organizational equilibrium *cannot be achieved without coordinated conflict among opposing forces.* The coordination is provided by a third party. As such, conflict is functional. Assael (1969) seems to offer support for this analysis in his attempt to distinguish between constructive and destructive conflict. His five basic requirements for constructive conflict are:

1. A critical review of past actions.
2. More frequent and effective communications between disputants, and the establishment of outlets to express grievance.
3. A more equitable distribution of systems resources.
4. Standardization of modes of conflict resolution.
5. Creation of a balance of power within the system.

The absence of these conditions, according to Assael, will produce destructive conflict. Constructive conflict is achieved by "conflict management" through the five requirements above.

CONFLICT IN THE UNIVERSITY

Although this paper began with the assumption that a university is a kind of organization, it is becoming increasingly clear that there are important dissimilarities between the modern university and the classical models of organization such as Weber's notions about bureaucracy. A recent article (Cohen, March, and Olsen, 1972) in *Administrative Science Quarterly* suggests that some university organizations can be described as "organized anarchies." The characteristics are three: (1) problematic preferences (the absence of a set of preferences to be employed in making choices); (2) unclear technology (the organization's own processes are not understood by its members); and (3) fluid participation (participants vary in the amount and time they devote to different domains and the decision makers for a particular kind of choice change capriciously). The authors' choice of a title for the article reflects succinctly these characteristics of the university, "A Garbage Can Model of Organizational Choice."

There is another important way in which universities differ from the bureaucratic model. Etzioni (1959) says that professional organizations (including the university) take on a dual authority—an administrative structure which follows the bureaucratic pattern and a professional authority expressed in the spirit of collegiality and professional autonomy. Etzioni also asserts a basic incompatibility between these two orientations.

Inspired by these and other notions, Darkenwald (1971) submitted a Likert-type scale measuring conflict in decision making between the department and central administration to 283 department chairmen at 54 institutions. The institutions represented high, medium, and low differentiation as measured by the Scale of Institutional Differentiation (which in turn was developed by Talcott Parsons and Gerald Platt). Differentiation is defined as the degree to which departments have boundaries, interests, and functions separate from each other. The greater the differentiation, the greater the department's functional autonomy. Size, quality, and degree of research orientation of the faculty are also components of differentiation. It was observed that the "major, highly differentiated university closely approximates the ideal model of the professional organization. The most salient organizational characteristic of the highly differentiated university is the subordination of the administrative authority structure, which functions mainly in a support capacity, to the professional authority structure" (p. 408).

Darkenwald's hypothesis of a curvilinear relationship between *conflict* (department vs. central administration) and organizational *differentiation* was supported by the data. Decision-making conflict between department and central administration "was no greater at major universities than at the smallest liberal arts college" (p. 411). Chairmen at the medium-differentiated institutions experienced the greatest conflict (significant at both the .025 and .001 levels).

The curvilinear relationship was explained as follows:

> With increasing levels of institutional differentiation—and, concomitantly, professionalization—conflict increases up to the point at which universities begin to take on the attributes of full-fledged professional organizations. At this stage, conflict begins to diminish. When either the professional or the administrative authority structure is dominant, internal conflict tends to be relatively low. When there is no clear subordination of one to the other, a struggle for power ensues and conflict is exacerbated. (p. 411)

Paul and Schooler (1970) examined the so-called "generation gap" between senior and junior members of university faculties. Questionnaires that asked each group to evaluate the other were returned by

125 senior faculty members and 140 recently hired faculty members, drawn from the rosters of the Academy of Management and the American Accounting Association.

About the differences between the two samples, the authors concluded:

> The significance of the ability to research and publish testifies to the strength of publish or perish doctrine with newly hired professors. With younger professors the ability to research and publish is the single most important indicator of competence. The senior professors see the newly hired people as preoccupied with research, given to technique-oriented approaches which detract from teaching and the establishment of student rapport. It is possible that the serious student protests of the past few years may cause a "back-to-the-student" emphasis, especially in the large universities. (p. 214)

The reference in the final sentence of the quotation to "serious student protests of the past few years" can serve as a transition to perhaps the most important aspect of conflict within the university. Lipset (Lipset and Schaflander, 1971) has recently produced a history of student activism in America and a detailed analysis of its most recent manifestations. He sets to rest with impressive evidence the popular but misguided notion of the generation gap. Nor does he consider size of institutions the crucial variable it was once thought to be. Quoting Keniston and Lerner, Lipset (1971) wrote that "actually 'there are fewer protests per 10,000 students at large universities than at small ones'." (p. 96). There is more of everything at a large university; size seems to play a role in conflict only to the degree that the university must be large enough to provide a "critical mass" of protest-prone people.

The three institutional correlates of student activism in the sixties which emerged from the research are, in Lipset's words: "(1) size, insofar as it may be regarded as a source of the critical mass, the number necessary to sustain a protest movement and demonstrations; (2) bureaucratization, or degree of impersonal treatment of students; and (3) the politically relevant or predisposing characteristics which students (and faculty) bring with them to [the] university" (p. 100).

In terms of psychological correlates of student activism, Lipset rejects the hypothesis supported by early studies that left-wing activists were an elite group. For example, it first surfaced that they made better grades than the average student. Later studies, comparing the left-wing with the right-wing activist, led Lipset to this conclusion: "In general, those who have the psychic energy to be active, whether as conservatives, moderates or leftists, tend to be somewhat more qualified academically, then passive students" (p. 109). Other supposed psychological correlates (e.g., that leftist activists "have more democratic values than other students") were also dismissed. After an excellent history of student activism in America—the "emphasis on teaching and close faculty contact with undergraduates was attacked as a source of student discontent" in the late 1800s (p. 140)—as well as a consideration of cross-cultural studies, Lipset seems to embrace a general thesis of *cyclical waves of activism and withdrawal,* that "the student population [now approaching eight million] is the most volatile and most easily mobilizable of all social strata" (p. 195).

If Lipset's thesis is correct, we shall see conflict (and perhaps violence) erupt again on the university campus. We became curious about how administrators, faculty, students, and staff at a university viewed conflict and conflict aftermath after having experienced it in recent years. Because of the organizational importance of such attitudes, Pondy (1969) argues that an understanding of the sources of attitudes toward conflict and the means of conflict resolution is essential. Two clinical studies of U.S. government organizations have suggested that anti-conflict attitudes (and behaviors) have led to serious organizational dysfunctions.

For example, Chris Argyris (1967) conducted a series of studies within the U.S. Department of State. The participants were 60 senior Foreign Service officers. Argyris reported what he regarded as causes of organizational ineffectiveness within the Department. These causes took the form of norms, or rules for correct behavior. Each norm was validated by at least a majority of the 60 officers. "The first norm cited," wrote Argyris, "was the tendency to withdraw from open discussion of interpersonal difficulties and conflict. This withdrawal eventually included *substantive* issues that might, if discussed forthrightly, create conflict or interpersonal embarrassment" (p. 8).

A closely related norm "also exists," continued Argyris, "suggesting that the appropriate response to aggressiveness is to withdraw and to judge the individual negatively but not tell him" (p. 8).

Irving L. Janis (1971) examined the historical background of U.S. disasters in Vietnam, the Bay of Pigs, Korea, and Pearl Harbor. He found in each case the phenomenon of "groupthink," an absence of conflict, a "mode of thinking that persons engage in when *concurrence-seeking* becomes so dominant in a cohesive ingroup that it tends to override realistic appraisal of alternative courses of action" (p. 43).

Janis also examined the background of two highly successful group enterprises in government: the formulation of the Marshall Plan and the handling of the Cuban missile crisis. He then formulated a series of recommendations designed to prevent the recurrence of groupthink. Taken together they give high priority to conflict, the open airing of objections and doubts. He warns, however, that conflict could result in serious disadvantages to the organization.

Although Janis limited his study to decision-making bodies in the U.S. government, he observed the symptoms of groupthink in business and industry and other fields where small, cohesive groups make policy.

If, then, attitudes toward conflict can be assumed to have serious consequences for an organization, it does seem appropriate to inquire into the attitudes toward conflict held by members of an organization—the university—which has experienced the phenomenon in intense degrees during recent years. It would seem equally appropriate to inquire into attitudes toward the *consequences,* if any, of that conflict—conflict aftermath—held by those who have experienced it. In an infrequent reference to conflict within the university, Pondy (1969) hypothesizes that the "occurrence of violent conflicts like university student riots probably indicates the absence or inadequacy of legitimate means whereby lower participants can initiate institutional change" (p. 502).

A CASE STUDY OF ATTITUDES TOWARD CONFLICT AND CONFLICT AFTERMATH AT A NORTHEASTERN UNIVERSITY

Background

The data considered in this chapter were gathered as part of a larger, diagnostic study of organizational communication within a northeastern state university of about 13,000 students. Some of the interviewees had been on the campus during the late sixties and early seventies. They seemed to agree that this particular university experienced less conflict than the campuses which dominated the headlines of the period, less perhaps than most campuses. Nonetheless, the university did witness a number of causes, movements, demonstrations, and in one instance, violence in the form of property destruction.

The issues were similar to those which emerged at most universities during this period: opposition to the war in Indo-China, the demand for increased student power, opposition to curricular requirements, and support for several faculty members whose contracts were not renewed. Certain unsanctioned methods were employed: confrontations, a student strike in the spring of 1969, interruptions in classes, and, of course, the destruction of property. Of the three models suggested by Pondy—the bargaining model, the bureaucratic model, and the systems model—the bureaucratic model seems to fit these conflicts best, particularly when one attempts to account for the issues over which unsanctioned tactics were employed. That is, overt and sometimes violent conflict seemed to erupt between parties to a superior-subordinate relationship—students versus the administration with the faculty divided. The central issue seemed to be the question of *autonomy*. Students were successful in championing a proposal which eliminated all curricular requirements except those specified by the department in which the student majored. The struggles against *in loco parentis* also seem to fit this model. The bargaining model of conflict over scarce resources could be used to explain confrontations over the establishment of ethnic studies, but even in these cases the bureaucratic model is at least equally applicable. The systems model seems not to apply at all.

Administrators and faculty reacted to these conflicts in what some might call a flexible manner and in what others might call an inconsistent manner. For example, the administration stood firm against a student movement to retain a faculty member who was not renewed by his department. On the other hand, the administration and faculty permitted students to become voting members of the university senate—the body which approved the student proposal on curriculum requirements. This institutional mode of conflict resolution might well have minimized the use of violence and other unsanctioned tactics on this campus.

During the fall of 1971, still another confrontation took place between students and the administration. Students asked for the establishment of a program in Puerto Rican Studies. The new administration, feeling that prior commitments on this issue had not been honored, complied with the student demands. Although it may well be coincidental, we were approached by the administration not long after this conflict episode about conducting a diagnostic study of communication within the university. By the time the study was begun, January of 1972, the campus was relatively quiet.

Method

The interviewees for the study were randomly selected (except that virtually the entire population of top administrators was included) by the university's computing center. The numbers within the subsamples may be found in Table 1.

Several categories require definitions. The administration included the president and four vice-presidents and their assistants. Directors are the head administrators of service subunits such as the computing center and the library. Nonteaching professionals are specialists such as laboratory technicians who are considered to be faculty members without class-

Table 1 Interviewee Samples [a]

	Number in Original Sample	Number Actually Interviewed
Administration	14	13
Directors	15	15
Deans	13	12
Chairmen	21	20
Governance	13	11
Faculty	80	74
Nonteaching Professionals	28	25
Students	150	123
Civil Service	41	29

[a] Tables 1, 2, 3, and 4 may differ in sub-sample responses because the number giving full responses to a question varied.

room responsibilities. Governance comprises student, faculty, and staff members who hold positions of leadership in various organs of the governance system. A lengthy interview guide and ten scales, pretested in classes and pilot interviews, gathered data about a wide range of topics such as perception of university goals, personal and systematic problems of communication, knowledge of the university's hierarchy, influences in university policy making, and the Burkeian concepts of order, mystery, and identification in the administrative hierarchy. The interviews were conducted by the faculty and students of the Department of Rhetoric and Communication during February, March, and April of 1972.

In regard to conflict, each interviewee was presented with five 7-point semantic differential scales with the following polar adjectives: undesirable-desirable; unnecessary-necessary; inappropriate-appropriate; bad-good; and wrong-right.[1] Because we wondered whether or not the unfavorable attitudes toward interpersonal *and* substantive conflict found by Argyris had penetrated the university, we purposely defined the concept in a way some would characterize as polite, drawing-room controversy; that is, conflict was defined as follows: "Consider conflict to be disagreement and debate over issues and values, not over personalities." The results may be found in Table 2.

Major Findings

All subsamples responded in the favorable or positive range of the scale (i.e., all means were larger than the assumed neutral point of four) in considering conflict. It does seem surprising that they are no higher

[1] The reliability of the scales was estimated by means of Cronbach's Alpha. The sample-by-sample coefficients were extremely high, ranging from .91 (students) to .99 (administration).

Table 2 Attitudes Toward Conflict

Sample		Undesir-able-desir-able	Unneces-sary-neces-sary	Inappro-priate-appro-priate	Bad-good	Wrong-right	Totals
Admin.	($n = 13$)	6.30	6.30	6.38	6.30	6.30	31.58
Dirs.	($n = 14$)	6.42	6.42	6.50	6.42	6.50	32.26
Deans	($n = 11$)	6.36	6.36	6.45	6.45	6.45	32.07
Chmn.	($n = 16$)	5.87	5.69	6.12	5.75	5.87	29.30
Gov.	($n = 11$)	5.72	5.90	5.72	5.63	5.27	28.24
Fac.	($n = 74$)	6.00	6.01	5.96	5.83	5.91	29.71
NTP	($n = 25$)	4.96	5.36	5.20	5.18	5.24	25.94
Stdts.	($n = 123$)	5.65	5.91	5.66	5.72	5.81	28.75
CS	($n = 29$)	4.65	5.27	5.34	5.27	5.10	25.63

than they are in some cases—keeping in mind the polite definition employed.

Interviewee responses were compared across the nine subsamples by utilizing the one-way analysis of variance procedure for unequal *n*s. Those persons in upper-echelon positions (upper-level administrators, deans, and directors) reported more favorable attitudes toward conflict, $\bar{X} = 32.00$, than did those individuals in more subordinate positions (chairmen, governance leaders, faculty, and students), $\bar{X} = 29.14$ ($t = 2.92$, $p < .01$). The mean for the former three groups was also greater than the mean for those persons lowest in the hierarchy (civil service employees and nonteaching professionals), $\bar{X} = 25.78$ ($t = 5.32$, $p < .002$). Chairmen, governance, faculty, and student attitudes toward conflict, $\bar{X} = 29.14$, were more favorable than the attitudes of civil service employees and nonteaching professionals, $\bar{X} = 25.78$ ($t = 3.91$, $p < .002$). The data would suggest that *the higher an interviewee's position in the hierarchy, the more favorably did he view conflict in the sense of disagreement and debate over issues and values.*

We are somewhat at a loss to explain these differences. At first examination, it would appear that administrative experience and theory would teach the deans, directors, and administrators the value of organizational conflict. Our notion of dynamic equilibrium, if correct, would also demand these persons to play a coordinating role in the management of conflict. This would be supported by the comments of a vice-president who talked at great length about the value of organizational conflict. He described universities as "the most conservative institution in existence," and characterized most academics as "liberal in their politics, but conservative in practice." He expressed his "great respect for such martyrs as Angela Davis and Bobby Seale." He continued to say that the "estab-

lishment would never permit changes" without the tactics of such radicals. A "first thrust toward change," he said, must come from radicals;
then comes "evolutionary change." Similarly liberal attitudes were expressed by other administrators.

We broadened the concept of conflict with our follow-up question,
"Has the conflict and unrest of the past few years within the university
produced changes?" (Interviewees were quick to observe and complain
loudly about this intended change in meaning. We assume, therefore,
that our intended meaning was elicited.)

A summary of the answers can be found in Table 3. The over-
whelming majority (almost 93 percent) of the 294 interviewees who
answered the question felt that the conflict and unrest had produced
changes within the university. What were the changes?

Table 3   Changes Produced by Campus Conflict
and Unrest

Sample		Yes	No	No Answer	
Adm.	($n = 13$)	13	0	0	
Dirs.	($n = 15$)	14	0	1	
Deans	($n = 12$)	9	1	2	
Chmn.	($n = 20$)	17	0	3	
Gov.	($n = 11$)	11	0	0	
Fac.	($n = 74$)	69	4	1	
NTP	($n = 25$)	24	0	1	
Stdts.	($n = 123$)	98	11	14	
CS	($n = 29$)	18	5	6	
Totals		273	21	28	$= 322$

We asked the interviewees to specify the changes they felt were effected by conflict and unrest. Each interviewee was then asked to amplify
his response by either giving specific examples of change or an explanation of why she or he felt no changes had been effected.

The most frequently mentioned change, cited by 123 people, was
increased student participation in decision making and increased sensitivity to student needs. The second change, mentioned by 67 interviewees,
was the creation of special areas and courses of study such as Puerto
Rican Studies, Afro-American Studies, and interdisciplinary programs.
The third change, mentioned by 62 interviewees, was the relaxation of
curricular requirements such as the CURE proposal, which eliminated
all degree requirements other than 120 hours and those courses required
for a major. The fourth change was S/U grading—mentioned by 58 interviewees. Fifth on the list of changes is a miscellaneous category, the es-

sence of which seems to be an increased awareness of, and interaction between, different groups within the university. This would include faculty-student and "administrative-others" relationships. (This change tended to be mentioned more often by administrators than by other groups.)

The sixth change, mentioned by 27, was the relaxation of dorm rules, dress codes, and other manifestations of *in loco parentis*.

The seventh change was mentioned by 22 interviewees; it is the establishment of the Educational Opportunities Program and the recruitment of minority students.

Twelve interviewees said that faculty participation in decision making had increased. (Two interviewees said that faculty participation had *decreased*.)

Eight interviewees felt that the conflict and unrest of the past few years had caused the administration to become too readily responsive to pressure. Other changes were mentioned with less frequency. Not all of these changes, of course, were characterized as desirable.

It is interesting to ask what motives generated the movement to promulgate such changes. It seems apparent once again that the bureaucratic model—not the bargaining and systems models—offers the best explanation: these changes seem to be motivated, almost without exception, by *a drive by persons in a subordinate position to seize a greater degree of autonomy in their organizational life.*

We followed up the question of conflict-produced changes by asking, "Is the change (or lack of change) you just mentioned desirable, undesirable, or both?" In Table 4 we find summarized the answers given by interviewees who felt that changes had been produced. In short, 45 percent felt that the changes were wholly desirable; 43 percent felt that the changes were both desirable and undesirable; only 12 percent felt that the changes were wholly undesirable. It is of interest (and of statistical significance: $\chi^2 = 12.70$, $p < .05$) to note that only 29 percent of the faculty characterized the changes as wholly desirable—compared to 61 percent of the administration and 56 percent of the students.

Which changes tend to be viewed as desirable, which as undesirable, and which as both? The first change—student participation—was seen as undesirable by 7 people (mainly in the sense that it had gone "too far"); 39 saw it as a mixed blessing, mainly because the same students are "used" over and over again on committees and councils. Seventy-seven saw this as a desirable change.

The second change—the inauguration of special studies—was seen as undesirable by 10 interviewees. Some were unhappy that they were created under conditions of administrative capitulation, and others questioned their legitimacy as academic studies. Twenty-five had mixed

Table 4 Desirability of Changes Produced
by Conflict

Sample	Desirable	Undesirable	Both
Adm.	8	0	5
Dirs.	10	1	3
Deans	5	1	3
Chmn.	7	4	6
Gov.	4	0	7
Fac.	20	13	36
NTP	8	2	14
Stdts.	55	8	35
CS	6	3	9
Totals	123	32	118

feelings, but 32 interviewees saw them as desirable changes.

The third change—relaxation of curricular regulations—was seen as a negative change by 12 interviewees (six students and six faculty members) because, they felt, too much freedom can be educationally dysfunctional. Twenty-three were ambivalent about this change, and 27 saw it as a positive advance.

S/U grading was mentioned by 58 interviewees. Twenty-four interviewees regarded this change as undesirable. Twenty were ambivalent toward S/U grading and only 14 interviewees praised the change.

Increased awareness and interaction between heretofore isolated groups were almost universally regarded as desirable. The only negative responses, ironically, were that this phenomenon had not been sufficiently contagious, that it had not spread to enough members of the university community.

The demise of *in loco parentis* was seen as undesirable by 6 (only one of whom was a student); 9 had mixed feelings, and 12 saw it as a positive change.

The establishment of the Educational Opportunities Program and the recruitment of minority students was mainly seen as good; only one perceived this as an undesirable change ("lowering of standards").

Increased faculty participation in university decision making was cited by none as an undesirable change. No one regarded the administration's increased susceptibility to pressure tactics as wholly desirable. Six saw it as undesirable and two as both undesirable and desirable.

It is worth the time to consider the rationale of those who thought no changes had resulted from the conflict and unrest of recent years. Only 21 people reacted this way; 13 saw this *lack* of change as undesirable—chiefly because what passed for changes were cosmetic in nature.

They felt that only the surface is different—and this they find to be undesirable as well as disappointing.

The changes wrought by both sanctioned and unsanctioned methods of communication appear, in most cases, to be perceived as either a mixed blessing or as wholly desirable.

An important reservation about this finding must be made. Only 29 percent of the faculty evaluated the changes as wholly desirable as compared to 61 percent of the administration and 56 percent of the students. Faculty members also were critical of the administration's tendency to "give in." There have been recent indications that some of the changes may be reversed (e.g., S/U grading). Furthermore, since the data were collected, a group of faculty members has begun to organize a "Faculty Forum" which will apparently serve as an advisory group without student participation. Other reversals of changes may well be effected. The campus may be in for a wave of withdrawal and a faculty-inspired reversal of past changes.

Other data gathered during the study were found to correlate significantly with attitudes toward organizational conflict. For example, attitudes toward conflict tended to be more favorable when subjects were able to identify correctly the various formal levels of the hierarchy in the university ($r = .22$, $p < .005$) and when the subjects were able to name the vice-presidents along with their titles ($rs = .16$ in both cases, $ps < .005$). The subjects were asked to respond to a semantic differential scale measuring their self-perceived aggressiveness in attempting to influence university policies. The more aggressive the subject perceived himself, the more favorable was his attitude toward conflict ($r = .18$, $p < .005$).

Attitudes toward conflict were also studied in relation to Kenneth Burke's constructs of identification, mystery, and order in the hierarchy of an organization (Burke, 1962). We investigated the possibility that attitudes toward conflict would be most favorable when subjects identified with the hierarchy of the university; i.e., members of an organization would be more likely to approach disagreement over issues when they perceived themselves as having more in common with the hierarchy as opposed to the lower levels of the organization.

Identification was measured by creating all possible pairs from seven personnel classes within the university (president, vice-president, dean, chairman, faculty, student, civil service employees). Using the paired-comparison technique, subjects were asked to select the person in each of the twenty-one pairs with whom he identified more or with whom he had the most in common. An arbitrary weight was assigned to each level—7 for president, 6 for vice-president, and so on. For each of the subsamples in the study, the proportion of times that the subsample identified with each of the seven personnel levels was multiplied by the level's weight, and a sum of the seven scores was computed for each subsample. Thus, the higher the identification score for a subsample, the more it identified with the hierarchy of the university. The mean identification scores and attitude toward conflict scores for the subsamples were converted to ranks (administration, directors, deans, chairmen, faculty, students, nonteaching professionals). The Spearman *rho* for the rank-ordered identification and attitude scores was .856, $p < .05$, indicating that the most favorable attitudes toward conflict were observed when subjects identified with the hierarchy of the university.

Burke hypothesized that members of an organization perceive the hierarchy of the organization on at least two continua: mystery and order. For example, the more ordered a hierarchy is perceived, the more mysterious it is also perceived. We reasoned that if perceived mystery is related to perceived order, the mystery should also be related to identification. That is, the more mysterious a hierarchy is perceived, the less the individual should identify with the hierarchy. Furthermore, attitudes toward conflict also should be related to mystery—the less mysterious the hierarchy is perceived, the less inhibited the individual should be in approaching the hierarchy in terms of "disagreement over issues"; i.e., the way conflict is conceptualized.

Perceived mystery and order in the hierarchy were each measured by four semantic differential scales derived from two factor-analytic studies. The mystery scales were mysterious-clear, public-secret, obvious-hidden, and visible-invisible. The order scales were ordered-unordered, organized-unorganized, arranged-unarranged, and structured-unstructured.

The mean mystery and order scores for the seven subsamples were converted to rank orders. The Spearman *rho* for identification and mystery was .893, $p. < .05$. High perceived mystery thus covaried with low identification regarding the hierarchy of the university (this does not appear as a negative correlation because in the scoring for mystery the lower score was assigned to high perceived mystery). *Rho* for attitudes toward conflict and mystery was .679. Although this relationship was in the expected direction (more favorable attitudes toward conflict when little mystery is perceived), the *rho* did not reach the .05 level of significance.

The data, therefore, seem to indicate that the more an individual knows about the hierarchy of his organization, the more he identifies with that hierarchy, and the more aggressive he perceives himself to be in attempting to influence policy, the more favorable will be his attitude toward conflict within the organization. The more mysterious he perceives the hierarchy to be, the less favorable will be his attitude toward conflict.

Conclusions, Interpretation, and Implications

We began with the assumption that organizational models of conflict have relevance to the special case of conflict within universities. The data seem to support that assumption. The "best fit" seems to be provided by Pondy's bureaucratic model of conflict in which it is hypothesized that the drive for autonomy will force those in a subordinate position to enter into manifest conflict with those in a superior position. Most instances of conflict mentioned by our subjects fell into this category. The bargaining and systems models were found not to apply. It should be noted, however, that manifest conflict may be either public or private. Our subjects seem to have been more concerned with the former than with the latter. We have good reason to believe that the bargaining model does apply to the private conflict between, say, a chairman and dean, in deciding how scarce resources such as faculty lines and graduate fellowships are to be distributed. Our questions, nonetheless, generated very little data of this sort. It is public conflict of the sixties and seventies that was salient in the memories of our subjects.

The data gathered suggest several tentative generalizations. Our subjects reported favorable attitudes toward conflict in the broad sense of disagreement and debate over issues and values. It was surprising, however, that some samples were *barely* favorable toward such a polite conceptualization. The subjects also felt that the conflict and unrest of the sixties and seventies did serve as change agents within their university. In regard to this conflict aftermath, the changes wrought by both sanctioned and unsanctioned methods were viewed by most as either mixed blessings or wholly desirable. The faculty, however, seems to be an exception to this generalization, and there is evidence that the faculty may now move to reverse some of these changes.

Attitudes toward conflict appear to be related to other variables. It appears, for example, that the higher the person's position in the hierarchy, the more favorably did he view conflict as defined in this study. Knowledge of the hierarchy seems to be related to a favorable attitude toward conflict. Self-perceived aggressiveness in attempting to influence university policies also seems to be related to a favorable attitude toward conflict. On the other hand, the higher the degree of mystery perceived in the hierarchy, the less favorable will be the attitude toward conflict.

What, then, can we say about the relationships between conflict and communication within organizations? First, it is difficult for us to conceive of *latent* conflict becoming *perceived* conflict without some form of communication. It is also difficult to imagine *manifest* conflict without some kind of communication, particularly when we consider that manifest conflict assumes that one party *knowingly* frustrates the goals of another party. In some cases communication can resolve the conflict satisfactorily. On the other hand, communication can clearly *exacerbate* conflict in certain situations. Whether the manifest conflict is public or private seems to be a critical factor. Our subjects seemed to be more willing to discuss public conflict than private conflict. It may well be easier in some ways to communicate conflictful messages in public (with the safety that numbers of colleagues provide) than in a private, one-to-one relationship. Parties to a public conflict may well be forced into more rigid positions and offer more resistance to compromise and change than the parties to a private conflict.

This factor also seems to be related to our findings about mystery and identification. If there must be order, there will be superiors and subordinates. The more ordered the system, the greater will be the number of layers of superiors and subordinates. The more layered the organization, the more mystery will exist between those at the bottom and those at the top—particularly when the sanctioned "channels" do not permit direct communication between the two parties. With high mystery there will be little identification between parties. High mystery and low identification will no doubt inhibit the willingness to communicate about a latent or perceived conflict. Perhaps, and this is pure speculation, these conditions may well make it impossible for those at the "bottom" to enter into *private* conflict with those at the "top." The only alternative may be in confronting the full weight of the hierarchy's mystery with the full weight of the numbers residing in the "lower" strata of the organization. Only the power of numbers can balance the power of the mystery. And because of the numbers, such communication will perforce be public. Nonetheless, changes effected by such behavior may not produce a conflict aftermath satisfactory to all parties. If not, the changes may be highly vulnerable to reversal. The faculty's recent interest in achieving such reversals in the university studied would seem to be an instance of this. Thus, the use of public, unsanctioned methods of conflict communication may be somewhat counterproductive in the long run. Like the role of conflict in organizations, and like the role of communication in resolving conflict, the use of public, unsanctioned methods of conflict communication will be both functional and dysfunctional.

It would be extremely useful to have comparative data on mystery, order, and identification from a number of universities and other organizations. No doubt there would be significant differences from organization to organization. Are there organizations with a low degree of mystery in the hierarchy? What conditions seem to exist in such organizations? Can an organization be consciously demystified? How do patterns of vertical communication differ in cases of low mystery as compared with high mystery? How do conflict facilitation and resolution differ in cases of high and low mystery?

Until the answers to these questions are available, we shall have to steel ourselves to the need for confronting the mystery of the hierarchy wherever it exists: in universities, associations, unions, and even governments. It will require courage, knowledge of the hierarchy, and aggressiveness in engaging it in private (and perhaps even public) conflict. And it will have to work both ways. The "lower" strata, by sheer numbers, must be reciprocally mysterious to the top hierarchy.

REFERENCES

ARGYRIS, C., *Some Causes of Organizational Ineffectiveness Within the Department of State.* Washington, D.C.: Department of State Occasional Paper, No. 2, 1967.

ASSAEL, H., "Constructive Role of Interorganizational Conflict," *Administrative Science Quarterly,* 14 (1969), 573–81.

BURKE, K., *A Rhetoric of Motives.* Cleveland,: World Publishing Company, 1962.

COHEN, M. D., J. G. MARCH, and J. P. OLSEN, "A Garbage Can Model of Organizational Choice," *Administrative Science Quarterly,* 17 (1972), 1–25.

DARKENWALD, G. G., JR., "Organizational Conflict in Colleges and Universities," *Administrative Science Quarterly,* 16 (1971), 407–12.

ETZIONI, A., "Authority Structure and Organizational Effectiveness," *Administrative Science Quarterly,* 4 (1959), 43–67.

GREGORY, C. O., *Labor and the Law.* New York: W. W. Norton, 1958.

JANIS, I. L., "Groupthink," *Psychology Today,* 5 (1971), 43.

LIPSET, S. M., and G. M. SCHAFLANDER, *Passion and Politics: Student Activism in America.* Boston: Little, Brown, 1971.

PAUL, R. J., and R. D. SCHOOLER, "An Analysis of Performance Standards and Generational Conflict in Academia," *Academy of Management Journal,* 13 (1970), 212–16.

PONDY, L. R., "Organizational Conflict: Concepts and Models," *Administrative Science Quarterly,* 12 (1967), 296–320.

———, "Varieties of Organizational Conflict," *Administrative Science Quarterly,* 14 (1969), 409–505.

RAVEN, B. H., and A. W. KRUGLANSKI, "Conflict and Power," in *The Structure of Conflict,* P. Swingle, ed., pp. 69–109. New York: Academic Press, 1970.

SCHELLING, T. G., *The Strategy of Conflict.* Cambridge: Harvard University Press, 1960.

TEDESCHI, J. T., "Threats and Promises," in *The Structure of Conflict,* P. Swingle, ed., pp. 155–91. New York: Academic Press, 1970.

7

The
Carrot and Stick
as
Handmaidens of Persuasion
in Conflict Situations

HERBERT W. SIMONS

Short of annihilating one's opposition, about the only way to realize one's interests in a conflict situation is to exert *social influence*. To influence another is to modify his (or her) beliefs, values, attitudes, or overt behavior in preferred ways. Influence may be exerted directly upon the opposition or it may be exerted indirectly, as when a litigant takes his case before a judge.

What are the means by which influence may be exerted in social conflicts? Are certain means of influence characteristically practiced by certain types of individuals? What, in particular, is the role played by persuasion in conflict situations? Is it clearly differentiable from other forms of influence or does it overlap with them?

As should soon become apparent, these seemingly innocuous questions have important normative implications; they are as much questions for the social critic as they are for the behaviorally oriented social scientist. In this paper, I should like to bring the contributions of both to bear upon the issues just raised. I hope especially to debunk several popular stereotypes about the practice of social influence in our society and to suggest relationships between influence by persuasion and influence by means of its alleged alternatives—what I have labeled, colloquially, the carrot and the stick. Before presenting my own position, let me indicate how these methods of influence are characterized by others.[1]

POPULAR CHARACTERIZATIONS OF THE CARROT, THE STICK, AND PERSUASION

Roughly synonymous with the carrot in academic jargon is what Gamson (1968) labels as an *inducement* or what Raven and Kruglanski (1970) call *reward influence*. It involves the promise or actual bestowal of a benefit to B, either by A or by someone acting in concert with A. The clearest example of an inducement involves the pledge or payment of money (or its equivalent), contingent upon appropriate behavior by B. However, the contingencies for reward need not be made explicit, and in Gamson's terms, the reward need not be quite so tangible as money. Thus, B may be induced by the promise of group acceptance or by the pledge of love from another. Contingent rewards are akin to what Skinner (1953) calls *reinforcements*. Seeking to secure a preferred level of output from B, A may *positively reinforce* B so as to increase the rate or strength of that output. Or A may induce changes in B through *negative reinforcement*. The reward in these cases is escape from or avoidance of a noxious situation, as when a prisoner's parole is made contingent upon good behavior. In either case, A "adds advantages" to B's situation (Gamson, 1968).

Roughly synonymous with the stick in scholarly discourse is what Gamson labels as a *constraint* or what Raven and Kruglanski label as *coercive influence*. Gamson speaks here of "adding disadvantages" to B's situation. This involves the threatened or actual introduction of a cost to B, either by A or by someone acting in concert with A. The clearest example of a constraint involves the threat or imposition of

---

[1] Terms like "influence," "power," and "authority" are used in a bewildering variety of ways by social scientists. Nor are they in agreement on "means" or "methods" of influence. For clarity's sake, I will confine myself largely to terms and definitions put forth in two respected treatments of social influence, by Gamson (1968) and Raven and Kruglanski (1970). Even here I will be obliged, in subsequent footnotes, to indicate differences in their approaches or to comment on subtle nuances in their treatments of influence that are not reflected in the text of this chapter.

physical punishment, coupled with a demand that B modify his behavior in specified ways. As with inducements, however, punishments may be psychological rather than physical and their cessation need not be linked specifically to particular outputs by B. Thus, as in the Skinnerian paradigm, B may not know what is expected of him, only that he should change his behavior. Kelman (1958) has labeled as *compliance* the behaviors produced by either inducements or constraints. As Gruder (1970) points out, it is not always easy to determine whether a compliant B has been induced or constrained. Minimally necessary for such determinations is knowledge of the history of the relationship between A and B. Thibaut and Kelley (1959) speak here of B's *comparison level,* "a standard by which the person evaluates the rewards and costs of a given relationship in terms of what he feels he 'deserves' " (p. 21). As Blau (1964) puts it,

> The crucial factor is the baseline from which an individual starts when another seeks to influence him and the only difference between punishment and rewards is in relation to this initial baseline, whether he is worse off or better off than he was before the transaction started. . . . A man who has reason to expect to remain in his job does not think of his regular earnings as distinctive rewards and the loss of income is a punishment for him. (pp. 116–17)

The third means of influence, persuasion, or rhetoric, is obviously of greatest interest to persons who study communication. Included within the range of acts labeled as "persuasion" are those in which A passively serves as a model or example for others and those in which A actively manipulates others. The range is also divisible in terms of those persuasive attempts which rely primarily on the information or perceived logic of the arguments presented, those which rely mainly on the credibility of the source, and those which rely chiefly on emotional appeals. Most successful persuasive communications involve combinations of all three, each in good amounts. (Karlins and Abelson, 1970; McGuire, 1969)

Although persuasion is often characterized as a weak sister in relation to its relatives within the influence family—note such expressions as "talk is cheap," "talk rather than substance," and "mere rhetoric"—it is nevertheless regarded by many as a more ethical method of influencing others. One generally shuns the coercive label like the plague, takes pains to deny that he is bribing others when he offers them inducements, and represents himself as a persuader—if possible, as someone using "rational persuasion." Persuasion is especially valued as an instrument of democracy. Democratic theory holds that persuasion is, or ought to be, the vehicle of collective decision making, the means by which ideas are tested, differences resolved, and action taken (e.g., J. S. Mill, 1947). Officials of government proudly proclaim that ours is indeed a system run by persuasion, from the moment that ordinary citizens petition their elected representatives to the moment when these same representatives take governmental action.[2] Inducements and constraints are said to have no place in ideally democratic forms of government; they are the coinage of the realm of corrupt governments or of totalitarian regimes.

Persuasion is typically defined in terms of two, and frequently three elements (e.g., Gamson, 1968; Bettinghaus, 1968; Minnick, 1968). First, there is the act itself, a communicated message from A to B. Usually the message is carried through verbal symbols as in a speech or essay, but it may be transmitted nonverbally or through symbolic acts such as saluting or waving the flag. Second, there is the potential or actual consequence. Persuasion changes minds; it modifies B's attitudes, beliefs, and values and not just his overt behavior. The third element frequently cited is intent to persuade, emphasized by some writers (e.g., Bettinghaus, 1968) to distinguish persuasion from purely expressive or consummatory acts.

On the basis of these defining elements, persuasion is differentiated from inducements and especially from coercive influence, the latter being viewed by most writers as antithetical to persuasion. Persuasion is to seduction as coercion is to rape. It offers choice or the perception of choice whereas coercion denies choice or the perception of choice. It leads to voluntary compliance whereas coercion leads to grudging compliance (e.g., Fotheringham, 1966; Bettinghaus, 1968).[3]

---

[2] Technically speaking, according to Gamson, the latter do not practice influence when they act as agents of a social system; instead, they practice "outcome modification" or "social control." Whether these added terms are useful I leave for the reader to decide. In any event, the means of outcome modification and social control described by Gamson can easily be reclassified as fitting within one or another of his categories of influence. For the sake of simplicity, I will not maintain his distinction in this chapter and will continue to count government officials among those using influence, whether they act in their own or the system's interests.

[3] Here, once again, not all theorists use terms in the same way. Although Gamson's use of "constraint" and Raven and Kruglanski's use of "coercive influence" refer to roughly the same phenomena, Gamson would probably argue that the latter's choice of terms is unfortunate. He points out that insofar as coercion involves restrictions on choice, any of the three means of influence (persuasion, inducements, or constraints) may be highly coercive. Hypnotism, for example (which he classifies as "persuasion"), may be considerably more coercive than threats (which he classifies as "constraints"). At least one rhetorician (Burgess, 1973) has made the same point. He distinguishes "coercive rhetoric," as in threats, from the actual use of force, and argues that good arguments, like threats, may be coercive in the sense that they are intellectually compelling. These useful insights notwithstanding, I will continue to use the terms "coercion" and "coercive influence" as Raven and Kruglanski use them and as I assume most other theorists use them.

By the examples they use to illustrate the term, most textbooks on persuasion tend to reinforce the prevailing view that coercion is intrinsically evil (e.g., Scheidel, 1967; Minnick, 1968). Simultaneously, they characterize "approved" figures in our culture as noncoercive. Coercion is almost always identified with thieves in the night or other nefarious scoundrels, rarely with soldiers at Valley Forge, for example, or the Philadelphia police. On the basis of the persuasion-coercion dichotomy, "moderate" protestors have been distinguished from "militant" protestors, "nice" bosses from "authoritarian" bosses, and the "mouths of diplomats" from the "mouths of guns." As his only examples of physical coercion, Scheidel lists the rack, the thumbscrew, the iron maiden, and the threat of being shot. To this list, Minnick adds bludgeons, beatings, and imprisonment. The examples certainly do not endear one to coercion.

Because "persuasion," "inducement," and "coercion" are politically sensitive terms, the question "Who practices each?" assumes more than academic significance. Merely by being affixed as labels to persons or acts, the terms may either enhance or help impugn the credibility of others and advance or weaken their causes.

Here Gamson (1968) introduces what I believe is a useful clarification, although it is not entirely free of problems.[4] He suggests that the prototypical case of persuasion—we will call it *pure persuasion*—involves an actor, A, who modifies the behavior of B solely on the basis of the appeals, arguments, or advice he offers, and *not* because of his power to reward or punish B directly. A ghetto leader, for example, would be engaged purely in persuasion if, in urging the mayor to release funds for a proposed housing program, he visualized for the mayor some of the positive or negative consequences that might result from adoption or nonadoption of the proposal. The ghetto leader might predict, for example, that unless better housing is provided, the ghetto residents will

[4] Problems arise in applying these definitional criteria to familiar cases. Does a salesman "induce" and not "persuade" because he rewards with a product or service in exchange for the customer's money? If so, what others regard as a prototypical case of "persuasion" is treated by Gamson as "non-persuasion." What, then, of the advertiser? Because he does not reward directly, is he a persuader? Or because he promises rewards on behalf of the sponsor, is he, like the salesman, an inducer and not a persuader? Similar questions arise with respect to Gamson's distinction between "constraint" and "persuasion." Does a newspaper editorial indirectly persuade or constrain the mayor when it urges its readers to petition him to fund a housing project? Gamson calls this a "constraint," and in a sense it is, but it seems odd not to classify it also as an instance of "persuasion." Other problems bearing more directly on social conflict will be taken up later in this chapter. Suffice it to say that despite these problems, the distinction does help to clarify matters. It helps us, for example, to distinguish between "fear appeals" and "threats." In the former, the source only predicts the adverse consequences for the receiver; in the latter, he also promises to help make them happen.

riot. Or he might prophesy that if funds for the housing program are provided, the ghetto residents will help reelect him. So long as the ghetto leader is not a potential or actual *cause* of these consequences (either by himself, or, indirectly, through his influence on those who follow him), then his is a case of *pure persuasion.* Should the leader state or imply, however, that he will help instigate the riot or bring out the vote, contingent upon whether or not the housing proposal is implemented, then the leader would be constraining or inducing and would not be engaging purely in persuasion.

The foregoing reference to "pure persuasion" raises the question whether there are any cases that are less than "pure." Are there, for example, ostensibly persuasive acts, the effectiveness of which rests as much on the power of the influence agent to induce or constrain as on the quality of his arguments? Were the student protestors of the sixties correct, for example, when they asserted that university administrators were masking their own use of coercion and inducements with the facade of appearing to act purely as persuaders? On the other hand, are there seemingly nonsymbolic acts that nevertheless have the effect of changing minds? Were the targets of militant protests correct in asserting that the building occupations, the bombings, and the riots were "coercion," pure and simple? Or might there be an implicit rhetoric—even an intentional rhetoric—in some acts of violence, and might that violence actually lead to attitude modification? Is persuasion of sorts involved in attempts at inducing behavior changes in others? Are there, in general, borderline cases that involve admixtures of persuasion and coercion or persuasion and reward influence? Consideration of these questions occupies the remainder of this chapter.

A STATEMENT OF POSITION

Contrary to the prevailing view of persuasion as clearly separable from constraints (i.e., coercive influence) and inducements (i.e., reward influence), I shall argue here that in conflict situations, *persuasion, broadly defined, is not so much an alternative to the power of constraints and inducements as it is an instrument of that power, an accompaniment to that power, or a consequence of that power.*[5]

By a social conflict I mean that state of a social relationship in

5 As I hope I have made clear in context, I mean by "power" the *capacity* to influence through constraints and inducements. This usage is similar to Raven and Kruglanski's sense of power as "potential influence" and to Gamson's notion of "influence in repose." It is somewhat more restrictive, however, in that it excludes the "power to persuade," insofar as that power does not in itself rest on the influence agent's capacity to reward or constrain.

which incompatible interests between two or more persons give rise to a struggle between them. The notion of a clash of interests presupposes something more than what is typically implied by such terms as "disagreement," "difference of opinion," or "controversy." The conflict may involve value differences or personal animosities, or competition for scarce resources, or some combination, but in any case, the personal interests of one or more parties must appear to be threatened. Thus, when a newspaper columnist argues that the auto workers are not paid enough, his column is controversial, it is true; and he may even be resting his case on deeply felt value premises, but he is probably not engaged in a genuine conflict because his own interests are not likely to be at stake. Let us suppose, however, that the same message had come from the head of the United Auto Workers in the midst of a bargaining session; furthermore, that the official had threatened a walkout if General Motors did not furnish large increases. This, too, would be a controversial act, but it would have the added quality of being an expression of genuine conflict.

Now, where a disagreement does not threaten personal interests, pure persuasion (free of coercive or reward influence) is generally the only means of influence that conflicting parties feel called upon to use because neither party is likely to suffer very much by failing to achieve his goals, or to achieve very much by offering inducements or imposing constraints. Some apparent conflicts turn out to be pseudo-conflicts, of course; with a bit of dialogue it is discovered that there is no real incompatibility of interests. Still, however applicable the model of pure persuasion may be for nonconflicts or pseudo-conflicts, it should not be viewed as the paradigmatic means of influence for genuine conflicts. *In a genuine conflict, power serves rhetoric and rhetoric serves power.*

This is not to say that the naked imposition of power in the form of bribes or raw coercion is the sole or principal means by which influence is exerted in conflict situations. Indeed, as Schelling (1960) has repeatedly emphasized, most conflicts are *mixed-motive* or *variable-sum* contests; they involve actors who are motivated to compete with the other while simultaneously being obligated to cooperate with the other. Concomitantly, each is impelled to induce or constrain while at the same time being impelled to participate in the give and take of persuasion. Thus, as in my earlier example of a conflict over money between the auto workers and the auto companies, each side is prepared to back up its demands and counterdemands with threats of strikes, layoffs, etc., but they simultaneously recognize that they are dependent on each other (for jobs and profit) and that they can raise their individual payoffs through cooperative efforts to achieve the highest possible joint payoffs. Each side offers inducements and threatens or imposes constraints but it also engages in a goodly amount of rhetoric, backed up by the power of rewards or punishments. And that, once again, is the main point I am trying to convey. In conflict situations, power and persuasion are handmaidens.

Specifically, I shall argue a two-part thesis here about persuasion in social conflicts, the bare outlines of which are stated below: (1) *Practically all acts that seem on the surface to be instances of coercive influence or reward influence also involve persuasive elements. Minimally, A must alter or reinforce B's beliefs about A's willingness and capacity to induce or constrain, but acts of inducement or constraint may also be designed to modify attitudes or values.* Protestors, in particular, frequently attempt to persuade by actions that others pejoratively label as "coercive." That the rhetorical intent, nature, or consequence of their acts often goes unnoticed is commonly a result of the fact that they lack what Weber (1947) called legitimate authority. (2) *Many acts that seem on the surface to be instances of pure persuasion are made effective because the influence agent has the greater power to constrain or induce. The mere possession of that power may serve as an effective backdrop for persuasion, especially if the influence agent is in a position of legitimate authority. Constraints or inducements may also be used to control or purchase the instrumentalities of persuasion—what I shall call communication resources.* That the rich and powerful in our society often escape pejorative labeling as "bribers" or "coercers" is frequently because their use of inducements or coercion is either subtle or approved.

ELEMENTS OF
PERSUASION IN ACTS COMMONLY
LABELED AS CONSTRAINTS OR INDUCEMENTS

Recall that the elements of persuasion, as traditionally defined, are: (1) communicated messages, whether verbal or nonverbal; (2) altered beliefs, attitudes or values, not just overt compliance; and (frequently) (3) deliberate intent. By any or all of these definitional criteria, acts commonly labeled as constraints or inducements have persuasive elements. It is true that some acts are *primarily* acts of constraint or inducement; furthermore, it is sometimes possible to separate out elements within a given act. Nevertheless, an examination of the acts themselves will reveal them to exhibit a combination of elements.

No attempt will be made in this section to present a comprehensive theory or to review, exhaustively, all of the research bearing on the subject at hand. I will try, however, to provide a sampling of combinational patterns, to highlight interesting research, and from time to time, to suggest normative implications.

The Role of Persuasion in
Establishing the Credibility of
Threats and Promises

Despite the fact that the concept of credibility looms large in the lexicon of communication theorists, relatively little study has been made of how threats and promises are made credible. In practically all social conflicts, A must persuade B that he has the *willingness* and the *capacity* to punish or reward. Admittedly, this is more a matter of altering beliefs than of changing deep-seated attitudes or basic values, but it is neverthe-less at least a peripheral use of persuasion.

The believability of threats and promises appears to be more a function of what one does nonverbally than of what one says verbally. This is nicely illustrated by the Woody Allen film *Take the Money and Run*. In typical gangster movies, of course, the bank robber looks like a bank robber, and by mauling those who get in his way, he leaves no doubt about his willingness and ability to coerce. The scene from the Woody Allen movie parodies the classic bank holdup. By contrast to truly credible bank robbers, poor, inept Woody is holding a rain-damaged pistol made of soap. Moreover, when he nervously hands the bank teller a note de-manding money, she calmly explains to him that he has not spelled "m-o-n-e-y" correctly.

The importance of nonverbal communication in establishing the credibility of threats has not been lost on militant protestors. In *Mau-Mauing the Flak Catchers,* Tom Wolfe (1970) presents a semi-fictionalized account of what one ghetto leader might have told his followers in prep-aration for their confrontation with OEO officials.

> Now don't forget. When you go downtown, y'all wear your *ghetto rags* . . . see . . . Don't go down there with your Italian silk jerseys and your brown suede and green alligator shoes and your Harry Belafonte shirts looking like some supercool toothpick-noddin' fool . . . Don't anybody give a damn how pretty you can look . . . You wear your *combat* fatigues and your leather *pieces* and your shades . . . your ghetto rags . . . see . . . and don't go down there with your hair all done up nice in your curly Afro like you're messing around. You go down there with your hair *stickin' out* . . . and *sittin' up!* I want to see you down there looking like a bunch of *wild niggers!* (pp. 99–100) [6]

[6] Copyright © 1970, Tom Wolfe, *Radical Chic and Mau–Mauing the Flak Catchers* (N.Y.: Farrar, Straus & Giroux), pp. 99–100. By permission of the publisher and the International Famous Agency.

Just as threats may be made credible by the infliction of small doses of punishment, probably the best way to make promises credible is to provide initial rewards as a sign of good faith. When a Skinnerian reinforces a pigeon (or monkey, or human) for making a desired response, he is, in effect, saying nonverbally to the pigeon that he can be depended upon for more food if the pigeon behaves appropriately. As with pigeons, human behaviors are subject to the Skinnerian principle of extinction if promises turn out to be "nothing but rhetoric."

Promises and threats are made more credible if A is perceived as unable or unwilling to alter the forces that he has set in motion. As applied to promises, for example, A may convince B of his sincere intent to reward by depositing the promised reward with a third neutral party, the agreement being that the third party must reward B if B fulfills the contract.

Schelling (1960) strongly emphasizes this point as applied to threats. How, for example, does A convince B of his willingness and capacity to seize from B a contested traffic lane? Not by "rational persuasion," but by pointing his car and looking the other way, or by owning a 1947 Plymouth with several dents in it, or by acting as though seizure of the lane is a matter of principle, or by appearing as though he is insane or mentally retarded. By abandoning rationality in the traditional sense, A compels B to be rational, or so he hopes.

Actually inflicting punishments or providing rewards incurs costs to the influence agent, either in their delivery or in the form of retaliatory punishments by others. The trick, therefore, is to issue credible threats and promises while expending the lowest possible costs. Hence, the use of such rhetorical ploys as bluffing, issuing vague rather than explicit promises, and packaging meager initial inducements so that they have the appearance of great worth ("selling the sizzle and not the steak"). Hence, also, the use of conditional threats that leave options open to B (Schelling, 1960). For example, A may couple his threats with the promise not to punish B if B complies.

There is considerably more that can be said about the role of persuasion in making threats and promises credible. Other research in this area is reviewed by Tedeschi (1970).

Implicit Appeals and Arguments in Ostensibly Coercive Acts

Beyond simply altering B's beliefs about A's willingness and capacity to constrain or induce, acts commonly viewed as nothing but coercive or nothing more than reward influence may actually be designed to modify

B's attitudes and basic values. Here the focus will be on persuasive elements in ostensibly coercive acts by protestors, and in the next subsection the appeals and arguments that may be contained implicitly in cases of inducement will be discussed.

The charges of officialdom notwithstanding, those who witnessed the confrontations and ghetto riots of the sixties should require little evidence for the claim that coercive acts may at the same time contain persuasive appeals and arguments. The protestors were frequently coercive—even violently so—but the violence was almost symbolic in nature, an act carrying a message. That the protestors could not hope to achieve their goals by force alone was evident from the relative power imbalance on the side of their targets. So as to leave no doubt about rhetorical intent, however, the protestors selected symbolic targets for their sit-ins, building occupations, burnings, and bombings, and they underscored the messages implicit in their nonverbal acts by their songs, speeches, and leaflets.

Adding to the potential effectiveness of the confrontational act are the self-incriminating responses that it frequently begets from its targets. The confronter seeks to delegitimize the opposition in the eyes of third parties by engaging him as reluctant actor in a drama of self-exposure.

The radicalizing possibilities inherent in confrontational tactics were thought through quite carefully by militants at Columbia during the Spring of 1968. Jerry Avorn (1969) has provided this evidence of deliberate intent to persuade.

> By the time of the IDA demonstration a new sub-group had come to dominate SDS. It became known as the "action faction," and advocated a new tactical approach—confrontation politics—to replace the dramatization-politicization style of the "praxis axis." The superficial dynamic of the tactic was simple: a physical confrontation . . . to discomfort the adversary who holds power, in this case the University administration. The tactical elegance of confrontational politics lay in the fact that the radicals had a good chance of winning whether the administration gave in to their substantive demands or overcame them by repression. The use of coercive force by the adversary . . . could be a powerful force to "radicalize" liberal or moderate students. For the crucial part of the SDS view is that while escalated tactics are necessary to bring pressure for change on substantive issues, the "radicalization" of large segments of the population is far more important. (p. 32–33) [7]

Commenting on the dilemma faced by targets of protest, Scott and Smith (1969) have this to say:

> The use of force to get students out of halls consecrated to university administration, or out of holes dedicated to construction projects seems to

---

[7] Jerry Avorn, ed., *Up Against the Ivy Wall: A History of the Columbia Crisis* (N.Y.: Atheneum Press: 1969), pp. 32–33. By permission of the publisher.

confirm the radical analysis that the establishment serves itself rather than justice. In this sense, the confronter who prompts violence in the language or behavior of another has found his collaborator. "Show us how ugly you are," he says, and the enemy with dogs and cattle prods, or police billies and mace complies. . . . Those who would confront have learned a brutal art, practiced sometimes awkwardly and sometimes skillfully, which demands response. But that art may provoke the response that confirms its presuppositions, gratifies the adherents of those presuppositions, and turns the power-enforced victory of the establishment into a symbolic victory for its opponents. (p. 8)

Ironically, coercive acts by extremist groups may serve an indirect persuasive function by bolstering the case for orderly social change. Andrews (1970) has put the matter well:

> Bred in the rational, Aristotelian tradition and nurtured in the ideal of a reasoning democracy, the teacher and critic of speaking reacts instinctively against the coercive purposes of disruption.
>
> But to deny coercion any place in the process of social change is perhaps to hope 'for the attainment of an ideal and not to describe realistically the rhetorical process. There is undoubtedly an intimate and compelling relationship between persuasion and coercion. The persuader, in his examination of alternatives, may find his position greatly strengthened when one alternative offered is the surrender to coercive demands. Even though his goals may be in some ways similar to the goals of the coercive rhetoricians, the persuader may well owe a large measure of his success to the revulsion toward or fear of the results of coercive methods. In short, while persuasion may be viewed by some as the antithesis of coercion, persuasion may often depend on its opposite to achieve its goals. (p. 187)

In support of his argument, Andrews cites the interplay of coercion and persuasion that led to the passage of the 1832 Reform Bill in England. Throughout the land, there was riot and destruction by the lower classes. Parliamentary opponents of reform were greeted with less than adulation in their own boroughs. With great accuracy, one Liverpool resident managed to toss a dead cat on to the top of Lord Sandon's head. In Bristol, the rioting that took place during Sir Charles Wetherell's visit was so intense that he was forced to flee for safety by scurrying over several rooftops. Meanwhile, in parliament, Whig MPs were sharply rebuked by Tories for submitting to the "universal bellow" of the violent masses. With good reason, the Duke of Wellington went so far as to accuse the ministry of having "coalesced with the mob," and even to have "encouraged" violent agitation for change. The response by the Whigs was predictable; a variation on what I have called elsewhere (Simons, 1970), the "brakeman" theme. Far be it for them to approve mob coercion; they were merely responding to it pragmatically. Macaulay claimed to support the reform measure because "unless the plan proposed, or some similar plan, be speedily adopted, great and terrible calamities will befall us" (Andrews, 1970, p. 192).

The brakeman theme is but one of many used by movement leaders who are caught between wanting to foment disruption by their supporters and wanting to avoid the coercive label. Awareness of the dilemma helps to explain, for example, why Rap Brown and Stokely Carmichael were so consistently ambiguous about the violent implications of the Black Power concept (Scott and Brockriede, 1969). To repudiate the use of force would have alienated militant supporters and rendered their movement less threatening to opponents. To openly acknowledge their willingness to coerce, would have fueled the arguments of those who sought to censure them on moral grounds. Compounding the problem for protest leaders is the fact that their opponents are ever ready to use the coercive tag even when the tactics employed are clearly noncoercive. Most of the marches and mass demonstrations organized by antiwar groups were no more disruptive than typical conventions by legionnaires, yet these groups were constantly pressed to justify their actions as noncoercive.

Coser (1956) has suggested that even the most blatant acts of collective violence may function symbolically to get attention, indicate ideological commitments, register hope or despair, or signal favorable or unfavorable attitudes toward others. There is always the danger, of course, that collective violence may produce backlash effects, but it may also arouse or reinforce group consciousness, mobilize support from third parties, and even evoke moral concern from those in power (Skolnick, 1969; Fogelson, 1971).

Thus far, I have discussed the use of coercion by protestors, but we should not lose sight of the fact that it is also employed by their targets. As hierarchical entities, universities and business organizations are inherently coercive; they confer coercive power to some, powerlessness to others. In crisis situations, these organizations, as well as government, can be violently coercive, considerably more so than protestors. That those in positions of authority do not (ordinarily) have to resort to blatant forms of coercion is partly due to their perceived legitimacy. The boss can be quite pleasant when ordering noxious tasks to be performed, precisely because he is the boss. No doubt, some exercises of coercive influence by authorities are entirely justified, but this does not take away from the fact that they are coercive. Nor does it mean that all such acts are justified. Later in this chapter, I hope to show how the exercise of constraints may be used to establish the perceived legitimacy of authority figures and how, once established, legitimacy may help to give coercive acts the appearance of being purely persuasive.

Apart from signaling a willingness and capacity to coerce in the future, the use of coercive force by authority figures generally serves a more direct and less symbolic function than coercion by protestors. Confinement in prison, for example, does not *carry* an implicit message as much as it *is* the message. As we will see in the next section, this is not necessarily true of the use of reward influence by those in power.

Persuasive Arguments and Appeals in Acts of Reward Influence

When A confers tangible benefits to B in payment for goods, services, or the promise of same, his reward carries no implicit message. When A's reward is manifestly noncontingent, however, and especially when it is symbolic in nature, chances are that it is serving a rhetorical function. Here I will discuss three common rhetorical functions—what I shall call the *obligating function,* the *ethos-building function,* and the *pacifying function.*

The Obligating Function. In conflict situations, unsolicited rewards are often A's way of committing B to respond in kind. "I've scratched your back," he seems to be arguing, "now it's your turn to scratch mine." Unilateral gestures of this sort are especially commonplace where trust levels between rivals are low and the opportunity for dialogue is at a minimum. In fact, as Raven and Kruglanski (1970) have suggested, one advantage of such rewards is that they open up the possibility for dialogue on a variety of topics, "thus promoting the exploration of the outcomes available in the relationship . . . including mutually satisfactory ways of resolving the existing conflict" (p. 90).

Warfare provides many examples of reward influence used to obligate adversaries. Inhibited from talking openly with the enemy, each side invokes *norms of reciprocity* (Thibaut and Kelley, 1959) through symbolic acts. Thus, on occasion, the North Vietnamese ceremoniously freed a few captured American pilots and the Saigon regime responded in kind by releasing some of its prisoners. Through an unspoken quid pro quo, truce arrangements were worked out in local areas and limitations were placed on what weaponry could be used in other areas. The persuasiveness of unsolicited rewards is increased when they lead third parties to pressure the enemy into responding in kind. Also adding to their persuasiveness is the implicit message that A will be justified in responding with greater ferocity on subsequent occasions should B fail to meet his tacitly imposed obligations.

Unfortunately, unsolicited rewards are highly unreliable as messages, both in terms of the clarity of their intent and in terms of the predictability of responses to them by adversaries. Thus, Averill Harriman, the chief American negotiator at the Paris Talks on Vietnam, and his successor, Henry Cabot Lodge, could disagree vehemently on the meaning of the withdrawal by North Vietnam of several combat divisions from South Vietnam. Was it conclusive evidence, as Harriman maintained, that the North was genuinely willing to accept a settlement? Or was it a ploy by the North, designed to intensify antiwar feeling in the United States and to pressure the Americans to withdraw before peace could be established? Raven and Kruglanski (1970) suggest that in interpersonal contexts, large rewards may beget even greater distrust than small rewards.

> Communicated promises of rewards are less likely to appear credible to the recipient to the extent that the rewards appear excessively large. Furthermore, sudden reception of considerable benefits might arouse suspicion and resentment, as when the rewards are interpreted as "bribes" or attempts at trickery. On the assumption that one is never given something for nothing, the individual's perceived salience of the outcomes at stake . . . is likely to increase. In addition, the feeling that the other side is being untruthful may instigate a strong feeling of resentment and lead to a resolution to resist the influencer on *interpersonal grounds.* (p. 92)

The Ethos-Building Function.   The first book in recorded history was a handbook on how to curry favor with the Pharoah by practicing the art of flattery (Gray, 1946). Centuries later, Aristotle was to suggest in his *Rhetoric* that in addition to appearing competent and trustworthy, the persuader could establish or improve his *ethos* by evincing good will toward his audience. Contemporary attitude-change researchers now speak of this variable as *expressed liking.* Numerous studies, reviewed by McGuire (1969) and others, have shown that expressed liking contributes significantly to attitude change. Mediating the change in attitudes is the recipient's increased attraction toward the source. In the language of psychological-balance theorists (e.g., Heider, 1958), the cognition, A likes B, places pressure on B to arrive at the balanced cognition, B likes A. As the next step in the process, B experiences psychological balance by arriving at the cognition, B likes what A likes.

As I indicated earlier, approval or expressed liking of others is treated by Gamson (1968) as a kind of inducement, but we have seen above that it may also be a persuasive appeal of sorts and that it may also lead to changes in attitudes toward advocated propositions. Here, certainly, is a type of inducement involving elements of persuasion.[8]

---

[8] In fairness to Gamson, he acknowledges that approval sometimes serves a rhetorical function—specifically, when the recipient regards it as rewarding for its own sake and not as an implicit promise of future rewards. Although this distinction adds clarity, it does not foreclose the possibility that the same act of approval may simultaneously serve to induce *and* persuade. An employee may recognize, for example, that his boss uses compliments as an implicit inducement for him to continue the good work; yet at the same time the employee may find it intrinsically gratifying.

Expressed liking becomes a psychological reward, but *ethos* may also be increased and attitudes toward propositions modified by bestowing more tangible rewards. This is certainly a major advantage that incumbent presidents have over their challengers in election contests. During the 1972 election campaign, for example, McGovern could declare that the war in Vietnam was not worth a single American life, but Nixon, by virtue of the power of presidency, could actually withdraw the bulk of American forces. By so doing, he was able to improve his own *ethos,* increase his chances of being reelected, and win support for other proposals and policies.

The Pacifying Function. Why don't more people rebel? That there are monstrous problems of urban decay, poverty, alienation, lawlessness, discrimination, and so forth, in our society, few would deny. That inequities are perpetuated through corporate subsidies, tax loopholes for the rich, and judicial indifference has been amply documented (e.g., Lundberg, 1968; Mintz and Cohen, 1971). Yet large numbers of the poor and the hapless in our society remain faithful to their political leaders and are proud of America's accomplishments.

Undoubtedly, there are many reasons for this anomaly, some of them to be discussed later in this chapter. Here I wish only to summarize the thesis presented by Murray Edelman (1964) in his book, *The Symbolic Uses of Politics.*

Edelman argues that the rewards provided to the mass of citizens by government (not just our own) are largely rhetorical in nature— rhetorical in the pejorative sense of "mere rhetoric" or "empty rhetoric." For that small handful with political clout, on the other hand, governmental rewards are real rather than symbolic or rhetorical; they confer money, power, status, and other concrete benefits.

Prime examples in support of Edelman's thesis are the regulatory agencies of our government, such as the Federal Drug Administration and the Federal Trade Commission. Manned by agents of the very industries they are supposed to regulate, these agencies convey the impression to the mass of citizens that government is working for them, yet in the small print of agency decisions—or even more importantly, in their "non-decisions" (Bachrach and Baratz, 1970), these agencies confer and maintain advantages to special-interest groups. Thus, for example, one agency, over a thirty-year period, permits the fat content of hot dogs and bologna to increase from 18.6 percent to 32.2 percent, while another agency does nothing to prevent the thousands of deaths and injuries that are caused by rigid or defective auto steering assemblies (Mintz and Cohen, 1971). Until pressure is applied, usually by such outsiders as Ralph Nader, information of this kind does not make the headlines. Instead, the press reports that the president has just appointed a new consumer's representative, and mentions only in passing that the appointee will have very little power.

Interestingly, Edelman suggests that most of us want things this way. The inducements offered to us by government are essentially symbolic because we are primarily rhetorical animals whose greatest need from government is not money, power, or status but symbolic identification with the drama of politics. To the average man, politics is a "spectator sport" on which he can project his desires, his fears, and his wishes. The primary requirement of the politician is not that he bestow tangible benefits but that he take dramatic action. Similarly, the television newscast need not present facts and figures about pressing problems but it must excite. As Edelman puts it:

> The parade of "news" about political acts reported to us by the mass media and drunk up by the public as drama . . . has the blurring or absence of any realistic detail that might question or weaken the symbolic meanings we read into it. It is no accident of history or of culture that our newspapers and television present little news, that they overdramatize what they report, and that most citizens have only a foggy notion of public affairs though often an intensely felt one. If political acts are to promote social adjustment and are to mean what our inner problems require that they mean, these acts have to be dramatic in outline and empty of realistic detail. (pp. 32–33)

Edelman's thesis is probably overstated but it undoubtedly contains more than a grain of truth. Whether we are willing or unwilling victims is not easy to determine. Whether the elites and "pols" of our society are quite so calculated and coldblooded as Edelman intimates is also not easy to verify. That some political inducements are essentially rhetorical in nature, and that they serve a pacifying function seems well supported. Once again, we see acts of reward influence involving persuasive or rhetorical elements.

Persuasive Effects of
"Forced Compliance"

Under "normal" circumstances of persuasion, attitude change precedes behavior change. A message is communicated, the receiver reevaluates his own thinking, modifies his attitudes, and then adjusts his overt behavior. Already, we have seen that acts of constraint and inducement may contain implicit arguments and appeals that lead recipients to modify attitudes and behavior in the "normal" sequence.

Can changes in behavior, evinced under conditions of "forced compliance," lead to changes in attitudes? The conventional wisdom holds that they cannot. Hence, the expression, "A man persuaded against his will is of the same opinion still."

Research in the last two decades has undermined this doctrine. Dissonance theorists (e.g., Festinger, 1957; Brehm and Cohen, 1962) have provided strong evidence for their hypothesis that discrepancies between attitudes and behavior, produced by pressuring subjects into performance of a noxious task, are likely to cause them to modify their attitudes. Such discrepancies apparently lead subjects to experience psychological discomfort with attendant pressures to reduce the dissonance.

Especially under conditions where they cannot justify compliance to themselves on other grounds, subjects apparently have little choice but to modify their attitudes. Thus, it is apparently *not* expedient to provide too much reward lest B resent the inducement as a bribe, cite the reward as sufficient justification for his counterattitudinal behavior, or regard attitude change as inconsistent with his view of himself as a person.

In Festinger and Carlsmith's (1959) famous study (some call it "infamous") subjects were induced to put spools on trays and turn pages for one hour. Payment for these noxious tasks was either $1 or $20, depending on whether the subject was in the high-dissonance or low-dissonance condition of the experiment. Following their performance of the task, subjects were induced on the basis of a phony but believable ruse to tell other subjects who had not yet participated that the task was fun. As predicted, subjects given only a $1 reward later indicated (to persons supposedly not associated with the experiment) that they enjoyed the task, while those in the $20 condition were considerably less enthusiastic.

The Festinger and Carlsmith study has been criticized on many grounds, one of which is that $20 was too obviously a bribe, but there have been variations on the experiment using smaller amounts that have yielded similar findings (e.g., Cohen, 1962, pp. 73–78; Carlsmith, Collins, and Helmreich, 1966). Consistent with the "forced compliance" hypothesis of dissonance theory, Smith (1961) and Zimbardo et al. (1964) found that a power figure who in other respects had made himself appear attractive to subjects was less successful at modifying attitudes following forced compliance than an unattractive power figure. The latter's unattractiveness presumably prevented subjects from rationalizing away the behavior-attitude discrepancy by convincing themselves that they complied for the sake of pleasing him. Additional research (e.g., Cohen, 1959; Brehm, 1962) suggests that too much coercion also will not modify attitudes because, as with induced individuals, the subject may then explain away his compliance on grounds that he acted against his will. These and other studies support the cognitive dissonance position.

Although contentions about the conditions under which subjects may be most readily persuaded following forced compliance remain a matter of lively debate, the studies on forced compliance leave little doubt but that "a man persuaded against his will . . ." *is not necessarily* "of the same opinion still." As McGuire (1969) has concluded, the question is no longer whether overt compliance tends to become internalized but "under what conditions it occurs in the greatest amount" (p. 180).

Once this inobvious principle is grasped, it helps explain a variety of cases of "self-persuasion." Draftees wounded in the Vietnam war report greater identification with the war effort than draftees who escaped unscathed. Antiwar sentiments would be dissonant with the conditions they now find themselves in while pro-war sentiments provide justification for their wounds. College administrators who have been pressured by protestors into approving Black Studies programs become advocates of these same programs once the programs are an accomplished fact. The *fait accompli* phenomenon also helps explain why presidents often find it easier to justify policies after they have been implemented rather than before. Those affected have little recourse except to modify their attitudes. Rationalized attitudes are also likely to be evidenced when persons are induced to change their life styles. Those who used to work side by side with a worker promoted to a supervisory position suddenly find that he is not the same friendly guy. His attitudes toward his former peers are modified following changes in his behavior, dictated by his new role.

Summing Up

I hope I have shown in this section that persuasive elements are quite frequently found in acts commonly viewed as pure coercion or pure inducement. Persuasion of sorts is used to make threats and promises credible. Persuasive appeals and arguments are implicit in many coercive acts, especially those performed by protestors, and they are also implicit in noncontingent, symbolic inducements. Finally, constraints and inducements can produce persuasive effects, both in terms of attitude change preceding behavior change and as a result of forced compliance.

Nothing that I have said until now should be construed as an endorsement of coercive influence or reward influence, either on moral or expediential grounds. It should be clear, however, that the popular stereotype of the militant protestor as purely coercive warrants reconsideration, as does the notion that only the most nefarious scoundrels practice coercion. Let us now consider some uses of constraints and inducements by those commonly viewed as "pure persuaders."

ELEMENTS OF CONSTRAINT AND INDUCEMENT IN OSTENSIBLY PERSUASIVE ACTS

As indicated earlier, our culture sharply distinguishes between persuasion and other methods of influence, reserving for the former category such instances as political speeches and religious sermons, legal briefs, and commercial advertisements. Thus, when the president calls upon us to endure sacrifices in time of war, or when a politician campaigns for reelection, each is supposedly engaging in pure persuasion.

Undoubtedly some communicative acts are purely persuasive, but we should expect this to be the exception in conflict situations. To be sure, it is often advantageous in these situations to give the appearance of being purely persuasive, but we should not be deceived by trappings and forms.

One important means by which influence agents may persuade us to *want* to do what we would not otherwise *choose* to do is to first convince us that they have legitimate authority over us and hence that we are duty-bound to obey them. The added advantage of legitimacy is that while leading us into performing noxious tasks, the authority figure may appear as the gentlest of persuaders. As I hope to show in the first part of this section, coercive and reward power (i.e., constraints and inducements) play a significant role in legitimizing persons and positions of authority.

Constraints and inducements are also used by those engaged in ostensibly persuasive acts to purchase or control the instrumentalities of persuasion. These functions of the carrot and stick are discussed in the second part of this section.

Ostensibly Persuasive Acts by "Legitimate Authorities"

Lest there be any doubts about the potential advantages to the influence agent of appearing as a legitimate authority, the findings from laboratory studies on the subject should quickly dispel them. In several studies, the experimenter's own legitimacy as a scientist was used to motivate compliance, and with great effect. Simply on the basis of such instructions as "The experiment requires that you continue," Milgram (1963) persuaded subjects to administer what they believed were dangerous electrical shocks to their peers. Pepitone (1958) encountered little resistance in getting subjects to sort out waste baskets filled with disgusting debris. Frank's (1944) subjects continued for a full hour in attempts at balancing a marble on a small steel ball. Orne (1962) has commented despairingly on his inability to find tasks so noxious that subjects would not perform them. Indeed, in one experiment (Orne and Evans, 1965), subjects picked up what they believed were poisonous snakes while others agreed to place their hands in nitric acid and to throw it in the face of a lab assistant.

Nor does obedience to unreasonable commands necessarily stop at public compliance. Recall that so long as they perceived themselves as having the opportunity for choice, conforming subjects in the "forced compliance" experiments (discussed earlier) tended also to modify their attitudes toward the noxious tasks. Other evidence suggests that compelling performance of such tasks may actually enhance the perceived legitimacy of the influence agent (Raven and French, 1958). Moreover, as Zimbardo (1972) has suggested, when receivers modify their attitudes or behaviors as a result of messages from legitimate authorities, they are more likely to make the attribution error of overestimating the extent to which they have had choice in the matter.

What exactly do we mean when we say that a source has legitimacy, or that he is a legitimate authority, or that he is exerting legitimate influence? A useful starting point is Raven's well-known definition of "legitimate influence" (Raven and Kruglanski, 1970):

> Legitimate influence by A over B stems from internalized values of B which dictate that A, by virtue of his role or position, has the right to prescribe behavior for B in a given domain, and B is obliged to comply. . . . Any compliance which has an "ought to" quality about it would fall into this category. (p. 74)

At first blush, it would appear that legitimate influence is a subcategory of influence by pure persuasion. B acts, not because he has been constrained or induced, but presumably because he has been persuaded that he *ought* to comply in light of A's *right* to prescribe behavior. Legitimizing A's directives is A's role or position. And legitimizing his position—conferring rights upon it—are values which B has freely internalized. B heeds presidential directives, for example, because the Constitution vests the presidency with certain powers. He respects the Constitution because he values the principles it embodies. If B has been fully persuaded of A's legitimacy, then A need not provide explicit persuasive arguments each time he issues a directive. Implicit in the directive is the message: "This directive should be executed because it issued from someone whom you freely accepted as a legitimate authority and whom you are thus duty-bound to obey."

Before we accept the view of legitimate influence as a subcategory of pure persuasion, we should look carefully at how positions of legitimate authority are established and maintained. Here, let me briefly record several observations about political legitimacy which I believe are applicable to other forms of legitimate authority as well.

1. *Political positions of legitimate authority are almost always established initially through the use of coercive influence.*

   Whether through the imposition of a Roman Peace upon colonized territories or through insurrection within one's own territory, establishment of the positions of emperor and king, president and prime minister, have traditionally been fought for by those with designs on power, rather than being granted by a willing public. Max Weber (1947) spoke of tradition and "legal-rational" factors as bases for legitimate authority, but this does not go far enough toward explaining how political forms are first established. Armed political takeovers are as much the rule for governments and governmental forms of which we approve as for those of which we disapprove. Witness, for example, our own American Revolution.

2. *The warrants for political positions of legitimate authority are themselves established and maintained by coercive and reward power.*

   In order to acquire and maintain social control, every ruling elite invents or fastens upon a chain of warrants by which to justify its rule. These consist, minimally, of appeals to supreme values and arguments linking the position of authority to those values. In its crudest form, the king maintains that the religion of his choice is the only religion and advances the view that he and he alone has Divine Rights, ordained by that religion, which legitimize his rule. So as to insure respect for this theocratic interpretation, heretics are punished, Holy Wars are fought against contenders, and a priestly class is induced to corroborate and reinforce the king's claims. Says Peter Berger (1967), every culture constructs an elaborate theodicy of good and evil by which to rationalize the power of some and the powerlessness of others. Underlying a given culture's theodicy are what Rokeach (1960) calls its primitive beliefs, the basic categories in terms of which it comes to know and name the world. These facticities (to use Berger's term), while appearing to have ontological significance, are actually cultural values which are passed off as fact or definition. Ultimately, it is through control over what people accept as basic beliefs that legitimate authority is firmly secured. In modern, industrialized societies, adds Berger, religious theodicies are replaced by secular equivalents. Thus, the Divine Right of kings is replaced by a doctrine of self-evident natural rights or by claims that a given regime's accession to power was justified by historical necessity.

   Crucial to the perpetuation of modern-day political power is control over the meanings of terms which help to justify the actions of a given social order and simultaneously serve to demean those who would challenge that order (Marcuse, 1964). Here we come full tilt back again to why it is that terms like "rational argument," "persuasion," "coercion," and "violence" are such politically sensitive terms, and to how it is that they have come to be applied so dichotomously and so selectively. As Skolnick (1969) has suggested, terms such as these tend to be "politically defined." Here is what the Skolnick Report has to say about the concept of "violence":

The kinds of acts that become classified as "violent," and, equally important, those which do not become so classified, vary according to who provides the definitions and who has superior resources for disseminating and enforcing his definitions. The most obvious example of this is the way, in a war, each side typically labels the other side as the aggressor and calls many of the latter's violent acts atrocities. The definition of the winner usually prevails. Within a given society, political regimes often exaggerate the violence of those challenging established institutions. The term "violence" is frequently employed to discredit forms of behavior considered improper, reprehensible, or threatening by specific groups which, in turn, may mask their own violent response with the rhetoric of order or progress. In the eyes of those accustomed to immediate deference, back talk, profanity, insult, or disobedience may appear violent. In the South, for example, at least until recently, the lynching of an "uppity" black man was often considered less shocking than the violation of caste etiquette which provoked it. (pp. 4–5)

3. *Coercive and reward power play a significant role in maintaining legitimate authority.*

Our civics textbooks notwithstanding, it seems fair to say that we heed an authority not only because of the lofty ideals that he or his position embodies, but also because of the coercive and reward power at his disposal. Not by accident, positions of legitimate authority tend also to be positions of power. The teacher may pass or fail us, the boss may promote or fire us, and the government may either help us to get along if we go along or it may put us in jail if we violate the law. Were authority based entirely on public acceptance of another's "right" to issue binding directives and our "duty" to comply, the authority's coercive and reward power would be unnecessary. But the fact is, of course, that legitimacy is largely sustained by the instrumental functions the authority performs, via his capacity to induce or constrain. On this point, many writers agree (e.g., Parsons, 1970; Gamson, 1968).

The importance of coercive and reward power in maintaining legitimate authority may be more fully appreciated when one recognizes just how difficult it is to present rational justification for granting legitimacy on non-instrumental grounds. Let us note well that each such grant, in the name of reason, places one in the paradoxical position of having surrendered the right to control the consequences of his own reason. The surrender, moreover, is to a faceless authority (a position or a role), and in advance of the authority's decisions or its consequences. One may argue that legitimacy ought to be granted in anticipation of the probable benefits to be provided by the authority (this, essentially, is what Parsons [1960] means by "political trust"), but then this argument becomes an instrumental justification for authority. One may also argue that legitimacy ought to be granted out of allegiance to a "social contract," but philosophical anarchists (e.g., Wolff, 1968) are fond of pointing out that we do not actually sign such contracts, and that even if we did, the signings themselves would require justification. Still another argument, offered especially by democratic theorists, is that the authority *is* us, in some metaphoric way. If this claim is taken to mean that democratic government derives its authority by consent of the governed, then, whether true or false, it is a descriptive statement, and not in itself a justification (Walzer, 1970). If the claim means that having been constituted by us the government will probably act for us, then this becomes, once again, an instrumental justification, and one not necessarily warranted for those who have been more often harmed than helped by governmental decisions.

My purpose has not been to show that all legitimate authority is actually illegitimate, only to suggest how difficult it is to justify claims to legitimacy on the basis of considerations independent of the carrot and the stick. I should add that even the most compelling theoretical justifications for legitimate authority are often inapplicable to specific regimes or persons. Thus, even if it is granted that democratic government ought to be regarded as legitimate in principle because (for example) it protects basic minority rights, what happens when a government labeled as democratic abridges those rights?

Not surprisingly, allegiances to governmental authority (and to other established institutions) are formed in children long before they learn *why* they should offer such allegiances. Easton and Dennis (1965) concluded from their massive study (a sample of over 12,000 children) of the political socialization of young children that the child "learns to like the government before he really knows what it is" (pp. 56–57):

> We find that the small child sees a vision of holiness when he chances to glance in the direction of government—a sanctity and rightness of the demigoddess who dispenses the milk of human kindness. The government protects us, helps us, is good, and cares for us when we are in need, answers the small child. (p. 44)

Other research on political socialization further supports the thesis that political authorities are granted legitimacy uncritically by children. Hess and Torney (1967) have provided strong evidence that the schools tend to reinforce an uncritical perspective:

> Compliance to rules and authorities is a major focus of civic education in elementary school. Teachers' ratings of the importance of various topics clearly indicate that the strongest emphasis is placed upon compliance to law, authority and school regulations. . . . Teachers tend not to deal with partisanship or to discuss the role and importance of conflict in the operation of the system, perhaps because of the position of the school in the community. . . . The school stresses ideal norms and ignores the tougher, less pleasant facts of political life in the United States. (pp. 219–20)

This is not to say that the political socialization of children is solely a product of formal programs of indoctrination. Eventually, the child comes to evaluate the government more critically, and on the basis of direct experience, but when he does, its coercive and reward power loom large in his evaluation. The data on attitudes toward political authorities by black children are especially interesting in this regard. They suggest that although surprisingly strong attachments are displayed by young children toward local governments and by teenage blacks toward the federal government, in general, white children identify considerably more with government and governmental authorities than do black children (Greenberg, 1970). Greenberg asserts that "as the black child more directly confronts his life in America, he comes increasing [sic] to reject America. Indeed, the lowest affect is displayed by the most perceptive black children, those aware of the unequal treatment of black people in general" (p. 181).

Still, it may be argued, if the granting of legitimacy is largely a function of the rewards and punishments meted out by authorities, why is it that blacks—especially oppressed blacks—should display any identification at all? One possible explanation, deducible from reinforcement theory, is that, on balance, blacks are more often helped than hurt by governmental actions. However appealing this notion may be, it is belied by the disadvantaged status of blacks in our society. Another possible explanation, discussed earlier in this chapter, is Edelman's thesis that our government compensates for its shoddy treatment of disadvantaged minorities by fulfilling their preeminent need for symbolic or psychological satisfactions. Related to this view is an explanation put forth by several persons who have had first-hand experience with thoroughly repressive regimes.

Bettleheim (1943) observed that many concentration camp victims seemed to emulate the mannerisms of their brutal Gestapo guards. Fanon's (1963) experience in colonial Algeria was that the colonized lost his own identity in the face of oppression and sought to capture an identity by becoming as much like his master as possible. Freire (1970) has echoed the same theme.

> Their ideal is to be men; but for them to be men is to be oppressors. This is their model of humanity. This phenomenon derives from the fact that the oppressed, at a certain moment of their existential experience, adopt an attitude of "adhesion" to the oppressor. . . . They live in the duality in which *to be* is *to be like,* and *to be like* is *to be like the oppressor.* (p. 33)

What emerges from the foregoing analysis is the conclusion that legitimacy is seldom granted on the basis of reasoned adherence to principles, but rather, that if we are at all critical in obligating ourselves to authorities, we do so on instrumental grounds—because of their coercive and reward power. We are persuaded to obey authorities but it is a kind of persuasion which is inseparable from constraints and inducements. And chances are that if we should later discover more noble reasons for accepting the authority of others, they will be after-the-fact rationalizations for our unalterable existence, much like the self-justifications offered by subjects in the experiments discussed earlier on "forced compliance." Stripped of its pretensions, the ostensibly persuasive act of calling upon us to "do our duty" is often a convenient cover—albeit a persuasive one—for those seeking to coerce us into doing what we would otherwise choose not to do. Once again, the carrot and stick are found to be handmaidens of persuasion.

Control Through Constraints and Inducements over the Instruments of Pure Persuasion

One reason that status and wealth tend to be self-perpetuating in our society is that "ins" and "haves" have greater control over the instruments of pure persuasion. Controls of this kind are all the more effective because they are subtle. Rather than risking censure by such blatant devices as using armed force against adversaries, or buying off politicians and judges, a powerful A may employ reward or coercive power to control the messages received by B or those whom B is attempting to influence.

Control over the instruments of pure persuasion is control over communication resources. In Lasswell's (1936) terms, it is control over who says what to whom, when, where, and how. That controls of this kind are exercised should require little evidence. Here, I will merely illustrate various types of control.

Electoral Controls. It has become a political axiom that in order to get elected to major office, one must either be wealthy or have rich friends. Contested presidential primaries cost several millions of dollars and election campaigns cost considerably more. In 1968, for example, Hubert Humphrey was reported to have spent $2 million on television in just the last two weeks of his campaign (Mendelsohn and Crespi, 1970). Campaign funds are used not only to purchase media time but also to hire skilled ghost writers, public relations experts, makeup men, and so on.

Controls Over Organizational Decision Making. Besides controlling skill and media resources, A may gain a persuasive advantage over B in a conflict situation by having greater access to decision centers or to channels through which ideas and information must flow. Powerful groups may gain the opportunity to have lobbyists testify at congressional hearings or, better still, at private meetings with congressmen. Less powerful groups may be denied the opportunity to testify. Within private organizations, the same facts of life obtain. Not everyone is given the opportunity to communicate directly with the president of the company, and in the event a worker wishes to complain about an immediate supervisor, he may be told that he must go through channels. In voluntary organizations, access to decision centers may be regulated informally or restricted by rigid membership requirements.

Conversely, A may control the information available to B or to those B is attempting to influence. If A is an authority figure, he may exercise control by making himself inaccessible. A particularly effective technique of social control is to deny B information and then, when he attempts to persuade others, to accuse him of being uninformed. With equal impunity, three presidents have used this technique against antiwar protestors, first by classifying politically embarrassing information, then by asserting that few would protest if they, too, had access to the secret documents.

Controls Over Discontent through Cooperation and Opportunities for Participation. Highly repressive regimes may inhibit overt expressions of discontent by denying access to channels or media, or by jailing or exiling protest leaders. More sophisticated governments, however, as well as those unable to succeed by coercion alone, may subdue discontent by bringing the discontented into the system—offering them inducements in return for cooperation, and inviting them to participate in governmental affairs. Although these acts may constitute real concessions, they are often rhetorical ploys, the functions of which are to fragment the opposition and steal its thunder (Gamson, 1968). Participation, especially, is a well-established method of producing counterattitudinal persuasion (McGuire, 1969).

Controls Over Consumer Demand. Much has been written in recent years about the subjugation of man to the impersonal demands of technology and bureaucracy. A persistent theme in the writings of such critics as Ellul (1964), Marcuse (1964), and Galbraith (1967) is that the modern organization can no longer afford the luxury of adapting to consumer demands. As a condition for its own survival, it must, if necessary, create those demands. Hence the vast expenditures of funds on market research, packaging, merchandising, advertising, and selling. Particularly when there is little difference among competing products, the organization's success is dependent upon its control over the instruments of persuasion (Packard, 1957).

Controls Over Basic Beliefs and Values. In the preceding section it was suggested that legitimacy is established and maintained, in part, through controls over primitive beliefs and basic values. Whether unwittingly or by design, controls of this kind tend to reflect, and in turn, reinforce, prevailing sentiments. Klapper (1960) has suggested that the entertainment media in our society, by dint of their profit-making motive, are compelled to give established values a "monopoly propaganda" position. It would not do, for example, for the heroine of a soap opera to be overtly promiscuous.

With respect to certain basic values, at least, materials used in the schools also tend to be one-sided. For example, a group calling itself Women on Words and Images (1972) has found that in the 134 elementary school readers it surveyed, boys outnumbered girls four to one in stories showing ingenuity, creativity, perseverance, strength, bravery, exploration, and so on, while girls exhibited such traits as docility, passivity, and dependency six times as often as boys. Not surprisingly, the group suggested that different controls be exercised over the instruments of pure persuasion in elementary schools.

SUMMARY, CONCLUSIONS, AND IMPLICATIONS

In keeping with the conventional wisdom, social scientists have generally held that persuasion is clearly separable from influence by means of the "carrot" (i.e., inducements, reward influence) and the "stick" (i.e., constraints, coercive influence). The overriding thesis of this paper has been that, however appropriate these distinctions may be for drawing-room controversies, they are inapplicable to social conflicts, situations involving struggles between opponents over incompatible interests. Instead, it was proposed that in social conflicts persuasion is an instrument of the power to reward or coerce, an accompaniment to that power, and/or a consequence of that power.

Six main arguments were advanced in support of the thesis:

1. Minimally speaking, the influence agent must establish persuasively the credibility of his threats and promises.
2. Ostensibly coercive acts—especially acts of protest—often carry implicit persuasive appeals and arguments.
3. The use of reward influence is often rhetorical in nature, designed either to obligate adversaries, establish ethos, or pacify potential opponents.
4. Changes in behavior, wrought by reward influence or coercive influence, frequently lead receivers to bring their attitudes into line with their behaviors so as to reduce dissonance.
5. Coercive and reward influence play significant roles in establishing and maintaining acceptance of "legitimate" authorities as legitimate.
6. Coercive and reward influence may be used to control those communication resources which constitute the instruments of pure persuasion.

Several of the observations made in this paper would appear to have important normative implications. Contrary to popular conceptions, it was suggested that persuasion is not practiced solely by "good guys"; that terms such as these tend to be politically defined and applied; that coercion may produce private compliance and not just grudging public compliance; that the power of constraints and inducements extends even to an influence agent's capacity to engage, effectively, in "pure persuasion"; and that the mechanisms of social control employed by professedly democratic governments are often rhetorical in the pejorative sense of the term. In general, these observations are consonant with the criticisms offered by the protestors of the sixties. Although, on the surface, those "inside the system" appear to influence by rational persuasion while those "outside the system" do not, closer examination reveals that the differences are often a matter of conspicuousness. One of the perquisites of authority is the capacity to mask the use of reward and coercive influence behind a cloak of reason, civility, and decorum.

Apart from its obvious normative implications, this paper raises a number of questions for research on the role of persuasion in social conflicts. How are threats and promises communicated most credibly? Through what verbal, nonverbal, and contextual means are norms of reciprocity invoked? What are the effects of threats and promises on attitudes toward value and policy propositions being advocated by influence agents? Under what conditions does coercion impair (or enhance) perceptions of legitimacy? What are the effects of confrontational tactics on the attitudes of targets? Most of the claims advanced in this paper should be regarded as tentative at this point. Considerably more empirical research is needed before they can be firmly established.

Finally, it seems clear that theories of persuasion are needed that are specifically geared to conflict situations. Elsewhere (Simons, 1972), I have suggested that compartmentalized thinking and an "establishment" bias have interfered with the development of such theories by scholars in speech communication.

What might be the basic underpinnings of such a theory? On the basis of the foregoing analysis, I would suggest that it incorporate at least the following assumptions:

1. All human acts and artifacts constitute potential or actual messages. Thus, even physical acts such as riots, bombings, and political payoffs may have symbolic meaning, apart from whatever direct impact they may have.
2. All communicated messages have potential or actual suasive effects. Thus, there is a rhetorical dimension to all human behaviors.
3. Persuasive messages in social conflicts always take on meaning from their social contexts. Repeatedly in this paper, we have seen that acts

such as confrontational protests made little sense apart from their contexts.

4. Influence in mixed-motive conflicts is neither a matter of the raw imposition of power nor of a friendly meeting of minds; instead, it is an inextricably intertwined combination of persuasive arguments backed up by constraints and inducements. In these social conflicts, once again, rhetoric serves power and power serves rhetoric.

A POSTSCRIPT:
IMPLICATIONS OF THE WATERGATE AFFAIR

No sooner had the finishing touches been given to this paper than the Watergate story broke in full fury. In so many ways, it illustrates my central thesis and its supporting arguments. Here I shall merely enumerate some of Watergate's more obvious lessons.

First, and most obviously, it illustrates how ostensibly persuasive acts may be made effective by the influence agent's use of inducements and constraints to control communication resources. The Committee to Reelect the President apparently went about this task with great thoroughness, if news reports are to be believed. Force was used to gather political intelligence, the opposition's candidates for the nomination were pitted against each other through espionage techniques, and public opinion was molded through bogus letters, telegrams, and advertisements in newspapers.

Second, Watergate illustrates the enormous power of legitimate authority while at the same time pointing up its fragility. The aura of the presidency was evidently sufficient to prevent the public from getting aroused about White House complicity when news of the bugging and burglary was first announced in June 1972. Within administrative circles, few dared to question the rightness or reasonableness of White House orders, even when compliance involved participation or complicity in criminal acts. Until pressure from the courts and from the press made action politically feasible, even Congress was effectively stymied on this and other questions of White House authority. For each audience, persuasive appeals to heed legitimate authority were combined with the president's power to reward and punish. Still, as we have seen, legitimacy does not rest exclusively on reward power or coercive power. Once the Watergate cover-up was exposed, and the trust on which legitimacy ultimately depends was undermined, power shifted quickly to the president's challengers. His legitimacy was shown to be at least partly a rhetorical force: a thing granted and not simply imposed; a persuasive appeal and not just a command.

Third, the Watergate scandal provides support for the "bring on repression" arguments put forth by protestors. Many who participated in one or another of the Watergate fiascos were apparently convinced that the protestors of the sixties still constituted an enormous threat to the American Way—and they justified their own actions in light of that perceived threat. Consistent with the theory of militant confrontations (discussed earlier), targets such as Mitchell and Haldeman eventually "completed" the protestors' rhetorical acts by responding in self-incriminating ways. For the protestors who beckoned the establishment figures to "Show us how ugly you are," the Watergate buggers, burglars, and other assorted bunglers could not have put on a better performance.

Finally, and most broadly, Watergate underscores the need to look at persuasion and inducements and constraints, not as isolated acts or as influence alternatives, but as complements of each other—and especially in conflict situations. We should learn from Watergate that even so apparently "pure" an area of persuasion as political campaign rhetoric cannot be studied apart from an examination of power relationships. By the same token, we should recognize that the power of inducements and constraints is not sufficient means of control in society—at least in a relatively free society such as our own.

REFERENCES

ANDREWS, J. R., "The Rhetoric of Coercion and Persuasion," *Quarterly Journal of Speech,* 56 (1970), 187–95.

AVORN, J., ed., *Up Against the Ivy Wall: A History of the Columbia Crisis.* New York: Atheneum Press, 1969.

BACHRACH, P., and M. S. BARATZ, *Power and Poverty: Theory and Practice.* Oxford: Oxford University Press, 1970.

BERGER, P. L., *The Sacred Canopy: Elements of a Sociological Theory of Religion.* Garden City, N.Y.: Doubleday, 1967.

BETTINGHAUS, E. P., *Persuasive Communication.* New York: Holt, Rinehart and Winston, 1968.

BETTLEHEIM, B., "Individual and Mass Behavior in Extreme Situations," *Journal of Personality and Social Psychology,* 38 (1943), 417–52.

BLAU, P. M., *Exchange and Power in Social Life.* New York: Wiley & Sons, 1964.

BREHM, J. W., and A. R. COHEN, *Explorations in Cognitive Dissonance.* New York: Wiley & Sons, 1962.

BREHM, J. W., "An Experiment on Coercion and Attitude Change," in *Explorations in Cognitive Dissonance.* J. W. Brehm and A. R. Cohen, eds., pp. 84–88. New York: Wiley & Sons, 1962.

BURGESS, P., "Crisis Rhetoric: Coercion versus Force," *Quarterly Journal of Speech,* 59 (1972), 61–73.

CARLSMITH, J. M., B. COLLINS, and R. L. HELMREICH, "Studies in Forced Compliance: I. The Effect of Pressure for Compliance on Attitude Change Produced by Face-to-Face Role Playing and Anonymous Essay Writing," *Journal of Personality and Social Psychology*, 4 (1966), 1–13.

COHEN, A. R., "Communication Discrepancy and Attitude Change: A Dissonance Theory Approach," *Journal of Personality*, 27 (1959), 386–96.

COSER, L. A., *The Functions of Social Conflict*. New York: Free Press of Glencoe, 1956.

EASTON, D., and J. DENNIS, "The Child's Image of Government," *The Annals of the American Academy of Political and Social Sciences*, 361 (1965), 41–57.

EDELMAN, M., *The Symbolic Uses of Politics*. Urbana, Ill.: University of Illinois Press, 1964.

ELLUL, J., *The Technological Society*, trans. J. Wilkerson. New York: Knopf, 1964.

FANON, F., *The Wretched of the Earth*, trans. C. Farrington. New York: Grove Press, 1963.

FESTINGER, L., *A Theory of Cognitive Dissonance*. Stanford, Cal.: Stanford University Press, 1957.

FESTINGER, L., and J. M. CARLSMITH, "Cognitive Consequences of Forced Compliance," *Journal of Abnormal and Social Psychology*, 58 (1959), 203–10.

FOGELSON, R. M., *Violence as Protest: A Study of Riots and Ghettos*. Garden City, N.Y.: Doubleday, 1971.

FOTHERINGHAM, W. C., *Perspectives on Persuasion*. Boston: Allyn and Bacon, 1966.

FRANK, J. D., "Experimental Studies of Personal Pressure and Resistance," *Journal of General Psychology*, 30 (1944), 23–64.

FREIRE, P., *Pedagogy of the Oppressed*, trans. M. B. Ramos. New York: Herder and Herder, 1970.

GALBRAITH, J. K., *The New Industrial State*. Boston: Houghton Mifflin, 1967.

GAMSON, W. A., *Power and Discontent*. Homewood, Ill.: Dorsey Press, 1968.

GRAY, G. W., "The 'Precepts of Kagemni and Ptah-Hotep,'" *Quarterly Journal of Speech*, 31 (1946), 446–54.

GREENBERG, E. S., "The Political Socialization of Black Children," in *Political Socialization*, E. S. Greenberg, ed., pp. 178–90. New York: Atherton Press, 1970.

GRUDER, C. L., "Social Power in Interpersonal Negotiation," in *The Structure of Conflict*, P. Swingle, ed. pp. 111–54. New York: Academic Press, 1970.

HEIDER, F., *The Psychology of Interpersonal Relations*. New York: Wiley & Sons, 1958.

HESS, R. D., and J. V. TORNEY, *The Development of Political Attitudes in Children*. Chicago: Aldine Publishing Co., 1967.

KARLINS, M., and H. I. ABELSON, *Persuasion: How Opinions and Attitudes are Changed*, 2nd ed. New York: Springer Publishing Co., 1970.

KELMAN, H. C., "Compliance, Identification and Internalization: Three Processes of Attitude Change," *Journal of Conflict Resolution*, 2 (1958), 51–60.

KLAPPER, J. T., *The Effects of Mass Communication*. Glencoe, Ill.: The Free Press, 1960.

LASSWELL, H., *Politics: Who Gets, What, When, How.* New York: McGraw-Hill, 1936.

LUNDBERG, F., *The Rich and the Super-Rich.* New York: Lyle Stuart, Inc., 1968.

MARCUSE, H., *One-Dimensional Man: Studies in the Ideology of Advanced Industrial Society.* Boston: Beacon Press, 1964.

McGUIRE, W., "The Nature of Attitudes and Attitude Change," in *The Handbook of Social Psychology,* Vol. 3, 2nd ed., G. Lindzey and E. Aronson, eds., pp. 136–314. Reading, Mass.: Addison-Wesley, 1969.

MENDELSOHN, H., and I. CRESPI, *Polls, Television, and the New Politics.* Scranton, Pa.: Chandler Publishing Co., 1970.

MILGRAM, S., "Behavioral Study of Obedience," *Journal of Abnormal and Social Psychology,* 67 (1963), 371–78.

MILL, J. S., *On Liberty,* A. Castell, ed. New York: Appleton-Century-Crofts, 1947.

MINTZ, M., and J. S. COHEN, *America, Inc.* New York: Dell Publishing Co., 1971.

ORNE, M. T., and F. J. EVANS, "Social Control in the Psychological Experiment," *Journal of Personality and Social Psychology,* 1 (1965), 189–200.

PACKARD, V., *The Hidden Persuaders.* New York: David McKay, 1957.

PARSONS, T., *Structure and Process in Modern Societies.* New York: The Free Press, 1960.

———, "On the Concept of Influence," *Public Opinion Quarterly,* 27 (1963), 37–62.

PEPITONE, A., "Attributions of Causality, Social Attitudes, and Cognitive Matching Processes," in *Person Perception and Interpersonal Behavior,* R. Tagiuri and L. Petrullo, eds., pp. 258–76. Stanford, Cal.: Stanford University Press, 1958.

RAVEN, B. H., and J. R. P. FRENCH, JR., "Legitimate Power, Coercive Power, and Observability in Social Influence," *Sociometry,* 21 (1958), 83–97.

RAVEN, B. H., and A. W. KRUGLANSKI, "Conflict and Power," in *The Structure of Conflict,* P. Swingle, ed. New York: Academic Press, 1970.

ROKEACH, M., *The Open and Closed Mind.* New York: Basic Books, 1960.

SCHEIDEL, T. M., *Persuasive Speaking.* Glenview, Ill.: Scott, Foresman, 1967.

SCHELLING, T. C., *The Strategy of Conflict.* Cambridge, Mass.: Harvard University Press, 1960.

SCOTT, R. C., and W. BROCKRIEDE, *The Rhetoric of Black Power.* New York: Harper and Row, 1969.

SCOTT, R. C., and D. K. SMITH, "The Rhetoric of Confrontation," *Quarterly Journal of Speech,* 55 (1969), 1–8.

SIMONS, H. W., "Requirements, Problems and Strategies: A Theory of Persuasion for Social Movements," *Quarterly Journal of Speech,* 56 (1970), 1–11.

———, "Persuasion in Social Conflicts: A Critique of Prevailing Conceptions and a Framework for Future Research," *Speech Monographs,* 39 (1972), 227–48.

SKINNER, B. F., *Science and Human Behavior.* New York: The Free Press, 1953.

SKOLNICK, J. H., *The Politics of Protest: A Task Force Report Submitted to the National Commission on the Causes and Prevention of Violence.* New York: Simon and Schuster, 1969.

SMITH, E. E., "The Power of Dissonance Techniques to Change Attitudes," *Public Opinion Quarterly*, 25 (1961), 629–39.

TEDESCHI, J. T., "Threats and Promises," in *The Structure of Conflict*, P. Swingle, ed., pp. 155–91. New York: Academic Press, 1970.

THIBAUT, J., and H. H. KELLEY, *The Social Psychology of Groups*. New York: Wiley & Sons, 1959.

WALZER, M., *Obligations: Essays on Disobedience, War and Citizenship*. Cambridge, Mass.: Harvard University Press, 1970.

WEBER, M., *The Theory of Social and Economic Organization*. Oxford: Oxford University Press, 1947.

WOLFE, T., *Radical Chic and Mau-Mauing the Flak Catchers*. New York: Farrar, Straus & Giroux, 1970.

WOLFF, R. P., *The Poverty of Liberalism*. Boston: Beacon Press, 1968.

Women on Words and Images, *Dick and Jane as Victims: Sex Stereotypes in Children's Readers* (pamphlet), 1972. Princeton, N.J., Box 2163.

ZIMBARDO, P. G., "The Tactics and Ethics of Persuasion," in *Attitudes, Conflict and Social Change*, B. T. King and E. McGinnies, eds., pp. 84–102. New York: Academic Press, 1972.

ZIMBARDO, P. G., M. WEISENBERG, I. FIRESTONE, and B. LEVY, "Communicator Effectiveness of Producing Public Conformity and Private Attitude Change," *Journal of Personality*, 33 (1963), 233–55.

8

Epilogue

GERALD R. MILLER

This volume's contributors have made beginning steps in dealing with the role of communication in a variety of potential conflict settings: the relative intimacy of interpersonal transactions, the asymmetrical climate existing between large, profit-making institutions and their customers, and the "ivy-covered" confines of the modern university. Moreover, the selections cover a near-gamut of research strategies and methodologies: Mortensen calls for a transactional approach to the study of communication and conflict; Jandt stresses the advantages of simulating social conflict; Steinfatt and Miller summarize and extend a body of research conducted in the tradition of tightly controlled laboratory studies; Tompkins et al. employ field research techniques to probe attitudes toward conflict within the university; Bowers makes use of the case study to illustrate the communication strategies available to institutions and their customers; and Simons provides a penetrating conceptual analysis of the relationships existing between persuasion and the use of threats and inducements. Each of the selections suggests potentially fruitful avenues of research for speech communication scholars intrigued with the place of communication in conflict situations.

Still, as Simons emphasizes in the Prologue, our efforts constitute but a modest beginning in unraveling the interwoven conceptual and operational threads that bind together communication and the conflict process. Appropriately, then, this epilogue will center on *issues raised* by the chapters, not on *problems solved* or *questions answered*. Although a tidy method of organizing these issues escapes me, I will, for the sake of convenience, lump them into two broad categories: definitional issues and methodological issues. Obviously, no claim is made for either exhaustiveness or exclusivity; instead, it will quickly become apparent that the two types of issues are inextricably related and that they are inseparable from numerous other theoretical and empirical questions.

DEFINITIONAL ISSUES

On Defining Social Conflict

In the Prologue, Simons correctly asserts that most contributors to this volume are dissatisfied with exclusively objectivist definitions of "social conflict." Obviously, social conflict is often closely linked with external stimulus features of the environment—usually, when one sees a fist speeding toward him, he is quick to parry the blow and to launch some form of countermeasure. But just as obviously, there are times when an approaching fist does not cognitively signal social conflict— for instance, the punches to the shoulder exchanged by adolescent boys may serve as affectionate greetings, agreed-upon means of asserting virility, or a mutual method of displacing excess sexual energies. Thus, the conditions necessary for social conflict would seem to consist of a subtle blend of environmental contingencies and human perceptions, a point underscored and developed nicely by Mortensen in his paper on a transactional approach to social conflict.

Even after granting this interplay between environment and actor, however, numerous thorny problems enter into the definition of the construct "social conflict." One such problem is illustrated by Simons' paper itself. Scorning so-called "drawing-room controversies" as instances of social conflict, Simons offers the following definition of the construct:

> By a social conflict I mean that state of a social relationship in which incompatible interests between two or more persons give rise to a struggle

> between them. The notion of a clash of interests presupposes something
> more than what is typically implied by such terms as "disagreement,"
> "difference of opinion," or "controversy." The conflict may involve value
> differences or personal animosities, *or competition for scarce resources,*
> [italics mine] or some combination, but in any case, the personal interests
> of one or more parties must appear to be threatened. (This volume,
> pp. 177–78.)

He goes on to argue that what he characterizes as "pure persuasion"—
persuasion that relies entirely on the rhetorical force of logical and emotional appeals with no resort to threats and inducements—may be useful
in pseudo-conflicts, but that in genuine conflicts, it does not provide a
viable means of influence. "In a genuine conflict, power serves rhetoric
and rhetoric serves power" (p. 178).

There is much to be said for Simons' analysis. Certainly, it underscores the inadequacy of an antiseptic, coercive-free, reason-governed
view of persuasion for dealing with most instances of social conflict.
Still, it seems to me that Simons has overgeneralized, that there are instances of genuine social conflict in which the only weapons for battle
are the logical and emotional force of the arguments employed. In
other words, I would hold that certain kinds of social conflicts are distinguished by the fact that neither party is clearly in a position to exercise coercive or reward power over the other; and furthermore, contrary
to what is suggested by Simons' position, that there can be, and often
is, a "winner" and a "loser" in such conflicts.

Consider the following illustrative situation. At a well-attended
cocktail party, two relative equals, A and B, with no prior animosities
toward each other, enter into a verbal dispute (or controversy, or disagreement) concerning the merits of a baseball players' strike. Because
neither has any financial ties with the game, there are no threats to
economic self-interest; because both are avid fans, each will suffer if
opening day is delayed. Even so, they disagree vigorously on the legitimacy of the strike, and as the exchange continues, others in the room
cease conversation and turn their attention to the argument. A seems
to be having all the best of it: he appears to have better command of the
facts of the situation; he marshals his arguments more skillfully; he presents his points more fluently. Soon onlookers are responding to A's
statements by murmuring, "Right," "Good point!" etc. B desperately
strives to turn the tide: his face grows ruddy; his voice grows louder; he
begins to hurl personal barbs at A. These barbs are greeted, in turn,
with disapproving glances and remarks by the bystanders; from B's perspective, the situation rapidly degenerates beyond redemption. As a result, B may retire to a corner and sulk; he may leave the party in a huff;
he may challenge A to "step outside"; or, as history has occasionally re-

corded in such circumstances, he may leave the party, obtain a gun, and return and shoot A.

What we have been privy to is a social conflict as real, if not as broad in its ramifications, as heated negotiations between Marvin Miller and the major league club owners. Given the circumstances described, both combatants at the cocktail party must rely primarily on their rhetorical skills to best the other. (Note that if the argument occurred between relative unequals, such as an employer and an employee, reward or coercive power might have been brought to bear.) *At stake is a very real, and relatively scarce social resource: the esteem and approval of others.* To argue that we do not often vie verbally for such approval would be to deny everyday experience. And when two or more people compete for social approval, incompatibility of interests often gives rise to a struggle for this scarce resource. Thus, a "drawing-room" controversy may indeed contain the seeds of social conflict, with "winner" and "loser" determined largely on grounds of argumentative acumen.

Some may contend that as long as B does not overtly acquiesce, A cannot be judged to have the upper hand in the conflict, nor can it be said that the conflict has been "resolved." With the first assertion I would disagree; with the second I would concur but append my belief that it is relatively trivial. In social conflicts of the type I have just described, one seldom plays to the opponent but rather gauges his success on the reactions of the human "M&M dispensers" who are overhearing the argument. No realistic academic debater ever feels he has convinced his opponent of the superiority of his position, but if the judge votes in his favor, he perceives he has emerged victorious from the conflict.[1] As for the second assertion, a process view of phenomena militates against the definitive "resolution" of most conflicts. To assert that a labor-management conflict has been "resolved" merely because the contesting parties agree to a two-year contract ignores that the competition of interests is an ongoing phenomenon and that the contract will have to be renegotiated two years later. Hence, whether or not B publicly capitulates, A perceives the conflict has been satisfactorily resolved *if* he gains the approval of other party-goers and *if* B does not later retaliate in one of the ways mentioned above.

Of course, not all transactions involving pure persuasion are instances of social conflict. People sometimes do match their argumentative

---

[1] I certainly do not agree with the notion that academic debate is a game devoid of social conflict. Tournament debating involves conflict over two scarce resources: trophies and the social approval that goes with them. Personal antagonisms run rampant; some coaches backbite each other; some debaters use any tactic from fabricating evidence to stealing opponents' file boxes; and spying is developed into a fine art, all because the conflicting parties perceive their self-interests as diametrically opposed.

wits for the sheer joy of it, for the learning that may result, or just to fill up available time. In such encounters, the participants usually do not feel their self-interests are threatened; hence, no social conflict occurs. But when parties to a verbal dispute perceive that their egos are on the line and that their first line of defense consists of their rhetorical skills, conditions are ripe for social conflict.

Even in cases in which persuasion is embedded in implicit or explicit threats and inducements—i.e., those cases which Simons holds are typical of "genuine" social conflict—the overriding motive of one or more of the combatants may be heightened esteem or broadly based social approval. Naturally, it would be a poor rhetorical strategy to articulate such a motive, so when matters of personal aggrandizement are paramount (and by no means am I adopting the cynical posture that such motives are always paramount), persuasive appeals are tailored to the social, political, and economic interests of the relevant constituency. Thus, it is not uncommon to draw the curtain on a cycle of social conflict where few tangible gains have been recorded for the socially oppressed constituency but where the social status of that constituency's leadership has been remarkably enhanced.

My prolonged discussion of Simons' position is not aimed at casting doubt on the major thrust of his remarks; rather, I have sought to underscore the remarkable definitional complexity of the term "social conflict." Moreover, I believe my distinctions and reservations are germane to several of the volume's chapters. None of the papers, save perhaps for Bowers and Tompkins et al., deal directly with conflicts of interest that have potentially profound social, political, and economic import. And in Bowers' case, the effect is cumulative, not particularistic; one would be hard-pressed to argue that a monthly change in the telephone bill for the Mount Vernon, Iowa, Fire Department is *in itself* likely to have much influence on the national psyche. As Bowers persuasively argues, it is the results of hundreds of such social conflicts that produce a collective mentality of fatalistic resignation and a belief that City Hall (or Sears, or GM, or IBM) is inviolable.

In addition, several of the papers—e.g., Steinfatt and Miller and Mortensen—focus primarily on experimental settings where the availability of *external* threats and inducements is largely lacking (the term "external" merits stress because in some of the studies reviewed by Steinfatt and Miller the experimental conditions themselves confer reward or coercive power on one or more of the parties), while other contributors define "conflict" in ways calculated to restrict it to what Simons calls "pure persuasion"—e.g., "Consider conflict to be disagreement and debate over issues and values, not over personalities" (Tompkins et al., this volume, p. 162).

Thus, if one accepts Simons' view in toto, it is tempting to assert that several of the chapters do not deal primarily with "genuine" social conflict. As I have attempted to indicate, I think this would be both a mistake and an oversimplification. Having been a long-time participant in the academic governance process, I am keenly aware that many "polite, drawing-room controversies" which occur in the presence of an audience can be aptly characterized as social conflicts. In such confrontations, a common ploy is to further batter the opponent's self-esteem by pointing out departures from the "rules" of pure persuasion; thereby, of course, gaining plaudits from the onlookers for possessing a keen rhetorical sense. To be sure, the genesis of the debate may lie in other perceived professional conflicts of interest, but once the battle is joined, the scarce social resources of esteem and approval become the locus of conflict. Tompkins et al. appear to be dead right, then, in stressing possible differences in the outcomes of debates that occur in private, as opposed to public, settings. Not only would the analysis I have presented suggest that there is a higher potential for "genuine" social conflict when the arena for pure persuasion is public, the results of extensive research in such areas as public commitment (McGuire, 1969) and group pressure (Cartwright and Zander, 1960) also reinforce this possibility.

Even when social conflict is initially spawned by competition for economic or political resources, the conflict may evolve to the stage where esteem or social approval becomes the primary consideration. Thus, Bowers mentions an alternative to abject surrender to the institution: the customer may continue to wage the battle long after it becomes economically unprofitable for him to do so. Such persistence may be partially explained by the blind rage fostered by perceived injustice, but it probably also results from the fact that the customer has made numerous pronouncements to friends and acquaintances concerning his determination to gain satisfaction from his complaint. To admit defeat, no matter what the savings in time and money, would be to risk the disapproval and derision of these friends and acquaintances; to carry the battle forward, regardless of temporal and financial costs, ensures their admiration and respect.

What is needed, then, to determine whether or not confrontations grounded primarily in pure persuasion are instances of genuine or pseudo-conflicts, is knowledge of the competing parties' phenomenological states. To the extent that they perceive that they are locked in combat for the scarce resource of others' social approval, they will view the situation as a real social conflict. *And at times, genuine conflict situations impose constraints that limit the combatants to pure persuasion; either threats or inducements are not available or their very use would invite social disapproval by the relevant audience.* Granted, the unavailability of threats or inducements is probably more characteristic of social conflicts between individuals than between large, competing political or economic groups. Still, to categorically relegate pure persuasion to the realm of pseudo-conflicts is to remove such individual confrontations from the scrutiny of the conflict researcher.

My remarks have touched chiefly on one issue associated with the definition of conflict. Certainly other questions could be raised. In the last analysis, of course, one's definition of "social conflict" will be partially dictated by the kinds of problems he wishes to pursue. Conversely, however, acceptance of a particular conceptual or definitional stance fixes one's research priorities. This continual interplay between construct definition and problem selection reinforces the need for frequent reassessment of the prevailing, "popular" definitions of a term such as "social conflict."

On Defining Communication

The conference that culminated in this volume was at least partially predicated on the assumption that speech communication researchers possess relevant interests and skills that should be brought to bear on the study of social conflict. Given this assumption, one might legitimately ask for a capsule summary of these interests. Although it is unlikely that all members of the field would agree, conferees at the 1968 New Orleans Conference on Research and Instructional Development put it this way: *"Spoken symbolic interaction is the central focus of study in the speech-communication area"* (Kibler and Barker, 1969, p. 18).

With but one reservation, I will accept this statement as a frame of reference for discussing the definitional views of "communication," whether explicitly stated or operationally implied, reflected by contributors to the present volume. The exception to be made concerns the term "spoken." Although there probably are (or at least were) good reasons for including it in statements concerned with defining the academic area of speech communication, our communicative interests in social conflict are somewhat more catholic. Thus, I will consider the extent to which the papers in this volume appear to share a central concern for the role of *symbolic interaction* in the process of social conflict. Lest the reader misunderstand my intent, I am not using the *centrality of symbolic interaction criterion* as a yardstick to measure whether each particular chapter passes muster; instead, it serves as a point of departure for considering some of the issues involved in defining "communication."

Mortensen's treatment of verbalized social conflict certainly focuses on dyadic symbolic interaction. Moreover, his attempt to identify differences in transactional patterns occurring in high- and low-conflict situations could provide useful basic data for the researcher interested in social conflict. Whether Mortensen has identified the most important parameters of verbal interaction and whether these parameters can be joined in some sort of functional predictive equation remain open questions. Still, the game is probably worth the candle, for an understanding of the verbal dimensions of a conflict relationship should both advance theoretical frontiers and contribute to therapeutic efforts aimed at de-escalating interpersonal conflict.

Similarly, most of the strategies identified by Bowers for use in social conflicts between institutions and their customers center on symbolic interaction. The customer's choice of such options as oral petition, written petition, appeals to superinstitutions, publicizing complaints, and collectivization relies heavily on the persuasive power of the spoken and written word—though in some of these strategies (e.g., appeals to superinstitutions and collectivization) threats and inducements are closely linked with message production. By the same token, symbolic interaction is an integral aspect of the institution's use of such strategies as avoidance, procedural counterpersuasion, substantive counterpersuasion, and adjustment.

I do question, however, whether such acts as trashing, bombing, or highjacking on the part of the customer, or wire-tapping, entrapment, or physical force on the part of the institution, should be labeled "communication strategies": in other words, I am concerned about how far we should extend the behavioral boundaries of the concept "symbolic interaction." To be sure, burning down buildings can be construed as having a rhetorical and/or a symbolic function; if nothing else, such acts signal the extent to which the party is willing to go to achieve redress of real or imagined grievances, and they forcefully underscore the party's willingness to carry out verbal threats and promises. Even so, there seems to be a useful distinction between statements that threaten arson and acts of arson themselves: the former are clearly symbolic and communicate a professed intent that may or may not be carried out; the latter are irrevocable actions, and once committed, they have no probabilistic dimension to them. This is not to say that these actions are divorced from communicative considerations, for in the arena of social conflict, the credibility of one's messages may hinge upon his willingness to engage in force or violence. But violent acts are extrinsic to symbolic interaction itself; they reinforce the integrity of symbolic interchange, rather than serving primarily as symbols per se.

The preceding assertion is, of course, an indication of my own definitional preferences, not a statement of fact. That many would disagree is attested to not only by several of the papers in this volume but also by the spate of articles and anthologies dealing with the "rhetoric" of everything from self-immolation to protest marching. Nevertheless, it seems unwise to me to permit our meanings for "symbolic interaction" such a broad latitude of acceptance. Carried to its teleological extreme, every behavior becomes rhetorical or symbolic; to use a purposefully absurd example, my aiming an angry kick at a rock and fracturing my toe becomes symbolic of an unconscious Freudian death-wish. Thus, the study of communication asserts a right of intellectual eminent domain over all the behavioral commerce of the world. Although such universality may be ego-satisfying, it neglects the twin needs of focus and priority in our study of human communication.

Some readers may contend that my argument has forced me to desert my professed interest in the nonverbal realm. Rather than accepting this contention, I would hold that I have sought to restrict the universe of nonverbal behaviors encompassed by "symbolic interaction." Certainly, I do not quarrel with the speech communication researcher's interest in such paralinguistic cues as tone, loudness, or fluency, nor am I bothered by a concern with the gestural behaviors that accompany speech acts. Even proxemics, when coupled with verbal exchanges, cause no problems. What does concern me is the possibility of construing "nonverbal communication" too broadly, thereby opening a Pandora's Box of conceptual and theoretical problems.

Of course, no one can or should be able to legislate what a researcher will or will not research. Hence, I have no doubt that students of speech communication will go on pursuing problems that I define as peripheral to the study of human communication, nor do I question the likelihood that such studies will contribute to our understanding of the process of social conflict. I simply depart from the view that such research takes communication as its major concern.

This departure provides a nice transition for my next point. At their present stage of development, the chapters by Jandt, Tompkins et al., and Steinfatt and myself seem, at best, only tangentially related to communication. Again, this is not to say that these contributors have failed to say something interesting, both in terms of the substance of their remarks and the avenues they suggest for future research, but only that their ideas merely lay the preliminary groundwork for subsequent exploration of the communication process.

Although Jandt makes a reasonable case for the methodological and pedagogical utility of simulating social conflict, he offers few clues concerning ways that communication might be analyzed in simulation situations. Without these guidelines, it may be relatively easy for the researcher to understand how to manipulate the initial inputs to the simulation and how to measure certain behavioral outcomes. What may escape him is a method for observing and measuring the communication transactions occurring during the simulation—the so-called "throughputs" of the system.

Tompkins et al. report useful data about the attitudes of various university groups toward ongoing conflict within the university. What is presently lacking is an attempt to come to grips with the communication behaviors that occur during university conflict or how these behaviors may vary within different situational contexts. Thus, their chapter deals with attitudes toward conflictful symbolic interaction, not conflictful symbolic interaction itself.

Steinfatt and I demonstrate rather clearly that under certain circumstances the opportunity to communicate is a necessary, though certainly not a sufficient condition for arriving at the best mutual solution to a potential conflict. Considering the constraints of prior gaming research, this demonstration has some value. But unquestionably, we need to look next at the communication that goes on during negotiations and to examine ways that various communication strategies and transactions affect the parties' success in reaching the best mutual solution.

The preceding comments are aimed at illustrating some of the issues involved in defining "communication." My intent has not been to nitpick, carp, or find fault with the chapters in this volume. As we have repeatedly stressed, a great deal of conceptual and definitional homework remains undone, for speech communication researchers have only recently begun to manifest an interest in the behavioral study of the role of communication in the process of social conflict. It is in the spirit of stimulating such homework that my remarks about definitional issues have been offered.

METHODOLOGICAL ISSUES

Transactional versus Unidirectional Approaches to Studying Communication and Conflict

Mortensen's appeal for greater use of transactional paradigms in studying communication and conflict has merit. To the extent that such paradigms can be successfully employed, it should be possible to capture more closely the process nature of communication, to identify the interactive effects of language exchanges on the users of that langauge. Such a goal is certainly worth pursuing.

Still, I am of the opinion that the unidirectional paradigm has been too quickly maligned by certain communication scholars. By "uni-directional" I mean an approach which concentrates on the manipula-tion of several communication variables in order to determine their individual or conjunctive effect on several dependent measures. Al-though for the most part the variables employed have not been com-munication-oriented, such a unidirectional approach typifies most of the game-theoretic research summarized in the paper by Steinfatt and myself.

One criticism of such research is that it is oversimplistic. Taken at face value, this criticism ignores the fact that it is often useful to abstract from a complex phenomenon, to reduce its complexity so that it can be studied more meaningfully. In fact, one is hard-pressed to suggest ways of studying the complex relationships between communication and social conflict without engaging in some kind of abstracting process. The cru-cial question, then, is whether the approach to reduction represented by the unidirectional paradigm is a useful one.

Critics of the paradigm answer this question negatively. One of the stock responses they invoke to support their disenchantment can be la-beled the "small amount of variance explained" argument. The argu-ment, alluded to in Mortensen's chapter, goes something like this: typi-cally, studies that manipulate two or three variables manage to account for only a very small proportion of total variance. This small amount of variance explained illustrates that communication is much too complex a process to offer up its behavioral secrets to such a simplistic research strategy. What is needed, say the critics, are more elaborate, multivariate approaches which enable the researcher to tap the marvelous complexity of human symbolic interaction.

One could respond to this argument by asserting that there are scientific criteria other than variance explained which should be used in evaluating the utility of a research paradigm. Rather than taking this route, I will meet the critics on their own grounds. Moreover, I will grant that most prior unidirectional studies have managed to explain only a small amount of the total variance and that as we throw more variables into the pot we usually manage to explain more of the vari-ance. (The latter fact, of course, is hardly startling.)

Where I do part company with critics of the unidirectional ap-proach is in their assumption that this small amount of variance ex-plained necessarily results from the insoluble complexity of the phe-nomena under investigation. A perfectly tenable alternative lies in the possibility that we have studied the wrong variables, or that the vari-ables we have chosen have suffered from poor conceptual and opera-tional explication. Using the single variable of *reinforcement schedules,* Skinner has been able to account for a rather large proportion of vari-ance in a number of behavioral environments. And it is the beautiful simplicity of Skinner's paradigm that most disturbs his detractors, for it violates the conventional wisdom about the intricate complexity of human behavior, both communicative and otherwise. Thus, an alternative to seeking ever more complex paradigms is to return to the conceptual drawing board and to hammer out a better set of constructs.

Perhaps an example will best illustrate my point. I suspect that two of the most important variables in determining the persuasive impact of a message, either in high- or low-conflict situations, are *physical attraction* and *means control*—the latter being roughly equivalent to what Simons calls "coercive and reward power." How much attention have communication researchers devoted to either variable? We have treated the area of means control like a scientific hot potato; primarily because, as Simons incisively points out, coercion violates our ideological predilections about the way persuasion *should* function in a democratic society. I do recall hearing one conversation about a study which found that among female communicators, physical attraction and persuasive effectiveness were positively correlated at greater than .90, though I have never been able to lay hands on the research. Interestingly, the study seemed to be viewed primarily as an amusing barroom anecdote capable of eliciting numerous suggestive comments: first, I suspect, because it seemed far too simple-minded for persons who get most of their professional brownie points from hatching up ostensibly complicated studies; second, because like means control, physical attraction as a persuasive device has an odious ideological ring. To the credit of the social psychologists, they have recently discovered what every layman has known for several thousand years; physical attraction is an important determinant of one's interactive success (see, e.g., Dion, Berscheid, and Walster, 1972).

Thus, I believe we should make new paradigmatic friends but keep the old. A variety of approaches should be used in the study of communication and social conflict, including the transactional paradigm proposed by Mortensen and the simulation techniques advocated by Jandt. But to support these new approaches is not to opt for the demise of unidirectional research. Such a death would be premature, for this approach has yielded valuable insights, and if better variables can be identified and operationalized, future studies may prove to be even more scientifically rewarding.

Laboratory versus Field Approaches to the Study of Communication and Conflict

Because there exists a voluminous literature which deals with the purposes and limitations of laboratory and field studies and which compares and contrasts the two approaches (see, e.g., Hovland, 1959; Miller, 1970; Redding, 1970), I will limit my comments to ways that laboratory and field studies seem to complement each other in studying the role of communication in the process of social conflict.

Tompkins et al. illustrate one valuable function of field research: the collection of descriptive data that enhances our understanding of some of the dimensions of "real-world" social conflict. As I have already emphasized, very little of the work thus far has dealt with descriptive indices of communication. Even so, it is important to understand people's attitudes toward conflict, particularly as they relate to relevant demographic variables, for these attitudes are likely to affect preferences in communication behaviors and strategies.

Field research can also aid in the identification of significant constructs, a task to which I have already assigned high priority. By observing communication and social conflict in natural settings, an ingenious person may inductively arrive at new category systems, or new classes of variables. After these systems have been formalized, their soundness and applicability can be tested by being held up to instances of ongoing social conflict, a procedure Bowers ably demonstrates in his paper.

Finally, valuable experimentation can also take place in the field, a fact that many researchers are prone to forget. Recently, field experimentation has experienced a revitalization, primarily because of the writings of such behavioral scientists as Campbell (1957; 1969). Speech communication researchers should not automatically equate experimental work on communication and conflict with the environs of the laboratory; instead, they should take advantage of opportunities to place their experiments in the more natural climate of the field.

Of course, there are times when field research does not permit the control needed to arrive at relatively unambiguous statements concerning relationships between variables. In such cases, the greater precision and control offered by the laboratory can be put to good advantage. Laboratory settings allow the researcher to construct the environment that he wishes to study, and they enable him to manipulate independent variables more unambiguously. These advantages are illustrated by the research discussed in this volume by Mortensen and by Steinberg and myself.

Elsewhere (Miller, 1973) I have metaphorically described the complementary roles played by laboratory and field research in the study of communication and social conflict. Perhaps those words best summarize the point I wish to make:

> But before one can embark on . . . a journey, he must choose a conveyance. The laboratory and the field represent two vehicles available to our traveler. To carry the analogy a step further, the laboratory can be likened

to a private limousine and the field to public transportation. In the cloistered confines of the former, the researcher can partially create an environment to study and to manipulate; if he wants a rear-seat bar or a private telephone, he may install them; if he tires of them, he may have them removed. The disadvantage, of course, is that he may lose touch with what is going on outside the curtained windows. In the din and clamor of the latter, the researcher's fellow travelers often jostle him with such bewildering confusion and rapidity that he becomes uncertain whether he is approaching his stop, or whether he has, in fact, passed it. Still, if he can keep his wits together, he can derive satisfaction from the knowledge that his ride has exposed him to a glimpse of reality not readily accessible to the limousine passenger. (pp. xiii–xiv)

A FINAL NOTE

Epilogues should be brief, and this one has become unmercifully long. Perhaps I can most effectively conclude by reasserting that the contributors to this volume have sought to break new ground, to raise more questions than they can answer. In a very real sense, their success will be determined by the behavior of others; specifically, by the amount of research and scholarship stimulated on the part of speech communication researchers and other like-minded colleagues. Certainly, plenty remains to be done.

REFERENCES

CAMPBELL, D. T., "Factors Relevant to Validity of Experiments in Social Settings," *Psychological Bulletin,* 54 (1957), 297–312.

———, "Reforms as Experiments," *American Psychologist,* 24 (1969), 409–29.

CARTWRIGHT, D., and A. ZANDER, eds., *Group Dynamics,* pp. 165–341. Evanston, Ill.: Row, Peterson, 1960.

DION, K., E. BERSCHEID, and E. WALSTER, "What is Beautiful is Good," *Journal of Personality and Social Psychology,* 24 (1972), 285–90.

HOVLAND, C. I., "Reconciling Conflicting Results Derived from Experimental and Survey Studies of Attitude Change," *American Psychologist,* 14 (1959), 8–17.

KIBLER, R. J., and L. L. BARKER, eds., *Conceptual Frontiers in Speech-Communication.* New York: Speech Association of America, 1969.

McGUIRE, W. J., "The Nature of Attitudes and Attitude Change, in *Handbook of Social Psychology,* Vol. 3., G. Lindzey and E. Aronson, eds., pp. 136–314. Reading, Mass.: Addison-Wesley, 1969.

MILLER, G. R., "Research Setting: Laboratory Studies," in *Methods of Research in Communication,* P. Emmert and W. D. Brooks, eds. pp. 70–104. Boston: Houghton Mifflin, 1970.

MILLER, G. R., Foreward, in *Conflict Resolution through Communication*, F. E. Jandt, ed., pp. xi–xv. New York: Harper & Row, 1973.

REDDING, W. C., "Research Setting: Field Studies, in *Methods of Research in Communication*, P. Emmert and W. D. Brooks, eds., pp. 105–59. Boston: Houghton Mifflin, 1970.

Bibliography [1]

FRED E. JANDT

ABUDU, M. J., et al., "Black Ghetto Violence: A Case Study Inquiry Into the Spatial Patterns of Four Los Angeles Riot Event-types," *Social Problems,* 19 (1972), 408–26.

ACKOFF, R. L., D. W. CONRATH, and N. HOWARD, *A Model Study of the Escalation and De-escalation of Conflict.* Vol. 1, Management Science Center, University of Pennsylvania, 1967.

ADELSON, A., *SDS.* New York: Scribner's, 1972.

ALGER, I., "The Superego in Time of Social Conflict," *Journal of Contemporary Psychotherapy,* 3 (1970), 51–56.

[1] This bibliography is based on Jandt's bibliography in *Conflict Resolution Through Communication* (New York: Harper & Row, 1973, pp. 452–70, the annotated bibliography "Conflict Theory and Communication," prepared by Thomas E. Harris and Robert M. Smith and distributed by the Speech Communication Module of the ERIC Clearinghouse on Reading and Communication Skills, and a new review of the literature for more recent and previously omitted items.

ALINSKY, S. D., *Reveille for Radicals.* New York: Random House, 1969.

———, *Rules for Radicals.* New York: Random House, 1971.

ALLEN, R. F., S. PILNICH, and S. SILVERIVEIS, "Conflict Resolution Team Building for Police and Ghetto Residents," *Journal of Criminal Law, Criminology and Police Science,* 60 (1969), 251–55.

ANDREWS, J. R., "The Rhetoric of Coercion and Persuasion," *Quarterly Journal of Speech,* 56 (1970), 187–95.

ARCHIBALD, K., ed., *Strategic Interaction and Conflict.* Berkeley, California: Institute of International Studies, 1966.

ARNOLD, W. R., "Criminality, Conflict and Adolescent Ambivalence," *Social Science Quarterly,* 49 (1968), 360–67.

ASSAEL, H., "Constructive Role of Interorganizational Conflict," *Administrative Science Quarterly,* 14 (1969), 573–82.

ATTHONE, J. M., JR., "Types of Conflict and Their Resolution: A Reinterpretation," *Journal of Experimental Psychology,* 59 (1960), 1–9.

AUBERT, V., "Competition and Dissensus: Two Types of Conflict and Conflict Resolution," *Journal of Conflict Resolution,* 7 (1963), 26–42.

AVORN, J., *Up Against the Ivy Wall.* New York: Atheneum Press, 1968.

AYOUB, V. F., "Conflict Resolution and Social Reorganization in a Lebanese Village," *Human Organization,* 24 (1965), 11–17.

BACH, G. and Y. BERNHARD, *Aggression Lab: The Fair Fight Training Manual.* Dubuque, Iowa: Kendall/Hunt Publishing Co., 1971.

BACH, G. R. and P. WYDEN, *The Intimate Enemy: How to Fight Fair in Love and Marriage.* New York: William Morrow, 1969.

BACHRACH, P. and M. S. BARATZ, *Power and Poverty: Theory and Practice.* Oxford: Oxford University Press, 1970.

BAILEY, N. A., "Toward a Praxeological Theory of Conflict," *Orbis,* 11 (1968), 1081–1112.

BAIN, H., et al., "Using the Analysis of Options Technique to Analyze Community Conflict," *Journal of Conflict Resolution,* 15 (1971), 133–44.

BALDWIN, D., "The Costs of Power," *Journal of Conflict Resolution,* 15 (1971), 145–55.

BARBU, Z., "Social Conflict and National Myth," *Listener,* 78 (1967), 116–17.

BARD, M., "A Community Psychology Program in Police Family Crisis Intervention: Preliminary Impressions," *International Journal of Social Psychiatry,* 15 (1969), 209–15.

———, and J. ZACKER, "Design for Conflict Resolution," *Proceedings of the American Psychological Association,* 5 (1970), 803–4.

BARKMAN, P. F., *Man in Conflict.* Grand Rapids, Mich.: Zondervan Publishing House, 1965.

BARKUN, M., "Conflict Resolution Through Implicit Mediation," *Journal of Conflict Resolution,* 8 (1964), 121–30.

BARRY, W. A., "Marriage Research and Conflict: An Integrative Review," *Psychological Bulletin,* 73 (1970), 41–54.

BARTH, R. T., "Intergroup Climate Characteristics, Perceived Communication Problems, and Unity of Effort Achieved by Task-interdependent Research and Development Groups," *Proceedings of the Academy of Management,* 1971, 250–54.

BASS, B. M. and G. DUNTEMAN, "Biases in the Evaluation of One's Own Group, Its Allies and Opponents," *Journal of Conflict Resolution*, 7 (1963), 16–20.

BATEMAN, M. M. and J. S. JENSEN, "The Effects of Religious Background on Modes of Handling Anger," *Journal of Social Psychology*, 47 (1958), 133–41.

BAY, C., "Political and Apolitical Students: Facts in Search of Theory," *Journal of Social Issues*, 23 (1967), 76–91.

BECK, D. F., "Marital Conflict: Its Course and Treatment as Seen by Caseworkers," *Social Casework*, 47 (1966), 211–21.

BECKER, J. and E. IWAKAMI, "Conflict and Dominance within Families of Disturbed Children," *Journal of Abnormal Psychology*, 74 (1969), 330–35.

BEER, S., "Operational Research Approach to the Nature of Conflict," *Political Studies*, 14 (1966), 117–32.

BEISECKER, T., "Verbal Persuasive Strategies in Mixed-motive Interactions," *Quarterly Journal of Speech*, 56 (1970), 149–60.

BELL, R. L., S. E. CLEVELAND, P. G. HANSAN, and W. E. O'CONNELL, "Small Group Dialogue and Discussion: An Approach to Police-community Relationships," *Journal of Criminal Law, Criminology and Police Science*, 60 (1969), 242–46.

BENNETT, L., JR., *Confrontation: Black and White*. Chicago: Johnson, 1965.

——, "Confrontation on the Campus," *Ebony*, 23 (1968), 27–34.

BENNETT, W., "Conflict Rhetoric and Game Theory: An Extrapolation and Example," *Southern Speech Communication Journal*, 37 (1971), 34–46.

BERGER, S. E. and J. T. TEDESCHI, "Aggressive Behavior of Delinquent, Dependent, and Normal White and Black Boys in Social Conflict," *Journal of Experimental Social Psychology*, 5 (1969), 352–70.

BERKOWITZ, L., "The Expression and Reduction of Hostility," *Psychological Bulletin*, 55 (1958), 257–83.

——, *Aggression: A Social Psychological Analysis*. New York: McGraw-Hill, 1962.

——, "Frustrations, Comparisons, and Other Sources of Emotion Arousal as Contributors to Social Unrest," *Journal of Social Issues*, 28 (1972), 77–91.

BERLE, A. A., *Power*. New York: Harcourt, Brace & World, 1969.

BERNARD, J., "Where Is the Modern Sociology of Conflict?" *American Journal of Sociology*, 56 (1950), 11–16.

——, "Parties and Issues in Conflict," *Journal of Conflict Resolution*, 1 (1957), 111–21.

——, "The Sociological Study of Conflict," *The Nature of Conflict: Studies on the Sociological Aspects of International Tensions*. UNESCO, Tensions and Technology Series. Paris: UNESCO, 1957.

BINGS, D. A. and E. G. WILLIAMSON, "Conflict Resolution on the Campus: A Case Study," *Journal of College Student Personnel*, 11 (1970), 97–102.

BIXENSTINE, V. E., N. CHAMBERS, and K. V. WILSON, "Effect of Asymmetry in Payoff on Behavior in a Two-Person Non-Zero-Sum Game," *Journal of Conflict Resolution*, 8 (1964), 151–59.

——, and J. W. GAEBELEIN, "Strategies of 'Real' Opponents in Eliciting Cooperative Choice in a Prisoner's Dilemma Game," *Journal of Conflict Resolution*, 15 (1971), 157–66.

——, C. A. LEVITT, and K. V. WILSON, "Collaboration Among Six Persons in a Prisoner's Dilemma Game," *Journal of Conflict Resolution,* 10 (1966), 488–96.

——— and K. V. WILSON, "Effects of Level of Cooperative Choice by the Other Player on Choices in a Prisoner's Dilemma Game, Part II," *Journal of Abnormal and Social Psychology,* 67 (1963), 139–47.

BLAKE, R. R. and J. S. MOUTON, "The Fifth Achievement," *Journal of Applied Behavioral Science,* 6 (1970), 413–26.

BLOOD, R. O.,JR., "Resolving Family Conflict," *Journal of Conflict Resolution,* 4 (1960), 209–19.

BLUMRASEN, W. "A Survey of Remedies for Discrimination in the Union and on the Job," *Industrial Relations Research Association: Proceedings of the 21st Annual Winter Meeting* (1969), 283–91.

BONACICH, P., "Putting the Dilemma Back into Prisoner's Dilemma," *Journal of Conflict Resolution,* 14 (1970), 379–87.

BORAH, L. A., JR., "The Effects of Threat in Bargaining: Critical and Experimental Analysis," *Journal of Abnormal and Social Psychology,* 66 (1963), 37–44.

BOSKIN, J., "The Revolt in the Urban Ghetto 1964–1967," *Annals of the American Academy of Political and Social Sciences,* 382 (1969), 1–14.

BOSMAJIAN, H. A., ed., *Dissent: Symbolic Behavior and Rhetorical Strategies.* Boston: Allyn and Bacon, Inc., 1972.

BOSTROM, R. N., "Game Theory in Communication Research," *Journal of Communication,* 18 (1968) 369–88.

BOULDING, E., *Conflict Management in Organizations.* Ann Arbor, Michigan: Foundation for Research on Human Behavior, 1961.

BOULDING, K. E., "Organization and Conflict," *Journal of Conflict Resolution,* 1 (1957), 122–34.

———, *Conflict and Defense: A General Theory.* New York: Harper & Row, 1962.

———, "Where Are We Going if Anywhere?" *Liberation,* 7 (1962), 17–21.

———, "Towards a Theory of Protest," *ETC: A Review of General Semantics,* 24 (1967), 49–58.

BOWERS, J. W. and D. J. OCHS, *The Rhetoric of Agitation and Control.* Reading, Mass.: Addison-Wesley, 1971.

BRAGER, G., "Commitment and Conflict in a Normative Organization," *American Sociological Review,* 34 (1969), 482–91.

BRIDEY, W. M. and M. HAZDEN, "Intrateam Reactions: Their Relations to the Conflicts of the Family in Treatment," *American Journal of Orthopsychiatry,* 27 (1957), 349–55.

BRITT, D. and O. R. GALLE, "Industrial Conflict and Unionization," *American Sociological Review,* 37 (1972), 46–57.

BRODY, E. A., "Social Conflict and Schizophrenic Behavior in Young Adult Negro Males," *Psychiatry,* 24 (1961), 337–46.

BROYLES, J. A., "John Birch Society: A Movement of Social Protest of the Radical Right," *Journal of Social Issues,* 19 (1963), 51–62.

BRUNSWICK, A. F., "What Generation Gap?: A Comparison of Some Generational Differences among Blacks and Whites," *Social Problems,* 17 (1970), 358–71.

BURGESS, P. G., "Crisis Rhetoric: Coercion versus Force," *Quarterly Journal of Speech,* 59 (1973), 61–73.

BURGESS, P. K., et al., "Aggressive Behavior of Delinquent, Dependent and Normal White and Black Boys in Social Conflict," *Journal of Experimental Social Psychology,* 7 (1971), 545–59.

BURKE, R. J., "Methods of Resolving Interpersonal Conflict," *Personnel Administration,* 32 (1969), 48–55.

———, "Methods of Managing Superior-subordinate Conflict: Their Effectiveness and Consequences," *Canadian Journal of Behavioral Science,* 2 (1970), 124–35.

———, "Methods of Resolving Superior-subordinate Conflict: The Constructive Use of Subordinate Differences and Disagreements," *Organizational Behavior and Human Performance,* 5 (1970), 393–411.

BURTON, J. W., *Conflict and Communication: The Use of Controlled Communication in International Relations.* New York: Free Press, 1969.

BWY, D., "Dimensions of Social Conflict in Latin America," *American Behavioral Scientist,* 11 (1968), 39–50.

CAPLAN, N. S. and J. M. PAIGE, "A Study of Ghetto Rioters," *Scientific American,* 219(2) (1968), 15–21.

CARTWRIGHT, D., "Influence, Leadership, Control," in *Handbook of Organizations,* ed., J. G. March. Chicago: Rand McNally, 1965, 1–47.

CARVER, T. N., "The Basis of Social Conflict," *American Journal of Sociology,* 13 (1968), 628–37.

CAVAN, R. S., "Family Tensions Between the Old and Middle Aged," *Marriage and Family Living,* 18 (1956), 323–27.

CENKNER, W., "Gandhi and Creative Conflict," *Thought,* 45 (1970), 421–32.

CHAPMAN, A. W., "Group Approach to the Reduction of Tensions and Conflict," *Journal of Human Relations,* 1 (1952), 39–47.

CHENEY, J., T. HARFORD, and L. SOLOMON, "The Effects of Communicating Threats and Promises Upon the Bargaining Process," *Journal of Conflict Resolution,* 16 (1972), 99–107.

CHERTKOFF, J. M., "Coalition Formation as a Function of Differences in Resources," *Journal of Conflict Resolution,* 15 (1971), 371–83.

COHEN, B. P., *Conflict and Conformity: A Probability Model and Its Application.* Cambridge, Mass.: M.I.T. Press, 1963.

COHNSTAEDT, M. L., "Process and Role of Conflict in the Community," *American Journal of Economics and Sociology,* 25 (1966), 5–10.

COLBURN, D. L., "Conflict and Conflict Resolution," in *Contemporary Studies in Social Psychology and Behavior Change,* ed., Joseph L. Philbrick. New York: Selected Academic Readings, 1966, 71–86.

COLE, S. G., "Conflict and Cooperation in Potentially Intense Conflict Situations," *Journal of Personality and Social Psychology,* 22 (1972), 31–50.

COLEMAN, J. S., *Community Conflict.* New York: Free Press, 1957.

COLLINS, R., "Functional and Conflict Theories of Educational Stratification," *American Sociological Review,* 36 (1971), 1002–19.

CONN, P. H., *Conflict and Decision Making: An Introduction to Political Science.* New York: Harper & Row, 1971.

CONRATH, D. W., "Experience as a Factor in Experimental Gaming Behavior," *Journal of Conflict Resolution*, 14 (1970), 195–202.

CONVERSE, E., "The War of All Against All: A Review of the Journal of Conflict Resolution," *Journal of Conflict Resolution*, 12 (1968), 471–532.

CORWIN, R. G., "Patterns of Organizational Conflict," *Administrative Science Quarterly*, 14 (1969), 507–20.

COSER, L. A., *The Functions of Social Conflict*. New York. Free Press, 1956.

——, "Social Conflict and Theory of Social Change," *British Journal of Sociology*, 8 (1957), 197–207.

——, "The Sociology of Poverty—To the Memory of Georg Simmel," *Social Problems*, 13 (1965), 140–48.

——, *Continuities in the Study of Social Conflict*. New York: Free Press, 1967.

COX, A., *Crisis at Columbia: Report of the Fact-Finding Commission Appointed to Investigate the Disturbances at Columbia University in April and May, 1968*. New York: Vintage Books (Random House), 1968.

COX, B. A., "Conflict in the Conflict Theories: Ethological and Social Arguments," *Anthropologica*, 10 (1968), 179–91.

DADRIAN, V. N., "On the Dual Role of Social Conflicts: An Appraisal of Coser's Theory," *International Journal of Group Tensions*, 1 (1971), 371–77.

DAHRENDORF, R., "Toward a Theory of Social Conflict," *Journal of Conflict Resolution*, 2 (1958), 170–83.

——, *Class and Class Conflict in Industrial Societies*. Palo Alto, Calif.: Stanford University Press, 1959.

——, "Conflict and Liberty: Some Remarks on the Social Structure of German Politics," *British Journal of Sociology*, 14 (1963), 197–211.

DANZGER, H., "A Quantified Description of Community Conflict," *American Behavioral Scientist*, 12 (1968), 9–14.

DARBONN, A., "Crisis: A Review of Theory," *International Journal of Psychiatry*, 6 (1968), 377–79.

DARKENWALD, G. G., JR., "Organizational Conflict in Colleges and Universities," *Administrative Science Quarterly*, 16 (1971), 407–12.

DAVIS, M. D., *Game Theory: A Nontechnical Introduction*. New York: Basic Books, 1970.

DE BERKER, P., "Staff Strain in Institutions," *British Journal on Delinquency*, 6 (1956), 278–84.

DE KADT, E. J., "Conflict and Power in Society," *International Social Science Journal*, 17 (1965), 454–71.

DELHEES, K. H., "Conflict Measurement by the Dynamic Calculus Model and Its Applicability in Clinical Practice," *Multivariate Behavioral Research*, (1968), special issue.

——, "Conceptions of Group Decision and Group Conflict Applied to Vector Space: A Research Model," *ACTA Psychologica Amsterdam*, 34 (1970), 440–50.

DENTON, F. H. and W. PHILLIPS, "Some Patterns in the History of Violence," *Journal of Conflict Resolution*, 12 (1968), 182–95.

DEREUCH, A. and J. KNIGHT, eds., *Conflict in Society*. Boston: Little, Brown, 1966.

DEUTSCH, M., "A Theory of Cooperation and Competition," *Human Relations*, 2 (1949), 129–52.

————, "Trust and Suspicion," *Journal of Conflict Resolution,* 2 (1958), 265–79.

————, "The Effect of Motivational Orientation Upon Trust and Suspicion," *Human Relations,* 13 (1960), 123–39.

————, "Conflicts: Productive and Destructive," *Journal of Social Issues,* 25 (1969), 7–41.

————, "Socially Relevant Science: Reflections on Some Studies of Inter-personal Conflict," *American Psychologist,* 24 (1969), 1076–92.

————, "Toward an Understanding of Conflict," *International Journal of Group Tensions,* 1 (1971), 42–54.

————, and R. M. KRAUSS, "The Effect of Threat Upon Interpersonal Bargaining," *Journal of Abnormal and Social Psychology,* 61 (1960), 181–89.

————, and R. M. KRAUSS, "Studies of Interpersonal Bargaining," *Journal of Conflict Resolution,* 6 (1962), 52–76.

————, and R. J. LEWICKI, " 'Locking-in' Effects During a Game of Chicken," *Journal of Conflict Resolution,* 14 (1970), 367–78.

DILLMAN, E., "A Source of Personal Conflict in Police Organizations," *Public Personnel Review,* 28 (1967), 222–27.

DODSON, D. W., "The Creative Role of Conflict Reexamined," *Journal of Intergroup Relations,* 1 (1959–1960), 5–12.

DOOB, L. W., *Resolving Conflict in Africa: The Fermeda Workshop.* New Haven: Yale University Press, 1970.

————, W. J. FOLTZ, and R. B. STEVENS, "The Fermeda Workshop: A Different Approach to Border Conflicts in Eastern Africa," *Journal of Psychology,* 73 (1969), 249–66.

DOUGLAS, A., "The Peaceful Settlement of Industrial and Intergroup Disputes," *Journal of Conflict Resolution,* 1 (1957), 69–81.

DRIVER, P. M., "Towards an Ethology of Human Conflict: A Review," *Journal of Conflict Resolution,* 11 (1967), 361–74.

DRUCKMAN, D., "Dogmatism, Prenegotiation Experience, and Simulated Group Representation as Determinants of Dyadic Behavior in a Bargaining Situation," *Journal of Personality and Social Psychology,* 6 (1967), 279–99.

————, "Prenegotiation Experience and Dyadic Conflict Resolution in a Bargaining Situation," *Journal of Experimental Social Psychology,* 4 (1968), 367–83.

————, "The Influence of the Situation in Interparty Conflict," *Journal of Conflict Resolution,* 15 (1971), 523–54.

DUBIN, R., "Theory of Conflict and Power in Union Management Relations," *Industrial and Labor Relations Review,* 13 (1960), 501–18.

DuBOIS, R. D. and M. S. LI, *Reducing Social Tension and Conflict: Through the Group Conversation Method.* New York: Association Press, 1971.

ECKHARDT, W., "Prejudice: Fear, Hate or Mythology," *Journal of Human Relations,* 16 (1968), 32–41.

————, "Psychology of War and Peace," *Journal of Human Relations,* 16 (1968), 239–49.

EDELMAN, M., "Escalation and Ritualization of Political Conflict," *American Behavioral Scientist,* 13 (1969), 231–46.

EHRLE, R. A., "Conflict: Costs, Benefits and Potentials," *Journal of Employment Counseling,* 8 (1971), 162–81.

EIBL-EIBESFELDT, I., *Love and Hate: The Natural History of Behavior Patterns.* New York: Holt, Rinehart & Winston, 1972.

EISENSTEIN, M. L., "Project Summary: Reducing Delinquency through Integrating Delinquents and Non-delinquents in Conflict Resolution," *Crime and Delinquency Abstracts,* 6 (1969), supplement, 33.

EISINGER, R. A. and M. J. LEVINE, "The Role of Psychology in Labor Relations," *Personnel Journal,* 47 (1968), 643–49.

ELDER, G. H., "Racial Conflict and Learning," *Sociometry,* 34 (1971), 151–73.

ELKIND, D., "Exploitation and Generational Conflict," *Mental Hygiene,* 54 (1970), 490–97.

EMSHOFF, J. R. and R. L. ACKOFF, "Prediction, Explanation and Control of Conflict," *Papers of the Peace Research Society,* 12 (1969), 109–15.

EPHRON, L., "Group Conflict in Organizations: A Critical Appraisal of Recent Theories," *Berkeley Journal of Sociology,* 6 (1961), 53–72.

ETZIONI, A., "Toward a Theory of Guided Societal Change," *Social Casework,* 49 (1968), 335–38.

EXLINE, R. V. and R. C. ZILLER, "Status Congruency and Interpersonal Conflict in Decision-making Groups," *Human Relations,* 12 (1959), 147–62.

FARBER, S. M., *Man and Civilization: Conflict and Creativity; A Symposium.* New York: McGraw-Hill, 1963.

FEIERABEND, I. K. and R. L. FEIERABEND, "Aggressive Behaviors Within Polities, 1948–1962: A Cross-national Study," *Journal of Conflict Resolution,* 10 (1966), 249–71.

FELLNER, C. H., "Provocation of Suicidal Attempts," *Journal of Nervous and Mental Disorders,* 133 (1961), 55–58.

FERENCE, T. P., "Feedback and Conflict as Determinants of Influence," *Journal of Experimental Social Psychology,* 7 (1971), 1–16.

FEUER, L. S., *The Conflict of Generations: The Character and Significance of Student Movements.* New York: Basic Books, 1969.

FINER, S. E., "Reflections on Violence," *New Society,* 14 (1967), 792–93.

FINK, C. F., "Some Conceptual Difficulties in the Theory of Social Conflict," *Journal of Conflict Resolution,* 12 (1968), 412–60.

FISH, K. L., *Conflict and Dissent in the High Schools.* Milwaukee: Bruce, 1970.

FISHER, B. A., "Decision Emergence: Phases in Group Decision-making," *Speech Monographs,* 37 (1970), 53–66.

———, "Process of Decision Modification in Small Discussion Groups," *Journal of Communication,* 20 (1970), 51–64.

FISHER, R., ed., *International Conflict and Behavioral Science.* New York: Basic Books, 1964.

FLOOD, M. M., "Some Experimental Games," *Management Science,* 5 (1958), 5–26.

FOA, U. G., "Cross-cultural Similarity and Difference in Interpersonal Behavior," *Journal of Abnormal and Social Psychology,* 68 (1964), 517–22.

FOGELSON, R. M., *Violence as Protest: A Study of Riots and Ghettos.* Garden City, N.Y.: Doubleday, 1971.

FOLEY, T. and J. T. TEDESCHI, "Status and Reactions to Threats," *Journal of Personality and Social Psychology,* 17 (1971), 192–99.

Foss, B. M., "The Variety of Human Conflict and Frustration and Their Consequences," *British Journal of Animal Behavior*, 4 (1956), 39.

Frey, R. L. and J. S. Adams, "The Negotiator's Dilemma: Simultaneous In-group and Out-group Conflict," *Journal of Experimental Social Psychology*, 8 (1972), 331–46.

Friedenberg, E. Z., "Current Patterns of Generational Conflict," *Journal of Social Issues*, 25 (1969), 21–28.

Frisch, M. J., "Democracy and the Class Struggle," *Ethics*, 74 (1963), 44–52.

Frohlich, W. D., "Age Differences in Ways of Resolving Interpersonal Conflicts: A Pilot Study," *Interdisciplinary Topics Gerontology*, 4 (1969), 158–66.

Gahagan, J. P. and J. T. Tedeschi, "Strategy and the Credibility of Promises in the Prisoner's Dilemma Game," *Journal of Conflict Resolution*, 12 (1968), 224–34.

Gallo, P. S. and C. G. McClintock, "Cooperative and Competitive Behavior in Mixed-motive Games," *Journal of Conflict Resolution*, 9 (1965), 68–78.

Galtung, J., "Institutionalized Conflict Resolution: A Theoretical Paradigm," *Journal of Peace Research*, 4 (1965), 348–97.

———, "Conflict as a Way of Life," *New Society*, 16 (1969), 590–92.

Gamson, W., *Power and Discontent*. Homewood, Ill.: Dorsey, 1968.

Gangrade, K. D., "Intergenerational Conflict: A Sociological Study of Indian Youth," *Asian Survey*, 10 (1970), 924–36.

Gans, H. J., "Ghetto Rebellions and Urban Class Conflict," *Academy of Political Science Proceedings*, 29 (1968), 42–51.

Garnett, J. C., "Conflict and Strategy," *Political Studies*, 14 (1966), 174–85.

Gassner, S. and E. J. Murray, "Dominance and Conflict in the Interactions Between Parents of Normal and Neurotic Children," *Journal of Abnormal Psychology*, 74 (1969), 33–41.

Geschwender, J. A., "Social Structure and the Negro Revolt: An Examination of Some Hypotheses," *Social Forces*, 43 (1964–1965), 248–56.

———, "Civil Rights Protest and Riots: A Disappearing Distinction," *Social Science Quarterly*, 49 (1968), 474–84.

Giffin, S. F., *The Crisis Game: Simulating International Conflict*. Garden City, N.Y.: Doubleday, 1965.

Gillis, J. S. and G. T. Woods, "The 16PF as an Indicator of Performance in the Prisoner's Dilemma Game," *Journal of Conflict Resolution*, 15 (1971), 393–402.

Glasgow, D., "Black Power through Community Control," *Social Work*, 17 (1972), 59–64.

Gluckman, M., *Custom and Conflict in Africa*. New York: Free Press, 1955.

Goffman, E., *Strategic Interaction*. New York: Ballantine Books, 1969.

Golavine, M. N., *Conflict in Space: A Pattern of War in a New Dimension*. London: Temple Press, 1962.

Goldberg, L. C., "Ghetto Riots and Others: The Face of Civil Disorder in 1967," *Journal of Peace Research*, 2 (1968), 116–32.

Goldin, P., "The School as Resistant Patient: A Model for the Participation of Mental Health Professionals in Reducing Racial and Ethnic Tensions," *Psychology in the Schools*, 7 (1970), 146–52.

GOLDMAN, R. M., "A Theory of Conflict Processes and Organizational Offices," *Journal of Conflict Resolution,* 10 (1966), 328–43.

———, "Confrontation at San Francisco State," *Dissent,* 16 (1969), 167–79.

GOLDSTEIN, J. W., "The Psychology of Conflict and International Relations: A Course Plan and Bibliography," *Journal of Conflict Resolution,* 14 (1970), 113–20.

GOODRICH, D. W. and D. S. BOOMER, "Experimental Assessment of Modes of Conflict Resolution," in *Family Process,* ed. N. W. Ackerman. New York: Basic Books, 1970.

GOODWIN, G. A., "Toward a Theory of Social Change," *Mosaic,* 1 (1966), 13–26.

GRANT, J., *Black Protest: History, Documents and Analysis, 1619 to the Present.* New York: Fawcett, 1968.

GREEN, R. T. and G. SANTORI, "A Cross-cultural Study of Hostility and Aggression," *Journal of Peace Research,* 6 (1969), 13–22.

GRIMSHAW, A. D., "Lawlessness and Violence in America and Their Special Manifestation in Changing Negro-white Relationships," *Journal of Negro History,* 44 (1959), 52–72.

———, "Violence: A Sociological Perspective," *The George Washington Law Review,* 37 (1969), 816.

GRINSPOON, L., "Private Conflict with Public Consequences," *American Journal of Psychiatry,* 25 (1969), 1074.

GUETZKOW, H. and J. GYR, "An Analysis of Conflict in Decision-making Groups," *Human Relations,* 7 (1954), 367–82.

GURR, T. R., *Why Men Rebel.* Princeton, N.J.: Princeton University Press, 1970.

———, "The Calculus of Civil Conflict," *Journal of Social Issues,* 28 (1972), 27–47.

GUTTER, H. C., "Conflict Models, Games and Drinking Patterns," *Journal of Psychology,* 58 (1964), 361–68.

HACON, R. J., *Conflict and Human Relations Training.* Elmsford, N.Y.: Pergamon, 1965.

HAHN, H., "Ghetto Sentiments on Violence," *Science and Society,* 33 (1969), 197–208.

———, "Cops and Rioters: Ghetto Perceptions of Social Conflict and Control," *American Behavioral Scientist,* 13 (1970), 761–79.

HALL, R. H., "Some Organizational Considerations in the Professional-Organizational Relationship," *Administrative Science Quarterly,* 12 (1967), 461–78.

HAMBLIN, R. L., D. A. BRIDGER, R. C. DAY, and W. L. YANCEY, "The Interference-Aggression Law," *Sociometry,* 26 (1963), 190–216.

HAMMOND, K. R., "Essays on Research Approaches to Potential Threats to Peace: New Directions in Research on Conflict Resolution," *Journal of Social Issues,* 21 (1965), 44–65.

———, "New Directions in Research on Conflict Resolution," *British Psychological Society Bulletin,* 19 (1966), 1–20.

———, F. J. TODD, M. WILKINS, and T. O. MITCHELL, "Cognitive Conflict Between Persons: Application of the 'Lens' Model Paradigm," *Journal of Experimental Social Psychology,* 2 (1966), 343–60.

HANSON, D. J., "The Idea of Conflict in Western Thought," *International Review of History and Political Science,* 5 (1968), 90–105.

HARVATH, W. J., "A Statistical Model for the Duration of Wars and Strikes," *Behavioral Science,* 13 (1968), 18–28.

HASSWELL, H. D. and R. ARENS, "Role of Sanction in Conflict Resolution," *Journal of Conflict Resolution,* 11 (1967), 27–39.

HAVENS, A. E. and H. R. POTTER, "Organizational and Societal Variables in Conflict Resolution: An International Comparison," *Human Organization,* 26 (1967), 126–31.

HAWKINS, J. L. and K. JOHNSEN, "Perception of Behavioral Conformity, Imputation of Consensus and Marital Satisfaction," *Journal of Marriage and the Family,* 31 (1969), 507–11.

HEILIZER, F., "Conflict Models, Alcohol and Drinking Patterns." *Journal of Psychology,* 57 (1964), 457–73.

HEIRICH, M., *The Spiral of Conflict: Berkeley, 1964.* New York: Columbia University Press, 1971.

HENDERSON, D., "Minority Response and the Conflict Model," *Phylon,* 25 (1964), 18–26.

HIMES, J. S., "The Functions of Racial Conflict," *Social Forces,* 45 (1966), 1–10.

HOBART, C. W., "Commitment, Value, Conflict and the Future of the American Family," *Marriage and Family Living,* 25 (1963), 405–14.

HOEDEMAKER, E. D., "Distrust and Aggression: An Interpersonal-International Analogy," *Journal of Conflict Resolution,* 12 (1968), 69–81.

HORAI, J. and J. T. TEDESCHI, "The Effects of Credibility and Magnitude of Punishment Upon Compliance to Threats," *Journal of Personality and Social Psychology,* 12 (1969), 164–69.

HOROWITZ, I. L., "Consensus, Conflict and Cooperation: A Sociological Inventory," *Social Forces,* 41 (1962), 177–88.

———, "The Treatment of Conflict in Sociological Literature," *International Journal of Group Tensions,* 1 (1971), 350–63.

HOWARD, J. W., JR., "Adjudication Considered as a Process of Conflict Resolution: A Variation on Separation of Powers," *Journal of Public Law,* 18 (1969), 339–70.

INDIK, B. P. and G. M. SMITH, "Resolution of Social Conflict Through Collective Bargaining: An Alternative to Violence," *The George Washington Law Review,* 37 (1969), 848–61.

ISARD, W., "Toward a More Adequate General Regional Theory and Approach to Conflict Resolution," *Papers of the Peace Research Society,* 11 (1969), 1–21.

JACKMAN, N. R., "Collective Protest in Relocation Centers," *American Journal of Sociology,* 63 (1957), 264–72.

JACKSON, H. M., "Social Progress and Mental Health," *Journal of Conflict Resolution,* 14 (1970), 265–75.

JACOBS, M. A., A. SPILKEN and M. NORMAN, "Relationship of Life Change, Maladaptive Aggression, and Upper Respiratory Infection in Male College Students," *Psychosomatic Medicine,* 31 (1969), 31–44.

JASINSKI, F. J., "Technological Delimitation of Reciprocal Relationships: A

Study of Interaction Patterns in Industry," *Human Organization,* 15 (1956), 24–28.

JAYAWARDENA, C., "Ideology and Conflict in Lower Class Communities," *Comparative Studies in Society and History,* 10 (1968) 413–46.

JOHNSON, D. F. and W. L. MIHAL, "Sex Differences in Interpersonal Conflict," *Psychonomic Science,* 28 (1972), 357–60.

JOHNSON, D. W., "Students Against the School Establishment: Crisis Intervention in School Conflicts and Organizational Change," *Journal of School Psychology,* 9 (1971), 84–92.

——— and R. DUSTIN, "The Initiation of Cooperation Through Role Reversal," *Journal of Social Psychology,* 82 (1970), 193–203.

———and R. J. LEWICKI, "The Invitation of Superordinate Goals," *Journal of Applied Behavioral Science,* 5 (1969), 9–24.

JOHNSON, R., "Intrapersonal and Interpersonal Conflicts of Black Personnel in Higher Education," *Journal of College Student Personnel,* 13 (1972), 311–13.

JOHNSON, T. A., "Newark's Summer, 1967," *Crisis,* 74 (1967), 371–80.

JOSEPH, E. D., "Memory and Conflict," *Psychoanalysis Quarterly,* 35 (1966), 1–17.

KADING, D., "Role of the Social Scientist Regarding Social Conflict," *Southwestern Social Science Quarterly,* 32 (1952), 271–76.

KADT, E. J., "Conflict and Power in Society," *International Social Science Journal,* 17 (1965), 454–71.

KAHN, R. L., "The Justification of Violence: Social Problems and Social Solutions," *Journal of Social Issues,* 28 (1972), 155–75.

——— and E. BOULDING, eds., *Power and Conflict in Organizations.* New York: Basic Books, 1964.

KAHN, S., *How People Get Power.* New York: McGraw-Hill, 1970.

KAHN-FREUND, O., "Intergroup Conflicts and Their Settlement," *British Journal of Sociology,* 5 (1954), 193–227.

KAMANO, D. K., "Relationship of Ego Disjunction and Manifest Anxiety to Conflict Resolution," *Journal of Abnormal and Social Psychology,* 66 (1963), 281–84.

KATZ, D., "Consistent Reactive Participation of Group Members and Reduction of Intergroup Conflict," *Journal of Conflict Resolution,* 3 (1959), 28–40.

———, "Group Process and Social Integration: A System Analysis of Two Movements of Social Protest," *Journal of Social Issues,* 23 (1967), 3–22.

KAUFMAN, C., "Some Ethological Studies of Social Relationships and Conflict Situations," *Journal of the American Psychoanalytic Association,* 8 (1960), 671–85.

KELLEY, H. H., "Experimental Studies of Threats in Interpersonal Negotiations," *Journal of Conflict Resolution,* 9 (1965), 79–105.

KILLIAN, L. M. and C. GRIGG, *Racial Crisis in America.* Englewood Cliffs, N.J.: Prentice-Hall, 1964.

KING, B. T. and E. MCGINNIES, eds., *Attitudes, Conflict and Social Change.* New York: Academic Press, 1972.

KINLOCH, G. C., "Parent-youth Conflict at Home: An Investigation Among

University Freshmen," *American Journal of Orthopsychiatry,* 40 (1970), 658–64.

KLEIN, A., ed., *Natural Enemies: Youth and the Clash of Generations.* Philadelphia: Lippincott, 1969.

KLEIN, S. M. and J. R. MAHER, "Decision-making Autonomy and Perceived Conflict Among First-level Management," *Personnel Psychology,* 23 (1970), 481–92.

KLINEBERG, O., "Black and White International Perspective," *American Psychologist,* 26 (1971), 119–28.

KNIGHT, D., H. CURTIS and L. FOGEL, eds., *Cybernetics, Simulation, and Conflict Resolution.* New York: Spartan Books, 1971.

KRAUSE, M. S., "Strategies in Argument," *Journal of Psychology,* 81 (1972), 269–79.

KRAUSS, R. M., "Structural and Attitudinal Factors in Interpersonal Bargaining," *Journal of Experimental Social Psychology,* 2 (1966), 42–55.

——— and M. DEUTSCH, "Communication in Interpersonal Bargaining," *Journal of Personality and Social Psychology,* 4 (1966), 572–77.

KRIEBEL, C. H. and L. B. LAVE, "Conflict Resolution Within Economic Organizations," *Behavioral Science,* 14 (1969) , 183–96.

LACHMAN, S. J. and T. F. WATERS, "Psychosocial Profile of Riot Arrestees," *Psychological Reports,* 24 (1969) , 171–81.

LAMMERS, C. J., "Strikes and Mutinies: Nine Comparative Studies of Organizational Conflicts Between Rulers and Ruled," *Administrative Science Quarterly,* 14 (1969), 558–72.

LANIGAN, R. L., "Urban Crisis: Polarization and Communication," *Central States Speech Journal,* 21 (1970), 108–16.

LAPREATO, J., "Class Conflict and Image of Society," *Journal of Conflict Resolution,* 11 (1967), 281–93.

———, "Authority Relations and Class Conflict," *Social Forces,* 47 (1968) , 70–79.

LARSON, A., "Politics, Social Change and the Conflict of Generations," *Midwest Quarterly,* 11 (1970), 123–37.

LASCUITO, L. A. and R. M. KORLIN, "Correlates of the Generation Gap," *Journal of Psychology,* 81 (1972), 253–62.

LENT, R. H., "Binocular Resolution and Perception of Race in the United States," *British Journal of Psychology,* 61 (1970) , 521–33.

LEVIN, G. and D. D. STEIN, "System Intervention in a School-community Conflict," *Journal of Applied Behavioral Science,* 6 (1970), 337–52.

LEVINE, R. A., "Anthropology and the Study of Conflict: An Introduction," *Journal of Conflict Resolution,* 5 (1961), 3–15.

LEVINGER, G., "Kurt Lewin's Approach to Conflict and Its Resolution," *Journal of Conflict Resolution,* 1 (1957), 329–39.

LEWIN, K., *Resolving Social Conflicts.* New York: Harper, 1948.

LIFF, Z. A., "Impasse: Interpersonal, Intergroup, and International," *Group Process,* 3 (1970), 7–30.

LINDSKOLD, S. and J. T. TEDESCHI, "Self-confidence, Prior Success, and the Use of Power in Social Conflicts," *Proceedings of the American Psychological Association,* 5 (1970), 425–26.

————, et al., "Reward, Power and Bilateral Communication in Conflict Resolution," *Psychonomic Science,* 23 (1971), 415–16.

LIPSET, S. M. and G. M. SCHAFLANDER, *Passion and Politics: Student Activism in America.* Boston: Little, Brown, 1971.

———— and S. S. WOLIN, *The Berkeley Student Revolt: Facts and Interpretations.* Garden City, N.Y.: Anchor Books (Doubleday), 1965.

LITTERER, J. A., "Conflict in Organization: A Re-examination," *Academy of Management Journal,* 9 (1966), (3), 176–86.

LITVAK, I. A. and C. J. MAULE, "Conflict Resolution and Extra-territoriality," *Journal of Conflict Resolution,* 13 (1969), 305–19.

LITWAK, E., "Models of Bureaucracy which Permit Conflict," *American Journal of Sociology,* 67 (1961–1962), 177–84.

LLOYD, K., "Urban Race Riots vs. Effective Anti-discrimination Agencies," *Public Administration,* 45 (1967), 43–53.

LOMAS, C. W., *The Agitator in American Society.* Englewood Cliffs, N.J.: Prentice-Hall, Inc., 1968.

LOOMIS, C. P., "In Praise of Conflict and Its Resolution," *American Sociological Review,* 32 (1967), 875–90.

————, "Wanted: A Model for Understanding and Predicting Change in Natural and Therapeutic Groups and Systems which Are Gemeinschaft-like," *Group Psychotherapy,* 21 (1968), 131–36.

LOOMIS, J. L., "Communication, the Development of Trust, and Cooperative Behavior," *Human Relations,* 12 (1959), 305–15.

LOWIE, R. H., "Compromise in Primitive Society," *International Social Science Journal,* 15 (1963), 182–229.

LUCE, R. D. and H. RAIFFA, *Games and Decisions.* New York: Wiley, 1957.

LUNGERG, G., "How to Live with People Who Are Wrong," *Humanist,* 20 (1960), 74–84

McCLEARY, R. D., "The Violence of the Privileged in the USA," *International Journal of Offender Therapy,* 14 (1970), 81–85.

McCLINTOCK, C. G. and S. P. McNEEL, "Reward Level and Game Playing Behavior," *Journal of Conflict Resolution,* 10 (1966), 98–102.

McGINN, N. F., E. HARBURG and G. P. GINSBURG, "Responses to Interpersonal Conflict by Middle Class Males in Guadalajara and Michigan," *American Anthropologist,* 67 (1965), 1483–94.

MACK, R. W., "The Components of Social Conflict," *Social Problems,* 12 (1965), 388–97.

———— and R. C. SNYDER, "The Analysis of Social Conflict—Toward an Overview and Synthesis," *Journal of Conflict Resolution,* 1 (1957), 212–48.

MACLENNON, B. W., "Mental Health and School Desegregation: An Attempt to Prevent Community Conflict," *Proceedings of the American Psychological Association,* 5 (1970), 801–2.

McNEIL, E. B., ed., *Nature of Human Conflict.* Englewood Cliffs, N.J.: Prentice-Hall, 1965.

————, "Violence Today," *Pastoral Psychology,* 22 (1971), 21–30.

MAHL, G. F., *Psychological Conflict and Defense.* New York: Harcourt, Brace & Jovanovich, 1971.

MAIER, N. R. and M. SASHKIN, "Specific Leadership Behaviors that Promote Problem Solving," *Personnel Psychology*, 24 (1971), 35–44.

MAJAK, R. R., "Political Integration Revisited: A Review of Three Contributions to Theory Building," *Journal of Conflict Resolution*, 11 (1967), 117–26.

MANAS, (Editors of). "The Psychology of Social Morality," *Liberation*, 11 (7), (1966), 33–34.

MANN, L. and V. A. TAYLOR, "The Effects of Commitment and Choice Difficulty and Predecision Processes," *Journal of Social Psychology*, 82 (1970), 221–30.

MANN, P. A. and I. ISCOE, "Mass Behavior and Community Organization: Reflections on a Peaceful Demonstration," *American Psychologist*, 26 (1971), 108–13.

MARLOWE, D., "Psychological Needs and Cooperation: Competition in a Two-person Game," *Psychological Reports*, 13 (1963), 364.

MARTIN, J. G., "Intergroup Tolerance: Prejudice," *Journal of Human Relations*, 10 (1962), 197–204.

MARTIN, R., "The Concept of Power: A Critical Defense," *British Journal of Sociology*, 22 (1971), 240–57.

MARWELL, G., "Conflict over Proposed Group Actions: A Typology of Cleavage," *Journal of Conflict Resolution*, 10 (1966), 427–35.

MASSIE, H. N., "Bedlam in the Therapeutic Community: The Disruption of a Hospital Therapeutic Community as a Pattern of Social Conflict," *Psychiatry in Medicine*, 2 (1971), 278–93.

MASON, H. L., *Mass Demonstrations Against Foreign Regimes: A Study of Five Crises.* New Orleans: Tulane University Press, 1966.

MAXIMEN, J. S., "Medical Student Radicals: Conflict and Resolution," *American Journal of Psychiatry*, 127 (1971), 1211–15.

MAZUR, A., "A Nonrational Approach to Theories of Conflict and Coalitions," *Journal of Conflict Resolution*, 12 (1968), 196–205.

MEAD, M., *Culture and Commitment: A Study of the Generation Gap.* New York: Natural History Press, 1970.

MEEKER, R. J. and G. H. SHURE, "Pacifist Bargaining Tactics: Some 'Outsider' Influences," *Journal of Conflict Resolution*, 13 (1969), 487–93.

MEGARGEE, E. I. and J. E. HOKANSON, *The Dynamics of Aggression.* New York: Harper & Row, 1970.

—— and E. S. MENZIES, "The Assessment and Dynamics of Aggression," in *Advances in Psychological Assessment*, ed., P. McReynolds, Vol. 2. Palo Alto, Calif.: Science and Behavior Books, Inc., 1971.

MEIER, A. and E. RUDWICK, "Negro Protest and Urban Unrest," *Social Science Quarterly*, 49 (1968), 438–43.

MELTZER, J., "The Urban Conflict." *Urban Affairs Quarterly*, 3 (1968), 3–20.

MENNINGER, K. A., *Man Against Himself.* New York: Harcourt, Brace & World, 1956.

MEYER, J. W. and P. E. HAMMOND, "Forms of Status Inconsistency," *Social Forces*, 50 (1971), 91–101.

MICHENER, H., et al., "Threat Potential and Rule Enforceability of Sources of

Normative Emergence in a Bargaining Situation," *Journal of Personality and Social Psychology*, 20 (1971), 230–39.

MILES, R. E. and J. B. RITCHIE, "Leadership Attitudes Among Union Officials," *Industrial Relations*, 8 (1968), 108–17.

MILLER, M. J., B. BREHMER and K. R. HAMMOND, "Communication and Conflict Reduction: A Cross-cultural Study," *International Journal of Psychology*, 5 (1970), 75–87.

MILLER, P. R., "Revolutionists Among the Chicago Demonstrators," *American Journal of Psychiatry*, 127 (1970), 752–58.

MINUCHIN, S., "Conflict-resolution Family Therapy," *Psychiatry*, 8 (1965), 278–86.

MISNER, G., "The Response of Police Agencies," *Annals of the American Academy of Political and Social Science*, 38 (1969), 109–19.

MITCHELL, H. E., J. W. BULLARD and E. M. MUDD, "Areas of Marital Conflict in Successfully and Unsuccessfully Functioning Families," *Journal of Health and Social Behavior*, 3 (1962), 88–93.

MONTGOMERY, D., et al., "Two Different Techniques for Reducing Conflict Between Groups," *International Journal of Group Tensions*, 1 (1971), 252–67.

MOON, H. L., "Of Negroes, Jews and Other Americans," *Crisis*, 74 (1967), 146–50.

MOORE, R. B., "Century of Color Conflict," *Negro Digest*, 17 (1967), 4–7.

MORAZE, C., "The Settlement of Conflicts in Western Culture," *International Social Science Journal*, 15 (1963), 230–56.

MORLEY, I. E. and G. M. STEPHENSON, "Interpersonal and Inter-party Exchange: A Laboratory Simulation of an Industrial Negotiation at the Plant Level," *British Journal of Psychology*, 60 (1969), 543–45.

MOSHER, D. L., R. L. MORTIMER and M. GREBEL, "Verbal Aggressive Behavior in Delinquent Boys," *Journal of Abnormal Psychology*, 73 (1968), 454–60.

MUDD, S., ed., *Conflict Resolution and World Education*. The Hague: Dr. W. Junk, Publishers, 1966.

MUELLER, W. J. and H. A. GRAFER, "A Stability Study of the Aggression Conflict Scale," *Journal of Consulting Psychology*, 30 (1966), 357–59.

MURPHY, R. F., "Intergroup Hostility and Social Cohesion," *American Anthropologist*, 59 (1959), 1018–35.

MURRAY, E. J. and M. M. BURKUN, "Displacement as a Function of Conflict," *Journal of Abnormal Psychology*, 51 (1955), 47–56.

MURRAY, H. A., "Studies of Stressful Interpersonal Disputations," *American Psychologist*, 18 (1963), 28–39.

MUSHKAT, M., "The Small States and Research Into Aspects of War and Peace," *International Journal of Group Tensions*, 1 (1971), 124–53.

NADER, L. and D. METZGER, "Conflict Resolution in Two Mexican Communities," *American Anthropologist*, 65 (1963), 584–92.

NADLER, E. B., "Social Therapy of a Civil Rights Organization," *Journal of Applied Behavioral Science*, 4 (1968), 281–98.

NAKAMYRA, C. Y., "Relations Between Children's Expression of Hostility and Discipline by Dominant Overprotective Parents," *Child Development*, 30 (1959), 109–17.

NEHRU, J., "Racism: That Other Face of Nationalism," *Journal of Human Relations,* 14 (1966), 2–16.

NELSON, L. and M. C. MADSEN, "Cooperation and Competition in Four Year Olds as a Function of Reward Contingency and Subculture," *Developmental Psychology,* 1 (1969), 340–44.

NEURINGER, C. and L. W. WANDKE, "Interpersonal Conflicts in Persons of High Self-concept and Low Self-concept," *Journal of Social Psychology,* 68 (1966), 313–22.

NICHOLSON, M., *Conflict Analysis.* New York: Barnes & Noble, 1970.

NIEBURG, H. L., *Political Violence: The Behavioral Process.* New York: St. Martin's Press, 1969.

NIERENBERG, G. I., *The Art of Negotiating.* New York: Hawthorn Books, Inc., 1968.

NORBECK, E., "African Rituals of Conflict," *American Anthropologist,* 65 (1963), 1254–79.

NORTH, R. C., H. E. KOCH and D. A. ZINES, "The Integrative Functions of Conflict," *Journal of Conflict Resolution,* 4 (1960), 335–74.

NYE, R. D., *Conflict Among Humans.* New York: Springer Publishing Company, Inc., 1973.

OPPENHEIMER, M., "Directions of Peace Research: Conflict or Consensus?" *Journal of Human Relations,* 13 (1965), 314–19.

———, "Southern Student Sit-ins: Intra-group Relations and Community-conflict," *Phylon,* 27 (1966), 20–26.

ORAN, P. G. and F. HEILIZER, "A Note on the Concept of Conflict," *Journal of Psychology,* 59 (1965), 35–43.

OSKAMP, S., "Comparison of Strategy Effects in the Prisoner's Dilemma and Other Mixed Motive Games," *Proceedings of the American Psychological Association,* 5 (1970), 433–34.

———, "Effects of Programmed Strategies on Cooperation in the Prisoner's Dilemma and Other Mixed-motive Games," *Journal of Conflict Resolution,* 15 (1971), 225–59.

———, and D. PERLMAN, "Factors Affecting Cooperation in a Prisoner's Dilemma Game," *Journal of Conflict Resolution,* 9 (1965), 359–74.

PAIGE, J. M., "Changing Patterns of Anti-white Attitudes Among Blacks," *Journal of Social Issues,* 26 (1970), 69–86.

PALLEY, H. A., "Community in Conflict: Family Planning in Metroville," *Social Service Review,* 41 (1967), 55-65.

PARSON, D. W. and W. A. LINKUGEL, eds., *Militancy and Anti-communication: Proceedings of the Second Annual Symposium on Issues in Public Communication.* Department of Speech and Drama, Speech Communication and Human Relations Division, The University of Kansas, 1969.

PARSONS, T., "Social Classes and Class Conflict in the Light of Recent Sociological Theory," *American Economic Review,* 39 (1949), 16–26.

———, "On the Concept of Influence," *Public Opinion Quarterly,* 27 (1963), 37–62.

PATCHEN, M., "Models of Cooperation and Conflict: A Critical Review," *Journal of Conflict Resolution,* 14 (1970), 389–407.

PAUL, R. J. and R. D. SCHOOLER, "An Analysis of Performance Standards and

Generational Conflict in Academia," *Academy of Management Journal,* 13 (1970), 212–16.

PINDERHUGHES, C. A., "The Universal Resolution of Ambivalence by Paranoia With an Example in Black and White," *American Journal of Psychotherapy,* 24 (1970), 597–610.

PLAITNER, P., *Conflict and Understanding in Marriage.* Richmond, Va.: Knox, 1970.

PLASTRIK, S., "Backlash, Violence and Politics," *Dissent,* 16 (1969), 373–75.

PLOSS, S. L., *Conflict and Decision-making in Soviet Russia and a Case Study of Agricultural Policy, 1953–1963.* Princeton, N. J.: Princeton University Press, 1965.

PODAIR, S., "How Bigotry Builds Through Language," *Negro Digest,* 16 (1967), 38–43.

POLLAY, R. W., "Intrafamily Communication and Consensus," *Journal of Communication,* 19 (1969), 181–201.

PONDY, L. R., "Organizational Conflict: Concepts and Models," *Administrative Science Quarterly,* 12 (1967), 296–320.

———, "Varieties of Organizational Conflict," *Administrative Science Quarterly,* 14 (1969), 499–505.

POPPLESTONE, G., "Conflict and Mediating Roles in Expanded Settlements," *Sociological Review,* 15 (1967), 339–55.

PORAT, A. M., "Cross-Cultural Differences in Resolving Union-management Conflict Through Negotiations," *Journal of Applied Psychology,* 54 (1970), 441–51.

PORSHOLT, L., "On Methods of Conflict Prevention," *Journal of Peace Research,* 2 (1966), 178–93.

PRESTON, M. G., et al., "Impressions of Personality as a Function of Marital Conflict," *Journal of Abnormal and Social Psychology,* 47 (1952), 326–36.

PRUITT, D. G., "Stability and Sudden Change in Interpersonal and International Affairs," *Journal of Conflict Resolution,* 13 (1969), 18–38.

PYLYSHYN, Z., N. AGNEW and J. ILLINGSWORTH, "Comparison of Individuals and Pairs as Participants in a Mixed-motive Game," *Journal of Conflict Resolution,* 10 (1966), 211–21.

RADLOW, R., "An Experimental Study of 'Cooperation' in the Prisoner's Dilemma Game," *Journal of Conflict Resolution,* 9 (1965), 221–27.

———, and M. F. WEIDNER, "Unenforced Commitments in 'Cooperative,' and 'Noncooperative' Non-constant-sum Games," *Journal of Conflict Resolution,* 10 (1966), 497–505.

RAPOPORT, A., *Fights, Games, and Debates.* Ann Arbor, Michigan: University of Michigan Press, 1960.

———, "Is Warmaking a Characteristic of Human Beings or of Cultures?" *Scientific American,* 213 (4) (1965), 115–18.

———, "Experiments in Dyadic Conflict and Cooperation," *Bulletin of the Menninger Clinic,* 30 (1966), 84–91.

———, "Violence in American Fantasy," *Liberation,* 11 (1966), 18–22.

———, "Prospects for Experimental Games," *Journal of Conflict Resolution,* 12 (1968), 461–70.

————, *Strategy and Conscience.* New York: Schocken Books, 1969.

————, and A. M. CHAMMAH, *Prisoner's Dilemma.* Ann Arbor, Michigan: University of Michigan Press, 1965.

————, and A. M. CHAMMAH, "Sex Differences in Factors Contributing to the Level of Cooperation in the Prisoner's Dilemma Game," *Journal of Personality and Social Psychology,* 2 (1965), 831–38.

RAPOPORT, L., J. D. PETTINELLI, and D. SUMMERS, "Assessing Potential Community Conflict,"*Proceedings of Annual Convention of American Psychological Association,* 5 (1970), 799–800.

RAVEN, B. H. and J. R. P. FRENCH, JR., "A Formal Theory of Social Power," *Psychological Review,* 63 (1956), 181–94.

Report of the National Advisory Commission on Civil Disorders. New York: Bantam Books, 1968.

REX, J., "The Plural Society in Sociological Theory," *British Journal of Sociology,* 10 (1959), 114–24.

————, and R. MOORE, *Race, Community, and Conflict: A Study of Sparkbrook.* New York: Oxford University Press, 1967.

REYNOLDS, M. B. and P. A. NICHOLSON, "General Systems, the International System and the Eastonian Analysis," *Political Studies,* 15 (1967), 12–31.

RICHMOND, A. H., "Conflict and Authority in Industry," *Occupational Psychology,* 8 (1954), 24–33.

RICKS, F., G. MATHESAN and S. W. PYKE, "Women's Liberation: A Case Study of Organizations for Social Change," *Canadian Psychologist,* 13 (1972), 30–39.

RINDER, I. D., "Identification Reaction and Intergroup Conflict," *Phylon,* 15 (1954), 365–70.

RINQUIETTE, E. L., "Mode of Conflict Resolution: A Replication and Extension," *California Mental Health Research Digest,* 3 (1965), 17–18.

————, "Selected Personality Correlates of Mode of Conflict Resolution," *Journal of Personality and Social Psychology,* 2 (1965), 506–12.

ROBERTS, T. B., "Freedom of the Mind: Humanistic Consciousness and Student Activism," *Journal of Human Relations,* 19 (1971), 188–211.

ROJCEWICZ, S. J., "War and Suicide," *Life Threatening Behaviors,* 1 (1971), 46–54.

ROSE, A. M., "Voluntary Associations Under Conditions of Competition and Conflict," *Social Forces,* 34 (1955), 159–63.

————, "The Comparative Study of Intergroup Conflict," *Social Quarterly,* 1 (1960), 57–66.

————, and C. B. ROSE, "Intergroup Conflict and Its Mediation," *International Social Science Bulletin,* 6 (1954), 25–43.

ROSENAU, J. N., "Intervention as a Scientific Concept," *Journal of Conflict Resolution,* 13 (1969), 149–71.

ROTHCHILD, D., "Ethnicity and Conflict Resolution," *World Politics,* 2 (1970), 597–616.

ROY, D. F., "Role of the Researcher in the Study of Social Conflict: A Theory of Protective Distortion of Response," *Human Organization,* 4 (1965), 62–71.

RUBENSTEIN, A., "Struggle Between Founders and Sons," *Encounter,* 31 (1968), 64–68.

RUSSELL, G. W., "The Perception and Classification of Collective Behavior," *Journal of Social Psychology,* 87 (1972), 219–27.

RUTHEFORD, B., "Psychopathology, Decision-making, and Political Involvement," *Journal of Conflict Resolution,* 10 (1966), 387–407.

SAMPSON, E. E., "Achievement in Conflict," *Journal of Personality,* 31 (1963), 510–16.

SANFORD, N., "Dehumanization and Collective Destructiveness," *International Journal of Group Tensions,* 1 (1971), 26–41.

SAPPENFIELD, B. R., "Repression and Dynamics of Conflict," *Journal of Consulting Psychology,* 9 (1965), 266–70.

SCANZONI, J.,"A Social System Analysis of Dissolved and Existing Marriages," *Journal of Marriage and the Family,* 30 (1968), 452–61.

SCHACHTER, S., et al., "Cross-cultural Experiments on Threat and Rejection: A Study of the Organization for Comparative Social Research," *Human Relations,* 7 (1954), 403–39.

SCHALLER, L. E., *Community Organization: Conflict and Reconciliation.* Nashville: Abingdon Press, 1966.

———, *The Change Agent.* Nashville: Abingdon Press, 1972.

SCHEFFIER, H. W., "Genesis and Repression of Conflict: Choiseul Island," *American Anthropologist,* 66 (1964), 789–804.

SCHELLING, T. C., *The Strategy of Conflict.* Cambridge: Harvard University Press, 1960. (Republished: New York, Oxford University Press, 1963.)

SCHERMERHORN, R. A., "Polarity in the Approach to Comparative Research in Ethnic Relations," *Sociological and Social Research,* 51 (1967), 35–40.

SCHIAMBERG, L., "Some Socio-cultural Factors in Adolescent-parent Conflict: A Cross-cultural Comparison of Selected Cultures," *Adolescence,* 4 (1969), 333–60.

SCHILLER, B. M., "Racial Conflict and Delinquency: A Theoretical Approach," *Phylon,* 30 (1969), 261–71.

SCHLENKER, B. R., et al., "The Effects of Referent and Reward Power Upon Social Conflict," *Psychonomic Science,* 24 (1971), 268–70.

SCHMIDT, S. M. and T. A. KOCHAN, "Conflict: Toward Conceptual Clarity," *Administrative Science Quarterly,* 17 (1972), 359–70.

SCHNEIDER, B., "Organizational Climate: Individual Preferences and Organizational Realities," *Journal of Applied Psychology,* 56 (1972), 211–17.

SCHROEDER, C. and S. R. SCHROEDER, "Decision Conflict in Children in a Risk Situation. *Psychological Record,* 20 (1970), 457–63.

SCHROEDER, P., "Relationship of Kuder's Conflict Avoidance and Dominance to Academic Accomplishment," *Journal of Counseling Psychology,* 12 (1965), 395–99.

SCHWARTZ, E. K., "The Interpreter in Group Therapy: Conflict Resolution Through Negotiation," *Archives of General Psychiatry,* 18 (1968), 186–93.

SCHWARTZ, N .B., "Conflict Resolution and Impropriety in a Guatemalan Town," *Social Forces,* 48 (1969), 98–106.

SCHWARTZ, S. H., K. A. FELDMAN, M. E. BROWN, and A. HEINGARTNER, "Some

Personality Correlates of Conduct in Two Situations of Moral Conflict," *Journal of Personality*, 37 (1969), 41–57.

SCODEL, A., "Induced Collaboration in Some Non-zero-sum Games," *Journal of Conflict Resolution*, 6 (1962), 335–40.

———, J. S. MINAS, P. RATOOSH, and M. LIPETZ, "Some Descriptive Aspects of Two-person Non-zero-sum Games," *Journal of Conflict Resolution*, 3 (1959), 114–19.

SCOTT, R. L. and W. BROCKRIEDE, *The Rhetoric of Black Power*. New York: Harper & Row, 1969.

———, and D. K. SMITH, "The Rhetoric of Confrontation," *The Quarterly Journal of Speech*, 55 (1969), 1–8.

SEARS, D., "Riot Ideology in Los Angeles: A Study of Negro Attitudes," *Social Science Quarterly*, 49 (1968), 485–503.

SEGAL, R., *The Race War: The World Wide Clash of White and Non-White*. New York: Viking, 1966.

SERENO, K. K. and C. D. MORTENSEN, "The Effects of Ego-involved Attitudes on Conflict Negotiation in Dyads," *Speech Monographs*, 36 (1969), 8–12.

SHARMANN, F., "On Revolutionary Conflict," *Journal of International Affairs*, 23 (1969), 36–53.

SHERIF, M., "Experiments in Group Conflict," *Scientific American*, 195 (11) (1956), 54–58.

———, "Superordinate Goals in the Reduction of Intergroup Conflict," *American Journal of Sociology*, 63 (1958), 349–56.

———, *Intergroup Conflict and Cooperation: The Robber's Cave Experiment*. Institute of Group Relations, University of Oklahoma, 1961.

———, and C. W. SHERIF, *Groups in Harmony and Tension: An Integration of Studies on Intergroup Relations*. New York: Octagon Books, Inc., 1966.

SHERMAN, M. H., N. W. ACKERMAN, S. N. SHERMAN, and C. MITCHELL, "Nonverbal Cues and Reenactment of Conflict in Family Therapy," *Family Process*, ed. N. W. Ackerman. New York: Basic Books, 1970.

SHOHAM, S., "Conflict Situations and Delinquent Solutions," *Journal of Social Psychology*, 64 (1964), 185–215.

SHORE, R. P., "Conceptions of the Arbitrator's Role," *Journal of Applied Psychology*, 50 (1966), 172–78.

SHUBIK, M., "Game Theory, Behavior, and the Paradox of the Prisoner's Dilemma: Three Solutions," *Journal of Conflict Resolution*, 14 (1970), 181–93.

SHURE, G. H., R. J. MEEKER, and E. A. HANSFORD, "The Effectiveness of Pacifist Strategies in Bargaining Games," *Journal of Conflict Resolution*, 9 (1965), 106–17.

SIEGEL, B. J., "Conflict, Parochialism and Social Differentiation in Portuguese Society," *Journal of Conflict Resolution*, 5 (1961), 35–42.

SIKES, M. P., "Police Community Relations Laboratory: The Houston Model," *Professional Psychology*, 2 (1971), 39–45.

SILVERT, K., *The Conflict Society: Reaction and Revolution in Latin America*. New York: American University and Field Staff, 1966.

SIMMEL, G., *Conflict and the Web of Group Affiliations*. New York: Free Press, 1964.

———, "The Poor." *Social Problems,* 13 (1965), 118–40.

SIMONS, H. W., "Confrontations as a Pattern of Persuasion in University Settings," *The Central States Speech Journal,* 20 (1969), 163–69.

———, "Requirements, Problems and Strategies: A Theory of Persuasion for Social Movements," *Quarterly Journal of Speech,* 56 (1970), 1–11.

———, "Persuasion in Social Conflicts: A Critique of Prevailing Conceptions and a Framework for Future Research," *Speech Monographs,* 39 (1972), 227–47.

SINGER, J. D., "Man and World Politics: The Psycho-cultural Interface," *Journal of Social Issues,* 24 (1968), 127–56.

———, and P. RAY, "Decision-making in Conflict: From Inter-personal to International Relations," *Bulletin of the Menninger Clinic,* 30 (1966), 300–12.

SINGER, S., "Factors Related to Participants' Memory of a Conversation," *Journal of Personality,* 37 (1969), 93–110.

SKOLNICK, J. H., "Social Control in the Adversary System," *Journal of Conflict Resolution,* 11 (1967), 52–70.

———, *The Politics of Protest: A Task Force Report Submitted to the National Commission on the Causes and Prevention of Violence.* New York: Simon & Schuster, 1969.

SMITH, C. G., "A Comparative Analysis of Some Conditions and Consequences of Intra-organizational Conflict," *Administrative Science Quarterly,* 10 (1965-1966), 504–29.

———, ed., *Conflict Resolution: Contributions of the Behavioral Sciences.* Notre Dame, Ind.: University of Notre Dame Press, 1971.

SMITH, D. H., "Communication and Negotiation Outcome," *Journal of Communication,* 19 (1969), 248–56.

SMITH, E. E., "Individual vs. Group Goal Conflict," *Journal of Abnormal and Social Psychology,* 58 (1959), 134–37.

SMITH, N., "On the Origin of Conflict Types," *Psychological Record,* 18 (1968), 229–32.

SMOCK, C., "An Inferred Relationship Between Early Childhood Conflicts and Anxiety Responses in Adult Life," *Journal of Personality,* 23 (1954), 88–98.

SNYDER, G., *Deterrence and Defense.* Princeton, N.J.: Princeton University Press, 1961.

SOLOMON, L., "The Influence of Some Types of Power Relationships and Game Strategies Upon the Development of Interpersonal Trust," *Journal of Abnormal and Social Psychology,* 61 (1960), 223–30.

SORENSON, R. C., "The Concept of Conflict in Industrial Sociology," *Social Forces,* 29 (1951), 263–67.

SPECTOR, S., "Teacher Reaction to Conflict Situations," *Journal of Educational Psychology,* 46 (1955), 437–45.

SPEER, D. C., "Marital Dysfunctionality and Two-Person Non-zero-sum Game Behavior: Cumulative Monadic Measures," *Journal of Personality and Social Psychology,* 21 (1972), 18–24.

SPERLICK, P. H., *Conflict and Harmony in Human Affairs: A Study of Cross Pressures and Political Behavior.* Skokie, Ill.: Rand McNally, 1971.

SPIEGEL, J. P., "Psychosocial Factors in Riots: Old and New," *American Journal of Psychiatry,* 125 (1968), 281–85.

STAGER, P., "Conceptual Level as a Composition Variable in Small-group Decision-making," *Journal of Personality and Social Psychology,* 5 (1967), 152–61.

STAGNER, R., "Personality Dynamics and Social Conflict," *Journal of Social Issues,* 17 (1961), 28–44.

———, and H. ROSEN, *Psychology of Union-Management Relations.* Belmont, Calif.: Wadsworth Publishing Co., 1965.

STANLEY, G. and D. S. MARTIN, "Eye-contact and the Recall of Material Involving Competitive and Noncompetitive Associations," *Psychonomic Science,* 13 (1968), 337–38.

STEINER, J., "Conflict Resolution and Democratic Stability in Subculturally Segmented Political Systems," *Res Publica,* 11 (1969), 775–98.

———, "Nonviolent Conflict Resolution in Democratic Systems: Switzerland," *Journal of Conflict Resolution,* 13 (1969), 295–304.

STEINFATT, T. M., "Communication in the Prisoner's Dilemma and in a Creative Alternative Game," *Proceedings of the National Gaming Council's Eleventh Annual Symposium.* Center for Social Organization of Schools, The Johns Hopkins University, Baltimore, 1972, pp. 212–24.

STEVENS, C. M., "A Note on Conflict Choice in Economics and Psychology," *Journal of Conflict Resolution,* 4 (1960), 220–24.

STOLL, C. S. and P. T. McFARLANE, "Player Characteristics and Interaction in a Parent-child Simulation Game," *Sociometry,* 32 (1969), 259–72.

SUGARMAN, B., "Tension Management, Deviance and Social Change," *Sociological Quarterly,* 10 (1969), 62–71.

SUMMERS, D. A., "Conflict, Compromise, and Belief Change in a Decision-Making Task," *Journal of Conflict Resolution,* 12 (1968), 215–21.

SUTTINGER, G., "Conflict Situations and Socially Aberrant Behavior of Juveniles," *Monatsschrift fur Kriminologie und Strafrechtsre form* (Berlin), 51 (1968), 241–54 (Refer *Crime and Delinquency Abstracts,* 6 (1969), 195).

SWINGLE, P. G., ed., *The Structure of Conflict.* New York: Academic, 1970.

———, and A. SANTI, "Communication in Non-zero-sum Games," *Journal of Personality and Social Psychology,* 23 (1972), 54–63.

SYKES, A. J. M. and J. BATES, "Study of Conflict Between Formal Company Policy and the Interests of Informal Groups," *Sociological Review,* 10 (1962), 313–17.

TALOR, A., "The Natural Course View of Conflict Resolution," *Psychological Reports,* 26 (1970), 734.

TANNER, R. E. S., "Conflict Within Small European Communities in Tanganyika," *Human Organization,* 23 (1964), 319–27.

TANTER, R., "Dimensions of Conflict Behavior Within and Between Nations," *Journal of Conflict Resolution,* 10 (1966), 41–64.

TAYLOR, R. W., "Logic of Research in Group and International Conflict," *Bulletin of the Research Exchange on the Prevention of War,* 1 (1953), 1–5.

TAYLOR, S. A., "Communication and Teacher-administration Negotiations," *Speech Teacher,* 22 (1973), 44–47.

TEDESCHI, J. T., T. BONOMA, and N. NOVINSON, "Behavior of a Threatener: Retaliation vs. Fixed Opportunity Costs," *Journal of Conflict Resolution,* 14 (1970), 67–76.

——, J. HORAI, S. LINDSKALD, and J. P. GAHAGAN, "The Effects of Threat Upon Prevarication and Compliance in Social Conflict," *Proceedings of the American Psychological Association,* 3 (1968), 399–400.

TEGER, A. I., "The Effects of a Campus Building Occupation on Attitudes and Images of the Conflict," *Journal of Applied Social Psychology,* 1 (1971), 292–304.

THEODORSON, G. A., "The Function of Hostility in Small Groups," *Journal of Social Psychology,* 56 (1962), 57–66.

THOMPSON, J. D., "Organizational Management of Conflict," *Administrative Science Quarterly,* 4 (1960), 389–409.

——, "Notes on Aggression," *Commentary,* 47 (1969), 63–65.

TILLMAN, J. A., JR., "The Nature and Function of Racism: A General Hypothesis," *Journal of Human Relations,* 12 (1964), 50–59.

TODD, F. J., K. R. HAMMOND, and M. M. WILKINS, "Differential Effects of Ambiguous and Exact Feedback on Two-person Conflict and Compromise," *Journal of Conflict Resolution,* 10 (1966), 88–97.

TOMPKINS, P. and E. V. B. ANDERSON, *Communication Crisis at Kent State: A Case Study.* New York: Gordon and Breach, 1971.

TRIPODI, T., "Cognitive Complexity and the Perception of Conflict: A Partial Replication," *Perceptual and Motor Skills,* 25 (1967), 543–44.

TRUITT, W. H., "Human Nature and the Cooperative Impulse," *Journal of Human Relations,* 14 (1966), 580–94.

TUBBS, S., "Two Person Game Behavior, Conformity-inducing Messages, and Interpersonal Trust," *Journal of Communication,* 21 (1971), 326–41.

TURK, A., "Conflict and Criminality," *American Sociological Review,* 31 (1966), 338–52.

VARELA, J. A., *Psychological Solutions to Social Problems: An Introduction to Social Technology.* New York: Academic, 1971.

VIDMOR, N., "Effects of Representational Roles and Mediators on Negotiation Effectiveness," *Journal of Personality and Social Psychology,* 17 (1971), 48–58.

VINCENT, J. E. and E. W. SCHWERIN, "Ratios of Force and Escalation in a Game Situation," *Journal of Conflict Resolution,* 15 (1971), 489–98.

——, and J. O. TINDELL, "Alternative Cooperative Strategies in a Bargaining Game," *Journal of Conflict Resolution,* 13 (1969), 494–510.

VITZ, P. and W. R. KITE, "Factors Affecting Conflict and Negotiation Within an Alliance," *Journal of Experimental Social Psychology,* 6 (1970), 233–47.

VON NEUMAN, J. and O. MORGANSTERN, *The Theory of Games and Economic Behavior.* Princeton, N.J.: Princeton University Press, 1944.

WAELDER, R., "Conflict and Violence," *Bulletin of the Menninger Clinic,* 30 (1966), 267–74.

WALKER, D., *Rights in Conflict.* New York: Bantam Books, 1968.

WALLACE, D. and P. ROTHAUS, "Communication, Group Loyalty, and Trust in the PD Game," *Journal of Conflict Resolution,* 13 (1969), 370–80.

WALLERSTEIN, I. and P. STARR, eds., *The University Crisis Reader: Confrontation and Counterattack.* New York: Random House, 1971.

WALMAN, B. B., "The Empty Bucket: An Editorial," *International Journal of Group Tensions,* 1 (1971), 5–25.

WALTON, R. E., "Interpersonal Confrontation and Basic Third Party Functions: A Case Study," *Journal of Applied Behavioral Science,* 4 (1968), 327–44.

———, *Interpersonal Peace-making:Confrontations and Third Party Consultation.* Reading, Mass.: Addison-Wesley Publishing Co., 1969.

———, "A Problem-solving Workshop on Border Conflicts in Eastern Africa," *Journal of Applied Behavioral Science,* 6 (1970), 453–89.

———, and J. M. DUTTON, "The Management of Interdepartmental Conflict: A Model and Review," *Administrative Science Quarterly,* 14 (1969), 73–84.

———, J. M. DUTTON, and T. P. CAFFERTY, "Organizational Context and Interdepartmental Conflict," *Administrative Science Quarterly,* 14 (1969), 522–42.

WALZER, M., *Obligations: Essays on Disobedience, War and Citizenship.* Cambridge, Mass.: Harvard University Press, 1970.

WANDERER, J. J., "An Index of Riot Severity and Some Correlates," *American Journal of Sociology,* 74 (1969), 500–505.

WARELL, L., "The Preference for Conflict: Some Paradoxical Reinforcement Effects," *Journal of Personality,* 32 (1964), 32–44.

WARREN, D. I., "Conflict Intersystem and the Change Agent," *Journal of Human Relations,* 13 (1965), 339–55.

———, "The Effects of Power Bases and Peer Groups on Conformity in Formal Organizations," *Administrative Science Quarterly,* 14 (1969), 544–46.

———, "Suburban Isolation and Race Tension: The Detroit Case," *Social Problems,* 17 (1969–1970), 324–39.

WASTOW, A. I., *From Race Riot to Sit-in; 1919 and the 1960's: A Study in the Connections Between Conflict and Violence.* Garden City, N.Y.: Doubleday, 1966.

WEDGE, B., "The Case Study of Student Political Violence: Brazil, 1964, and Dominican Republic, 1965," *World Politics,* 21 (1968-1969), 183–206.

WEINGART, P., "Beyond Parsons? A Critique at Ralf Dahrendorf's Conflict Theory," *Social Forces,* 48 (1969), 151–95.

WELLER, L., "The Effects of Anxiety on Cohesiveness and Rejection," *Human Relations,* 16 (1963), 189–197.

WESTHUES, K., "The Drop In Center: A Study in Conflicting Realities," *Social Casework,* 53 (1972), 361–68.

WHITE, H., "Management Conflict and Sociometric Struggle," *American Journal of Sociology,* 67 (1961), 185–99.

WHITING, B. B., "Sex Identity and Physical Violence: A Comparative Study," *American Anthropologist,* 67 (1965), (special issue), 123–140.

WHYTE, W. F., *Pattern for Industrial Peace.* New York: Harper, 1951.

WILLIAMS, J. "Race, War, and Politics," *Negro Digest,* 16 (1967), 4–9.

WILLIAMS, R., "Social Change and Social Conflict: Race Relations in the United States, 1944-1964," *Social Inquiry,* 35 (1965), 8–25.

WILLIAMS, R. M., "Conflict and Social Order: A Research Strategy for Complex Propositions," *Journal of Social Issues,* 28 (1972), 11–26.

WITTES, G. and S. WITTES, "A Study of Interracial Conflict," *American Education,* (June 1970), 7–11.

WOLFE, J. and P. HORN, "Racial Friction in the Deep South," *Journal of Psychology,* 54 (1962), 139–52.

WOLFE, T., *Radical Chic and Mau-Mauing the Flak Catchers.* New York: Farrar, Straus and Giroux, 1970.

WOODMANSEY, A. C., "The Internalization of External Conflict," *International Journal of Psycho-Analysis,* 47 (1966), 349–55.

WORELL, L., "The Preference for Conflict: Some Paradoxical Reinforcement Effects," *Journal of Personality,* 32 (1964), 32–44.

YATES, A. J., *Frustration and Conflict.* New York: Wiley, 1962.

YATES, H. W., "A Strategy for Responding to Social Conflict," *Pastoral Psychology,* 22 (1971), 31–41.

ZAND, D. E. and W. E. STECKMAN, "Resolving Industrial Conflict—An Experimental Study of the Effects of Attitudes and Precedent," *Industrial Relations Research Association: Proceedings of the 21st Annual Winter Meeting,* 1969, 348–59.

ZAWONDY, J. K., *Man and International Relations; Contributions of the Social Sciences to the Study of Conflict and Integration.* San Francisco: Chandler, 1966.

ZEIGLER, H. and R. C. ZILLER, "The Neutral in a Communication Network Under Conditions of Conflict," *American Behavioral Scientist,* 13 (1969), 265–81.

ZINNES, D. A., "Comparison of Hostile Behavior of Decision Makers in Simulation and Historical Data," *World Politics,* 18 (1966), 474–502.

————, "Introduction to the Behavioral Approach: A Review," *Journal of Conflict Resolution,* 12 (1968), 258–67.

ZURCHER, S. L., JR., A. MEADOW, and S. L. ZURCHER, "Value Orientation, Conflict and Alienation from Work: A Cross-cultural Study," *American Sociological Review,* 30 (1965), 539–48.

Index